A Sufi Message of Spiri
Volume VIII
(Revised editio

CW00505192

SUFI TEACHINGS
THE ART OF BEING

A SUFI MESSAGE
OF SPIRITUAL LIBERTY
VOLUME VIII
(Revised edition)

SUFI TEACHINGS
THE ART OF BEING

HAZRAT INAYAT KHAN

Element
Shaftesbury, Dorset • Rockport, Massachusetts
in association with
The International Headquarters of
the Sufi Movement, Geneva

© The International Headquarters
of the Sufi Movement, Geneva

First published by Barrie and Rockliff (Barrie Books Ltd.) 1963
Subsequent reprints by Uitgeverij Servire BV, Katwijk, Netherlands

Revised edition first published in Great Britain in 1991
by Element Books Limited
Longmead, Shaftesbury, Dorset
in association with
The International Headquarters
of the Sufi Movement,
Geneva

Revised edition first published in the USA in 1991 by
Element, Inc,
42 Broadway, Rockport, MA 01966

Cover design by Max Fairbrother
Typeset by Selectmove Ltd, London
Printed and bound in Great Britain by
Billings Ltd, Hylton Road, Worcester

British Library Cataloguing in Publication Data
Inayat Khan, Hazrat *1882–1927*
A Sufi Message of spiritual liberty.–Rev. ed.
Vol.8, Sufi teachings, the art of being
1. Sufi life
I. Title
297.44

ISBN 1–85230–097–3

Library of Congress Data Available

CONTENTS

Contents

PREFACE

Following the recent re-edition of Volume II of *The Sufi Message of Hazrat Inayat Khan*, this edition of Volume VIII has been revised to an even larger extent. This calls for an explanation of the editorial approach which will equally be applied to the other volumes of this series – both the re-issues and the volumes with which it is hoped to extend the series.

In the first place the revised and enlarged edition of *Sufi Teachings*, which has proved to be one of the most widely read books of the whole series, will now be brought out in two parts. In addition to Volume VIII a new Volume XIV will appear shortly. This means that the new edition has been enriched with many new lectures on a variety of related subjects, unpublished hitherto.

Commenced in 1960, *The Sufi Message of Hazrat Inayat Khan* included the books earlier published individually as well as numerous previously unpublished lectures and teachings. It proved to be a highly successful publication amongst English readers throughout the world. Its sophisticated editorial method included such elements as the "telescoping" of lectures on identical subjects and other ways of condensation and omission of materials to avoid duplication; the insertion into the main text of answers given to questions after lectures, and sometimes the questions themselves; a generally felicitous adjustment of the spoken word to the printed page. However, this "literary" method has in some cases led to arbitrary stylizing of unclear passages, to narrowing down the number of possible interpretations and to interruptions of a line of thought in order to elucidate a single point. In other words, it resulted in often very aesthetic versions, but left deviations of the original texts unaccounted for.

For the purpose of the present edition, therefore, the revision has entailed a renewed analysis of all the relevant manuscripts. Again: Hazrat Inayat Khan's teachings on the

philosophy and practice of mysticism were developed in
lectures, not in written articles or chapters. Their oral character is part of their highly personal tone, with all its
distinctive vivacity and charm. The present edition is aimed
at following that style of speech and teaching as closely as
is possible in the transition of pronouncement to page. The
consequences of this novel approach can be summarised as
follows.

Repetitions of subject or expression have not always been
avoided; in the few cases where omissions still occur (e.g.
of similes or stories) those have been accounted for. Texts
have been entirely "unscrambled": combined lectures or
paragraphs again separated out and questions and answers
lifted from the main body of the text. It should be noted,
moreover, that in Hazrat Inayat Khan's work repetition has
its particularly positive advantages. Firstly, of course, as a
natural method of instruction. Beyond that there is the
specifically mystical value of impregnating the consciousness:
in the practices of all mystical orders repetition is seen
as vital. However, in Hazrat Inayat Khan's lectures on
the same subjects repetition never really remains repetitive:
almost always he develops his theme along different lines,
evolving complementary rather than similar ideas, varying
shades of meaning and intent, sometimes proceeding into
quite different directions! Here too, his expertise in and
love for music should be borne in mind: he maintained a
lifelong preference for its distinctive method: themes and
motifs within one melodic and rhythmic pattern are to be
elaborated in innumerable variations; jointly constituting one
reality of intense and profound musical perception – and so,
in Sufi discourse, of mystical perception.

Another instance of the different editorial approach with
regard to oral utterance may be cited. Over and over again
Hazrat Inayat Khan in his lectures employs "*you*", in the
earlier edition often transformed into "one"; and it is precisely
the personal impact, the didactic effect, a lightening liveliness
joined to the depth of his vision, that he then aims at. It also
accentuates an aphoristic element of his style, in line with the
ancient Indian *sutra* tradition.

In any editorial version of Hazrat Inayat Khan's works, considerations such as the above should be kept in view if the shape and content of his lectures are to be grasped more fully. There are others as well.

Readers increasingly will become familiar with the characteristic combination of depths of mystic awareness and vision and a florid rhetoric style, which then suddenly return to practice and actuality by a rapid change of style and tone rather than mood. Then suddenly may emerge anecdotes, similes, colloquialisms etc. Best of all: there is Hazrat Inayat Khan's humour, his sometimes very comic intent, brightening the depth of dignity of his address. Often, it increases the ever-present tinge of Indian English, all the better illustrating the stylish and stylized Urdu underlying an English proficiency acquired relatively late.

An expression of that brilliance of spirit which Hazrat Inayat Khan himself was fond of describing as the mark of a "dancing soul", he often applies such humour for special effects or in driving a point home. Humour also serves as a main element of qualification, of emphasizing or recalling the relativity of anything expressed. However, often Hazrat Inayat Khan's humour is subtle and sudden, requiring full attention – sometimes also experience or some biographical knowledge – for timely enjoyment!

In Sufism humour has always gone together with mysticism. To Hazrat Inayat Khan happiness and serenity, joy and peace, are the soul's most essential characteristics, belonging together as do music and mysticism, ecstacy and meditation. The qualifying function of humour leads to a further point. The *Sufi Teachings* never are dogmatic. As so frequently in oriental spirituality, contradictions merely are regarded as duly representing various aspects of one Truth. Paradoxes are central to an advanced understanding. Hazrat Inayat Khan did everything to avoid that his Sufi mysticism would turn into yet another system; above all, it was not to become a closed circuit: it was deliberately to be kept as open-ended as at all possible. Any fixed expression would risk anew to become limitative, doctrinal, concrete. Therefore, too, his Sufi lectures were fully intended as oral transmission, by evocation rather than definition, of mystic insight and instruction: "Truth is what cannot be said in words".

In searching for an authentic as possible written representation of Hazrat Inayat Khan's Sufi philosophy and mysticism, the findings and reflections described above have furnished the main editorial guidelines. This new stage is further marked by the series' transition to a new publisher and a modification of appearance. Also to be changed is the serial title to be given to the volumes revised in accordance with this new editorial approach. For these nothing could be more appropriate than restoring to them the original name by which Hazrat Inayat Khan himself earlier described his life's work:

A Sufi Message of Spiritual Liberty

HEALTH AND ORDER OF
BODY AND MIND

CHAPTER I

Health

1

JUST AS for every illness there is a remedy, so for every disaster there is a reconstruction. Any effort, in whatever form and however small, made towards reconstruction or towards the betterment of conditions is worthwhile, but what we need most is the understanding of that religion of religions and that philosophy of philosophies which is self-knowledge. We shall not understand the outer life if we do not understand ourselves. It is the knowledge of the self that gives the knowledge of the world.

What is health? Health is order. And what is order? Order is music. Where there is rhythm, regularity, cooperation, there is harmony, there is sympathy. Health of mind and health of body therefore depend upon preserving that harmony, upon keeping intact that sympathy, which is going on in mind and in body.

Remember that life in the world, and especially if lived amidst the crowd, will test and try our patience every moment of the day, and it will be most difficult to preserve that harmony and peace which are all happiness. What is the definition of life? Life means struggle with friends and battle with foes; it is all the time giving and taking, and it is most difficult to keep the sympathy, to keep the harmony which are health and happiness.

Where are we to learn it? All education, learning and knowledge are acquired, but this one art is a divine art and man has inherited it. Absorbed in outer learning he has forgotten it, yet it is an art which is known to his soul, yet it is his own being, it is the deepest knowledge of his heart. No progress in whatever line will give a man that satisfaction his soul is craving for, except this art which is the art of life, the art of being which is the pursuit of his soul. In order to serve the reconstruction of the world the only thing possible and the only thing necessary is to learn the art of being, the art of life, for oneself and to be an example oneself before trying to serve humanity.

What is Sufism? It is that art which has just been spoken of, the art through which the music and symphony of life can be preserved, and through which man can enable himself to become the proper servant of God and humanity.

2

Health is an orderly condition caused by the regular working of the mechanism of the physical body. The regular working of the physical body depends upon the weather, diet, the balance between action and repose, and the condition of the mind.

Many think that it is some deformity of the body, a curve in the spine or a cavity in the brain, that affects the mind; few realize that very often the mind produces an irregularity in the spine or in the brain, thereby causing an illness. The ordinary point of view regards an illness as a physical disorder which can be cured by means of material remedies. Then there is another point of view: that of people who think deeply and who say that by not taking notice of an illness, or by suggesting to oneself that one is well, one can be restored to health.

This point of view can be exaggerated, when some people claim that illness is an illusion, that it has no existence of its own. The ordinary point of view can also be exaggerated when one thinks that medicine is the only means of cure and that thought has little to do with actual illness. Both these persons, the one who looks at it from the ordinary point of view and the other who sees from a deeper point of view, will find arguments for and against their idea. Some people go as far as to say that medicine must not be touched by those who have faith, and some affirm that an illness is as real as health. It is in the absence of illness that a person can easily call pain an illusion, but when he is suffering, then it is difficult for him to call it an illusion.

The question who is more subject to illness, a spiritual
person or a material person, may be answered thus: a spiritual
person who discards physical laws is subject to illness as much
as a material person who discards spiritual laws. No doubt a
spiritually inclined person is supposed to have less chance of
being ill, because his spirit has become harmonious through
spirituality. He creates harmony and radiates it; he keeps to
the realm of nature, in tune with the Infinite. Nevertheless,
a spiritual person's life in the midst of the world is like
the life of a fish on the land. The fish is a creature of the
water; its sustenance, its joy, its happiness are in the water.
A spiritual soul is made for solitude; his joy and happiness are
in solitude. A spiritual person, set in the midst of the world
by destiny, feels out of place, and the ever-jarring influences
of those around him and the continually striking impressions
which disturb his finer senses, make it more likely that he will
become ill than those who push their way in the crowd of the
world and are ready to be pushed away.

A spiritual soul is an old soul according to the Eastern
terminology. Even a spiritually minded young person shows
the nature of the aged, but at the same time spirituality
is perpetual youth. A spiritual person admires all things,
appreciates all things, enjoys all things to their fullness.
Therefore if one says that the spiritual person is like an old
person it is true, and if one says the spiritual person is like a
young person it is true also.

People have lost the conception of normal health these
days when the standard of normal health is below the real
conception of health. To be healthy is not only to be muscular:
to be really healthy is to be able to enjoy and appreciate life
fully. To be healthy means to be thoughtful; the one who can
feel deeply shows the sign of health.

It is not surprising if a material person becomes ill, nor
is it amazing if a spiritual person is unwell. The former
becomes ill because he has lost his rhythm, the latter is ill
because he could not keep to a rhythm which is not his
own. Be one spiritual or material, since one has to live in
the midst of the world, one shares the conditions of all
those who are far and near, and one subjects oneself to the

influences, desirable or undesirable, coming from all around. One cannot close one's eyes, nor can one close one's heart, to the impressions which continually fall upon one. The best one can do is to keep a careful watch against all that comes upon one causing irregularity, inharmony and disorder, to be resigned to all one has to pass through, and to be courageous in order to overcome all that keeps one back from health and perfection.

3

Health is a most important subject. There is a Hindustani proverb: Health is a thousand gifts. The other interests of life should sometimes be sacrificed to health.

If the veins and tubes of the body are stopped up, this causes disease. If they are stopped up by water, it causes colds and coughs. If they are stopped up with air – that is by poisonous gases – one gets rheumatism and similar diseases. If they are stopped up by a sort of rust, these are the germs that cause disease. There are surroundings, there are circumstances, there are germs that may cause disease, but the disease comes in proportion to the welcome one gives it.

One way is giving it too much sympathy. If a child has a headache, and the mother says: "Oh, poor child, you must lie down on your bed and I shall bring you an apple and an orange", the apple and the orange are brought to the headache, the bed and the sympathy are given to the headache to welcome it. If it is given such a welcome, it will make its abode there. There are some people who love their self so much that they say, "Oh, poor self, what a pity it is that you should be ill, that you should suffer". Self-pity is a great cause of disease.(1)

Then there is fear. If there is a dog in your street, and you show the dog that you are afraid, it will attack you. So it is with disease. I know this through my own experience. When I used to go about in India to give concerts, I used to think, "What will happen if I have a cold on the day of the concert? If it comes before it does not matter, but if it comes on the day of the concert, it will be terrible". And on the day of the concert the cold came and went into my throat. Until I learned the way of it the cold would always come. Another thought is, "What will become of me? I am well this week, but how shall I be next week? I may be ill. I am well this year, but next year I may be ill. I must take some precautions".

A rich lady whom I knew in Paris once wrote to me saying, "Murshid, I cannot come to your lecture". I went to see her, expecting to find her very ill. She said, "I cannot go out of the house or see anyone; the doctor forbade me". I asked, "Have you any pain?" "No", she answered, "I do not know; but the doctor told me not to go out". I said, "Is your doctor a god, is he a prophet or a messenger of God, that he has brought you a message of sickness?"

Question: Why does illness come upon us?
Answer: Illness comes because we allow it to come. We allow it either consciously or unconsciously, and it stays there where it finds a welcome, sympathy, a bed prepared for it, a doctor to attend to it.

Illness always comes from something bad: bad atmosphere, bad food, bad surroundings.

CHAPTER II

Physical Condition

I ONCE asked a very great Murshid which was best suited for psychic and occult powers, strength or weakness of the body. No doubt there are people who, when they were sick and weak, found themselves able to see things which, being well, they could not see. But this kind of psychic power has no scope for development, because there is no strength. We sometimes think that in order to have psychic powers we should become ethereal, delicate and weak, but physical strength is needed. If it were not so, God would not have manifested Himself as man. If this physical world were not needed it would never have been created. At whatever time of life, a person, whatever his constitution, should spend twenty minutes a day developing his bodily strength. How to develop physical strength is a very extensive subject and it would take a long time to study it.

Physical weakness produces many bad effects and prevents a person, however great his spiritual progress may be, to do what he wishes. There is weakness of the heart, of the body and of the brain. Weakness of the heart makes a person at one moment very happy, at another very sad. Small things make him instantly very joyful or very sad. To make the heart strong one should eat living food: that is fresh food. By drinking alcohol, which is dead matter, the worst matter is put into the heart, and its condition becomes very bad.

Weakness of the body makes a person unable to keep still, to have repose. To make the body strong a balance of activity and sleep is needed, a balance of work and repose, and physical exercices should be done. When you work there must be activity and no slowness, and when you rest there must be slowness and no activity. How many useless words do we speak, how much energy do we waste in useless actions. We should expend our energy on what is worthwhile, and not waste it in useless actions.

Good and righteous actions, good feelings – all the things people teach their children – are necessary. In reality it does not matter to God whether you are good or bad, righteous or unrighteous, but by a pious and good life man keeps himself, his body and brain, in good condition.

Weakness of the brain produces heat. In such a condition, however nice, however good a person may be, he is at one moment very hot-tempered, then cold as snow, then hot again. To worry very much, to repent very much, to sorrow very much, to think that life is a great burden upon us, to make a great thing out of every small event, of every small responsibility – it all weakens the brain. Normal deeds and actions and normal rest strengthen the brain.

Remember that all things pass. If worry comes – it is a passing thing. Keep it away, and if it is already there, help it to go; do not hold on to it. If you are good, the world will not understand you, and the better you become, the less the world will understand you. So you have a choice: to be like the world, or to be good and let the world misunderstand you. Let your joy and your satisfaction be within you.

The Sufis have ways of exciting the heart and making it quiet. They excite it when there is benefit in exciting it; they make it quiet when there is benefit in making it quiet. They let the brain be active, and let it rest.

CHAPTER III

Physical Culture

THERE ARE two tendencies: the tendency towards activity, which has brought man from the Unconscious to the manifestation, and the tendency towards inactivity, which takes him back there. It is a mistake, often made by ascetics, to give all attention to the inactive tendency and to neglect the physical altogether. Our physical body is our means of experiencing this world, and it is necessary to keep it in good order. To do this three things are needful: one is to keep the circulation in good order by physical practices, another is purification, and the third is development of the muscles.

It is very necessary to keep the circulation in good order. There must be balance: so much activity, so much sleep; so much eating, so much activity. If there is too much activity, the circulation cannot be good. There must be a balance of activity and repose, and there must be a balance of eating and work. I do not say, "Eat very little", I say, "Eat much and do much work".

It is a mistake to think out of an idea of delicacy that by eating little we shall become very wonderful. We should not think that we can only eat at certain hours; if it is wanted, we should be able to eat at any hour. We should not think that we cannot eat certain things; we should not think, "This is too heavy for me, I cannot eat it".

We should do whatever movement occurs in the course of our occupations, not thinking, "I shall be tired", but thinking that we are able to do it.

It is necessary to keep our life pure, and the five purifications should be done very carefully: the purification by air, the purification by water, the purification by earth, the purification by fire, and the purification by ether (2). A person is often inclined to neglect that which does not bring an immediate result that he can see with his eyes. But these purifications should be done very exactly. Washing face and hands is not enough: every tube and vein of the body must be kept clean. The postures and positions that are taught, the posture of the *dhikr*, of the *fikr*, of *shaqhl**, have the effect of making the blood flow through certain veins. If this is done there is no disease.

The muscles develop during the whole of life, while the bones do not continue to grow. They become solid, while the muscles develop. Whatever your age may be, you should have ten minutes or a quarter of an hour a day in which to do physical exercises. All physical practices, like standing on the hands or on the head, on both feet or on one foot, taught by the Sufis, are taught for this purpose.

* Spiritual Sufi practices to be done under the guidance of a teacher

CHAPTER IV

Control of the Body

A PERSON'S body usually goes quite out of control. If he wishes to hold up one foot, his foot will not obey him; for one moment it will go up, but after that it will not obey any more. If he goes to the photographer who says, "Steady", he begins to move at once. The word "steady" alone makes him shake, because it reminds him of his helplessness. Without the word "steady" he was all right, but his word brought his weakness before him, and weakness of the body expresses weakness of mind.

In India you will see people standing upon their heads, walking upon their hands, standing on one foot for hours. A person may say, "What a crazy practice! Of what use can this be? They must be mad." No, they have seen the madness of the whole world, and they try another madness. Their "madness" is knowledge. They remain in the same posture for hours and hours. If one of them folds his arms, he remains for hours with his arms folded. If he holds up his hand, he remains holding up his hand for hours. If he closes his eyes, he remains with his eyes closed for hours. If he does not speak, he does not speak for days and days.

When a person has been alone for some time, he begins to move. He moves his foot or his hand, or he drums on the table. He wants to feel that he is alive, and the consciousness realizes that it is alive by its activity, the activity of the body and of the mind. When the activity of the body is made to cease and the activity of the mind is stopped, then the consciousness has a chance of realizing that it is alive without the life of the body and of the mind. When the body is brought under control, and when the mind is controlled so that we can keep it on one thought as long as we like and make it blank as long as we like, then the soul, which is imprisoned in the body, is set free; it is not bound to mind and body. The whole world is open for it.

Then we realize that we are not this limited self, that we are not separate from God, not different, but that we are the same as God, that we have the same existence, the same immortal, unchanging life beyond all the changes of this material world. In this way we can become perfect, as the Father in heaven is perfect.

CHAPTER V

Balance

1

WHEN LOOKING at the world with the eyes of the seer, we shall see that people who are called wise and people who are called foolish are much nearer to each other than they are ordinarily thought to be: because of their unbalanced state their different occupations are much nearer to each other than they usually appear. The person who sees the good in others will see more and more good. The person with a fault-finding tendency will see so many faults that at last even the good seems bad in his eyes; the eyes themselves are bad.

There is much more chance of a fall for a person who is running than for one who is walking. The activity itself brings about a fall; the activity tends to grow more and more, and by this balance is lost. Sometimes a person has no balance in telling the truth. He says, "I tell the truth", and he is regardless of whether it is harmonious with his surroundings, whether people are prepared to receive it. He says, "I tell the truth, and I want to fight with everybody because I tell the truth!" Therefore the lesson of repose is the most important one to be learned.

Philosophy itself – the greatest, the highest thing in the world, the knowledge of God – has often been lost through lack of balance. This is why in the Bible, in the Vedanta, in the Qur'an the truth, told so plainly, is nevertheless told in a veiled manner. If the prophets, the masters had spoken the truth in plain words, the world would have gone to the left instead of to the right. It has been my own experience that philosophy, when plainly expressed, is understood quite differently than when it is expressed in a veiled manner.

When we speak we become inclined to speak more and more, and we become so fond of speaking that we speak regardless of whether anyone wishes to listen. We say what we do not really wish to say; afterwards we think, "Why did

I insult that person? Why did I tell my secret to somebody else?" Sa'adi the great Persian poet, says, "O, intelligent one, of what use is thine intelligence, if afterwards thou repentest?"

Whatever we do, whether good or bad, increases in us more and more. If one day a person thinks about music for five minutes, the next day that thought will continue for half an hour. If one day he thinks about poetry for ten minutes, the next day that thought will continue for an hour. If a person has a little thought of bitterness, unconsciously the thought will grow until his mind is full of bitterness. Every sin comes about in this way. Zarathustra distinguishes three kinds of sin: the sin of thought, the sin of speech and the sin of action. To have a thought of bitterness, the thought of evil, is like doing evil; to speak evil is like doing evil, and when a person commits an evil action, then the evil is concrete.

We have balance of thought, when we can see things not only from our own point of view, with the ideas and the feelings in which we are trained, but from all sides. The one-sided person has no balance.

Suppose you are very patriotic and see everything from the point of view of patriotism, and you go to an ironmonger and demand that he should sell you some things at a certain price. But the ironmonger is a poor man and, even for a patriotic purpose, he cannot sell the things at that price. After all he is an ironmonger and he thinks of his trade; he cannot be expected to see with your patriotic eyes. One person thinks only of patriotism; another says, "God save the trade". A third, who is a musician, says, "They are mad, crazy! Music is the only thing that matters". The poet says, "Poetry is the only thing in the world". Each thinks only of that in which he is active. A pious person exaggerates his piety so much that there is nothing in him but piety, which at last becomes hypocrisy.

One will ask: What is balance, and how can we achieve it? First there is the balance of activity and repose, of sleeping and waking. If a person thinks that by sleeping very much he will become great and so sleeps very much, he will become a monster instead of a man, because the body, which is given in order to experience the world, is not used. If one does not sleep at all, in a few days one will have a nervous break-down. If one fasts very much, certainly one will become very ethereal, one will see into the other world, into the other planes; if one has learned the way of inspiration, inspiration will come. But this body, these senses will become weak, so that one will not be able to experience the world for which they were given. Extremity is undesirable in everything, whether good or evil. The *madzubs* in India are those mystics who go to the extreme of spirituality. Their external self is so much forgotten that they leave the experience of the world altogether.

To sleep and wake, to eat and fast, to be active and to be still, to speak and to be silent – that is to have balance. The Sufi teaches control of the activity of the body, the balance of the body, by pose, posture and movements, which include *namaz*, *wazifa* and *dhikr*. He teaches the balance of the mind by concentration. To sit at home and close the eyes is not concentration. Though the eyes are closed, the thoughts go on. The right object of concentration must be chosen.

By concentration and meditation a person experiences ecstasy, the greatest happiness and bliss. Guidance of the Murshid is needed for this, otherwise the balance will be lost. A disciple was taught a practice by the Prophet Muhammad through which he experienced ecstasy. After some days he came bringing fruit and flowers which he offered to the Prophet, thanking him greatly and saying, "The lesson that you taught me has been of such great value to me; it has brought me such joy. My prayers, which used to last a few minutes, now last all day". The Prophet said, "I am glad that you liked the lesson but, please, from to-day leave it".

By control of the self a person experiences the higher plane in which all beings are one. The guidance of the teacher, the Murshid, is needed; no one can accomplish this by himself. And if anyone could, he would become so much interested in what he experienced there, that he would become absent from this world; absent-mindedness, even lunacy and many other evil consequences would result.

Ecstasy is the greatest happiness, the greatest bliss. A person always thinks, "I am this which I see; this small

amount of flesh and blood, bones and skin is I". By ecstasy the
consciousness is freed from this body, from this confinement;
it experiences its true existence above all sorrow, pain and
trouble. That is the greatest joy. To experience it, and to
keep control of the body and the senses through which we
experience all the life of this world – that is to have balance.
That is the highest state.

2

It is not only strength or nervous energy that enables man
to stand on the earth; besides muscular strength and nervous
energy there is balance. It is balance which enables man to
stand and walk without falling. In the absence of balance man
will not be able to stand or walk in spite of his muscular
strength and nervous energy.

When we think of the mind – is it reasoning, is it far-
reaching imagination which makes man thoughtful? No, it
is balance. There are many whose imagination reaches so
far that they can float in the air for hours together, and
there are others whose reason is so powerful that they can
go round and round and round, and end nowhere. If there is
anything that makes man thoughtful, it is not great reasoning
or far-reaching imagination: it is balance.

Is it the deep feeling of the heart, or is it living in a spiritual
ecstasy that makes a person illuminated? No, neither of these
things. A person can be in ecstasy, see visions, phenomena,
and yet he may not be called spiritual. A person may have
religious ideas, he may live a pious life, have lofty ideals,
and even then he may not be called an illuminated soul. This
shows that in order to make the body as it ought to be, to
keep the mind in order, and to maintain it to that pitch, it is
balance that is necessary.

When we study nature, we find that the growth of plants
and the life of trees all depend upon balance. And when we
think of the cosmos and study the condition of the stars
and planets, the main thing we realize is that the one holds
the other, thereby producing balance. All destruction caused
in nature, such as volcanic eruptions, floods, earthquakes,

comes from lack of balance. As long as nature holds its balance, the abyss in the heart of the earth can remain as it is; people can walk over it without any damage. Storms and famine, all the difficult conditions caused by nature, show that balance is missing; all the different plagues that come to mankind are caused by the lack of that balance which is the security of the health of humanity.

What we call art also comes from a balanced sense of line and colour, and what we call genius in science comes from the balance between perception and conception.

What do we learn from all this? That the secret of the existence of the individual as well as of the whole cosmos lies in one thing, and that is balance. It would not be exaggerated if I said that success and failure are caused by balance and by the lack of it. Progress and lack of progress can be explained as coming from balance and lack of balance.

There is another idea connected with what we call balance. Life is movement, balance is something that controls it, but perfect balance controls movement too much, bringing it to the pitch of inertia. For instance, if the strength of the right hand were equal to the strength of the left hand, if the right leg and the left leg were equal, man would not be able to work or to walk. If each of the two eyes had the same power of sight, a person would not be able to see. In this way balance controls everything, but too much balance destroys it, because too much balance brings stillness. The ordinary balance, which is not complete, brings about success.

Now the main idea is to know how balance is to be obtained and to be retained. In answer to the first question, how balance is to be attained, I would say that balance is naturally there, so there is no need to attain it. The question is only how to maintain balance and not how to attain it. The influence of our way of life in this active world always puts us off balance. No matter what direction we take in life, no matter what our occupation, our business in life, there is always difficulty in maintaining balance.

The Sufis therefore have found a key to it, and that key is to isolate oneself within, and thereby to gain a complete balance within oneself. I have already said that perfect balance means destruction of action, but when we think that from morning till evening our life is nothing but action, we naturally cannot keep that balance. By keeping a few minutes for a process of meditation, of silence, we can touch that complete balance for a moment, and then, naturally, in our active life a balance is maintained. Very often people make the mistake of thinking that by the help of meditation or silence they can bring about success in activity. If it brings about a successful result, it is only because complete balance in meditation makes one capable of maintaining the balance necessary for activity.

Success, failure, progress, standstill, one's state of being, it all comes from the condition that a person is experiencing within himself. A man of common sense will say, "For this reason or for that reason you have met with success or failure". A person who is clairvoyant will say, "Because a spirit or a ghost has said this or that, the conditions must be worse or better". The astrologer will say, "Because this star is in its house or not in its house, you are experiencing such or such conditions". But according to the Sufi idea the condition of life around one depends absolutely on the condition of one's inner self. So what is needed to change the conditions in outer life, or to tune oneself, is to work with one's inner self in order to bring about the necessary balance.

Once balance is lost, it is very difficult to bring it about again. In the first place it is often difficult to keep balance in everyday life, and once it is lost there is little hope of success, of happiness, or of progress. It is just like a clock getting out of order; it cannot work as long as it is not brought into a proper balance again – and the same is true for the condition of the soul. If a person has lost his wealth, has become a spendthrift, has become thoughtless, all these things are signs of his loss of balance. To be too sad, to be too busy, to be too lazy, all these things are signs of lack of balance. All that can be called too much, is always out of balance.

Balance is the security of life, not only in our outward life, but even in maintaining meditation and contemplation. People in the East have always considered balance to be the principal thing to maintain in life. All different exercises they have prescribed, whether in the form of religion or in the form of devotion, whether in the philosophical or in the psychical realm, are all meant to maintain balance.

3

Balance must be maintained between what is physical and what is eternal by being conscious of both. One must not dive so deep into eternity that one does not know what time it is, nor be so immersed in the physical that one is unaware of immortality. As there is night and day, so there is the change of consciousness from the physical to the spiritual, and from the spiritual to the physical. By keeping a balance between these two conditions a person leads a complete life.

Balance is something which is as rarely found among mystics as among others. When we become interested in something, it is our nature to want more and more of it, whether it is spirituality or something material. If we become very spiritual and are not material [enough], we lose the world. If we were not meant to live in this world, we would not have been sent here.

CHAPTER VI

Balance in Solitude

ALL THE prophets, all the great ones have sought solitude. Christ was in solitude for a long time in the caves of the mountains. Moses was in solitude on Mount Sinai. Buddha had to have solitude for a long, long time before he could give his message to the world. The Prophet Muhammad was for a long time in solitude on Mount Hira. Why this solitude?

You may see by the experience of your own life what solitude does. If you try to go out all day to talk with acquaintances and friends, you will find that each day so much is gone from your speech; first because of your exaggeration, for if you speak you begin to exaggerate. Then, if you speak to amuse people, you may say what is not true: you add to what you are saying. Then out of politeness you embellish what you say: you say what you do not mean.

To everyone the wish comes to go home, to be with one or two people whom one likes, or to be alone. When you are silent thoughts are less, feelings are less, and the mind has a rest. When people come – people whom you like or undesirable people – the impression of their words and actions falls upon you and your peace of mind is broken.

A part of your time should be given to solitude. The more you cultivate solitude, the more you will like it, but when very much time is spent in solitude, people become unbalanced. The *madzubs* in India are very great people, often they are *Nabi* or *Qutb**. They attain a very high degree of spirituality, they have control over the elements, but part of their power, as the world demands it of them, is lost to the external world. I think that it is most desirable to be well-balanced: to spend so much time with others, and so much time in solitude.

* high degrees in the Spiritual Hierarchy

CHAPTER VII

Balance in Greatness

ONE WAY of being great is to take all we can. The more we take the greater we become, and all the world will call us great. Another way is to give all we can. In the Bible we read, "If a man takes away your coat give him your cloak as well."

The question arises: How much can we give? The more we give the more will be taken from us. When Shams-e-Tabriz had given his skin, the worms and germs also took his flesh and blood. They did not say, "This man has given his skin, let him have the comfort that he may still have"; they took all.

We who are giving the message of liberty cannot give a message from which the world will run away. If we say, "Give all", the world will run away from such a message. The world will say, "If I give all, I shall have nothing to eat, I shall have nothing with which to cover myself. I must at least have something to eat and I must be covered".

There is a story told of our Murshid Farid Shakr Ganj(3) who was worshipping in the jungle. His way of worship was the ascetic way; he hung himself up in a well by his feet, head down, and in this way he practised. The animals did not come near him, but the birds came and ate his skin and his flesh. He let them eat, because he was practising this moral, but when they came near his eyes he warded them off with his hand and said, "O bird, I would also give thee mine eyes, if thou wouldst bring them first in the presence of the Beloved, that they might have a glimpse. Then thou couldst eat".

We must not give away the soul, the intelligence, the power of distinguishing. If we give these, we are like the tree: everyone may eat its fruits. Our arms were not given to us that we should fold them, but that we should work; our feet were not given to us that we should be motionless, but that we should walk. Our power of distinguishing is given to us that we may distinguish, and by distinguishing we also may learn not to distinguish. We must take a middle course: we must distinguish when to give, when not to give, to whom to give, to whom not to give.

CHAPTER VIII

Life's Mechanism

BY LIFE'S mechanism I mean environment. Life's mechanism has a great deal to do with one's success or failure. This is not unknown to individuals who think about it. Nevertheless not everyone thinks deeply enough to know to what extent it has its effect upon his life. The mystic always teaches that one should treat oneself as a patient and cure oneself of one's weaknesses, but condition is something which is to be thought of also from a practical point of view. This is not only a practical ideal that I give you, but it is supported by the words of Christ. One should not wonder why a man cannot accomplish soon enough what he wishes to accomplish in life, when it is even difficult for the Creator to do so. It is to teach this philosophy and secret that Christ has said, "Thy will be done on earth as it is in heaven". What does it mean? It means: Thy will is easily done in heaven, and I wish people would help so that it should be done as easily on earth.

If one had to swim across the sea, to journey by swimming, it would take great courage, great perseverance and great faith to make that journey, and one would not even know when one would arrive at one's destination. But when a ship is made it becomes convenient to journey; then one does not need to exhaust one's faith and perseverance to such an extent: there is a means enabling one to attain one's object. A mechanism, therefore, is the most necessary thing for the attainment of every object. If one wishes for comfort in the home, one wants a mechanism for it. If one has a business or an industry, a certain amount of organization improves the conditions. In a state a government answers the purpose of keeping order and peace. When it is cold one needs warm clothes, while in summer one needs a different environment.

Now that is easy to understand, but it is most difficult to make the right mechanism. In the first place there are so many who do not have their object clearly in mind. They will go on day after day not knowing what they really want, thinking differently every day about what they want. That deprives them of the mechanism which can only be produced after knowing one's definite object in life. Then again by too much enthusiasm, by too much arranging of the mechanism, one spoils one's affair, defeats one's purpose. And at other times through lack of mechanism one falls short, for the mechanism does not answer the purpose one holds.

No one can ever say that he has sufficient knowledge of this subject, for in treating oneself one must have one's own knowledge, but in arranging a mechanism one has to deal with many different natures. And how much more knowledge of human nature and of life must one possess in order to make the right mechanism! People have often come to me and said, "I have been able to manage myself as I was instructed, and I have been able to keep up my concentrations and meditations as I was told, yet I am not near to reaching my purpose". What is lacking is not practice or self-training, but what is lacking is the mechanism – which is another necessity. For instance if a person says, "I have been able to discipline myself, and now I can meditate fairly well. Shall I now sit at the seaport and meditate that I am in New York? Shall I arrive there?" Or a person with self-discipline will meditate, "All the wealth that is in the bank will come into my house". Will it come? Even if he continued for a thousand years to meditate upon the bank he will not get its wealth.

In this objective world there is a necessity of an objective mechanism in order to produce certain results, and if people going on the spiritual path will not see this side of it, with all their goodness and spirituality they will prove to others their lack of balance, and then the practical man has a reason to laugh at the mystical-minded person.

Therefore the work of the Sufi movement is not only to guide souls towards the higher ideal, but also to keep their eyes open on the way in order that they may see it with open eyes. We shall only give an example to those who have no belief in spiritual ideas by striking a balance throughout our lives. A person may take good care of himself and concentrate upon good health, and yet his environments may cause him illness. That cannot be helped; it is not lack of spirituality in

that person: it is lack of materiality. Does that not show that
we ought to balance the two? There is no great exaltation
when a person has become so spiritual that he levitates in the
air, if he is then no better than a balloon. If he can stand very
well on the earth, then he has accomplished something. It is
not of every man that we can say that he stands on his own
feet. Nothing is worse in this world than to be dependent,
and if spirituality will make a man more dependent – in other
words, at the mercy of other people in the practical things of
life – then spirituality is not to be wished for. Spirituality is
mastery, both materially and spiritually to be able to manage
oneself and to be able to keep the mechanism right.

Now what I have to say to my *mureeds* is that it is very easy
to make your Murshid contented and pleased – even with as
small a number as we are just now – only by knowing that
it is our sacred duty and our spiritual responsibility to make
ourselves as much as we can an example of the teaching that
the Sufi movement wishes to spread. In order to become
examples of this I do not ask you to work wonders, or to
be so good that it would be difficult for you to live in the
world. Only, as an example, you should strike a balance.
You should talk about higher things standing on the earth,
standing upon your feet. It is then that people will listen to
you, and then they will trust the movement.

At this time when a reconstruction of the world is necessary
it is our humble service at this juncture to contribute what is
most needed for this reconstruction. Therefore we should all
consider ourselves soldiers for this cause, discipline ourselves
and make the mechanism in life which is necessary for the
attainment of our object. For the very reason that we are few
we are more responsible for our existence. We must stand by
one another, we must do for one another all we can in every
way, that we may not easily be blown away by the wind.
In order to arrive at that balance and force and stability we
must not only meditate, but we must practise these things in
our everyday life.

CHAPTER IX

Harmony

IT IS harmony which makes beauty; beauty in itself has no meaning. An object which is called beautiful at a certain place and time is not beautiful at another place or at another time. And so it is with thought, speech and action: that which is called beautiful is only so at a certain time and under certain conditions which make it beautiful. So if one can give a true definition of beauty it is harmony. Harmony in a combination of colours, harmony in the drawing of a design or a line is called beauty, and a word, a thought, a feeling, an action that creates harmony is productive of beauty.

The question arises from where comes the tendency to harmony and from where comes a tendency to disharmony. The natural tendency of every soul is towards harmony, and the tendency towards inharmony is an unnatural state of mind or affairs. The very fact that it is not natural makes it void of beauty. The psychology of man is such that he responds both to harmony and inharmony. He cannot help it, because he is naturally made so; mentally and physically he responds to all that comes to him, be it harmonious or inharmonious.

The teaching of Christ, "Resist not evil", is a hint not to respond to inharmony. For instance, a word of kindness, of sympathy, an action of love and affection finds response, but a word of insult, an action of revolt or of hatred creates a response too, and that response creates more inharmony in the world. By giving way to inharmony one allows inharmony to multiply. At this time one sees in the world the greatest unrest and discomfort pervading all over. Where does it come from? It seems to come from ignorance of this fact that inharmony creates inharmony and will multiply inharmony.

A person who is insulted, has the natural tendency to think that the proper way of answering is to insult the other person still more. By this he gets the momentary satisfaction of having given a good answer, but he does not know what he has done by his good answer. He has given response to that power which came from the other and these two powers, being negative and positive, create more inharmony.

"Resist not evil" does not mean: receive evil into yourself. "Resist not evil" only means: do not send back the inharmony that comes to you, just as a person playing tennis would send back the ball with his racket. But at the same time it does not suggest that you should receive the ball with open hands.

The tendency toward harmony may be likened to a rock in the sea: through the wind, through the storm the rock stands in the sea; each wave comes with all its force and yet the rock remains still, it stands, it bears all, letting the waves beat against it.

By fighting inharmony one increases it, by not fighting it one does not give fuel to the fire which would rise and cause destruction. No doubt the wiser you become, the more difficulties you have to face in life, because every kind of inharmony will be directed at you for the very reason that you will not fight it. However, with all these difficulties you must know that you have helped to destroy that inharmony which would otherwise have multiplied. This is not without advantage, for every time you stand against inharmony like the rock in the sea, you increase your strength, although outwardly it may seem a defeat. But the one who is conscious of the increase of his power will never admit that it was a defeat, and as time passes the person against whom he has stood firm will realize that it was he who was defeated.

Life in the world has a constantly jarring effect. The finer one becomes the more trying it will be, and the time comes when, if a person is sincere and good-willing, kind and sympathetic, life becomes worse for him. If he is discouraged by this, he goes under. If he keeps his courage, then he will find in the end that it was not disadvantageous, because his power will some day increase to that stage, to that degree at which his presence, his word, his action will control the thoughts and feelings and activities of all. He will get that heavy rhythm, the rhythm that will make the rhythm of everybody else follow it. This is the attribute which in the East is called the quality of the master-mind.

In order to stand firm against the inharmony that comes from without, one must first practise to stand firm against all that comes from within, from one's own self; for one's own self is more difficult to control than other people, and when one is not able to control oneself and one has failed to do so, it is most difficult to stand firm against the inharmony from without.

Now the question arises: what is it that causes inharmony in oneself? It is weakness; physical weakness or mental weakness, but it is always weakness. Very often, therefore, one finds that it is bodily illness that causes inharmony and inharmonious tendencies. Besides, there are many diseases of the mind which the scientists of to-day have not yet discovered. There are two cases: a person, who is perhaps very ill, is considered insane, and, on the other hand, illnesses of the mind are not taken into account. Persons who suffer from these illnesses are considered sane, and no attention is given to the defects which come from these diseases of the mind. So they never have a chance to notice the disease in themselves, and they are continually finding faults with others. If they are in an office, if they are in a good position, if they are at home, everywhere they cause inharmony. Nobody understands the cause, for to be treated as insane the person must first be recognized as insane.

Health of the mind is so seldom discussed. In fact, as there are more solicitors, more lawyers, more barristers, more courts and more judges, so there are more cases. Consequently prisons increase, and what is the outcome? After a person has gone to prison and has come out of it, he has forgotten where he was; he follows again the same path, for the disease has not been found out. In court a person is judged, but what is the matter with him psychologically, what caused him to do what what he did, is not discovered. There are thousands of people in prison, because something is wrong in their mind. If they were kept in prison for a thousand years they would not improve. Nothing but injustice is awarded to them by putting them in prison. It is just like putting a person in prison because his body is ill.

The cause of every discomfort and of every failure is inharmony. What would be the most useful thing in education at the present time is to give the sense of harmony to children, and to develop it in them. It will not be so difficult as it appears to bring harmony to their notice. What is necessary is to point out to the youths the different aspects of harmony in the different aspects of life's affairs.

The work of the Sufi message, a message of love, harmony and beauty, is to awaken in humanity the consciousness of the true nature of love, harmony and beauty. The training which is given to those who become initiated in the inner cult is to cultivate these three things which are the principal factors in human life.

Question: How should we deal with criminals?
Answer: I would suggest that those who are accused of a certain fault should first – before being brought before the judge – be taken to a jury of psychologists in order to see what is the matter with them. Then, after a person is judged, he should again be taken to this jury.

Question: In what way could they be cured of their fault?
Answer: Instead of being sent to a prison, I think that they should be sent to a special school intended for criminals. (4)

Question: At what age should we begin to develop harmony in a child?
Answer: At the very beginning of a child's growth.

Question: By what means does one develop the sense of harmony in a child?
Answer: I would develop harmony in a child's manner, in his action, in his speech, first believing that he naturally has love for harmony. The inharmony he shows is not in his nature, and it is not difficult to put out what is not in his nature. With my personal experience – not only with children but with persons of all ages and of great variety – I should like to say that never for one moment I think that anything wrong belongs to anyone's nature. I think that it

is only something outside which has got hold of him and which can be taken off some time or other. Therefore I believe that there is hope for everyone, and if a person were accused of being the very worst individual yesterday, to-day I would look at him with hope and think he had gone far from yesterday.

Besides, I consider that to accuse a person of a fault, or to think of a person that he is wrong or inharmonious, creates in him that which you are thinking of. But I must tell you that it is difficult even for me. It is denying something which is before you, and which is not only standing still but active. It is just like saying of a person, who is cross by nature and who is cross with you, "No, he is not cross".

Question: That will change it?

Answer: It is the same with Christian Science. Of course a person who practises Christian Science likes so much to put his science into words that he makes people revolt against him. But as far as the idea goes, it is a most splendid idea. Denying a thing is destroying a thing, and to admit a certain thing is giving it a root. Even saying, "I have an enemy, and he is so bad to me", is really giving that enemy a strength from your own spirit. But when you put it out of your mind thinking, "Well, I have a good wish for everyone, I do not wish to look at anything that is disagreeable", it does not give the other that strength.

Question: Could you please give us a more definite idea about the way in which harmony in reasoning and action should be developed in children?

Answer: There are two faults that a child commits in speaking, not knowing that they are faults. One fault is that it sometimes likes to reason in a way in which a child should not reason: when there is no consideration of manner. In that way it creates inharmony, because it says something in a form in which a child ought not to speak. Secondly the child gets into a habit of saying something which psychologically is not right, which has no good results. This idea is very much considered in the East, but it is an idea that should be considered wherever humanity exists. There are many words which have power behind them, there are many words which cause bad effects. A child in its play does not consider what it says. It simply says things and does not feel backward to reason about somebody's death or illness, which psychologically may be wrong, besides being suggestive. If in play a child says to another child, "I shall cut off your head", another will perhaps take a knife and do it!

Now as to action – a child is full of activity, and in a moment one child is like a hundred children. He is always active, without knowing what to do. So he is destructive, he spoils things. If you stop him from doing one thing, he goes to another, and in order to stop that in him which is destructive and would make him do wrong things, you should awaken the desire for harmony in him.

Besides, for a child to consider others, the comfort of others, the importance of the word of others, are all necessary things. There is a saying in the East: good manner in a child means good luck, bad manner means bad luck. One can easily understand the reason of it: good manners attract love, affection and goodwill from all sides, and that helps the child to be good. Whenever a grown-up person sees a child with good manners, his first impulse is to think, "May he be blessed, may he succeed in life". That goodwill coming from grown-up people is not taken by a child if he disturbs them; he is deprived of that blessing.

It seems to me that the first lesson of religion should teach children to consider another, the friend, the well-beloved people at home. If children are not trained in this, they cannot understand religion when they grow up. I mean religion in the true sense of the word, not a special form of religion. Religion in the world of to-day is the betterment of the soul. A good time will only come when the coming generations will try to strive after the improvement of the soul.(5)

CHAPTER X

Mastery

IF YOU are the master of a great factory, and all the machines work by your will, are you happy, restful and peaceful when you come home? You may be the master of a whole army, or of a whole nation, or of many nations – when you are at home, are you peaceful and happy? The answer is "no", and this shows us that another mastery is needed. A man may be the master of a whole army, but if he has a stroke of paralysis all his mastership is gone and he can do nothing. It shows us that this mastership is passing. Mastery of the self is needed. It is not more difficult to gain than the other mastership, but a man will never give as much will-power and spend as many years to master the self, as he does to master a factory, because the results are much less tangible. A factory means: so many pounds to-morrow. The results of the other mastery are much subtler, much less perceptible.

This mastery is taught to those who are born to be masters, to those who are inclined this way; it is taught by repose and by control of the activity which keeps everything in this universe in movement.

This mastery is difficult to gain in the world. At every step it becomes more difficult, but you cannot run away to the caves in the mountains; you must stay where you are. If you ran away and lived in the caves in the mountains, the attractions of the world would draw you back again. In running away there is no safety; you would try to be content in the mountains, but your eyes would long to see the world again, your taste, which was used to different food, nice food, would not be satisfied with leaves and fruits.

Life in the world, which brings a person into contact with all sorts of undesirable people and affairs, makes spirituality more difficult, but at the same time it affords a test of the will and of spirituality. One may be more spiritual in a cave in the mountains, in silence and in solitude, but there one will never be able to test one's spirituality: whether it is strong enough to bear the contact of a contrary environment. To be ready for all responsibilities and all activities, to have a family, friends and cares, to pay attention to friends, to serve friends and enemies, to say to the worldly person, "I can do all that you do, and more than that", and at the same time remain spiritual – that is the greatest spirituality.

To be without cares or occupations may make spirituality easier, but when the mind is not occupied, very undesirable thoughts and desires come. It is mostly those who have no work and no occupation who lead an undesirable life. Those who have an occupation, or who have a master whom they must please, have less opportunity of following what is not desirable.

Reading the life of Shiva, the Lord of all the Yogis, one will see that after a long, long time of Yoga he was tempted. Likewise Vishvamitre Rishi, after a very long time of Yoga in the wilderness, was tempted by the fair ones from Indra, the decree of whose court has always been to hinder the advancement in spirituality of the rare ones. Though Machandra was a very great Yogi, he also was tempted and taken away from the desert by Mahila, a Hindu queen. Brought to her court he was married and made king, and among the flattering surroundings and luxurious environments he lost all his great powers achieved in the heart of the wilderness. It is easier to gain mastery in the wilderness, away from all temptations, but the mastery you gain in the world is of much more value; for the former is easily thrown down by a slight stroke, while the latter, achieved in the crowd, will last for ever.

The world will always call you away, because whatever a person does he wants to take his friend with him. If he drinks, he will say, "Come and drink with me". If he gambles, he will say, "Come, let us gamble together, and enjoy ourselves". If he goes to the theatre, he will say, "Come with me, let us go to the theatre, we shall enjoy it". So the world, busy with its selfish, unimportant occupations, will surely drag you towards itself.

This can only be overcome by the will. A person must have a will, and he must have confidence in his will. This idea is pictured by Hindu poets as a swimmer swimming against the tide. They picture the world as *Bhavasagara*, the sea of life, and the swimmer in it is the mystic, who attains perfection by swimming against the tide, who in the end arrives on the shore of perfection.

In all our business and occupations we should keep our thought fixed upon God. Then, in all our business, whatever it is, we shall see only God. Our mistake is that we take responsibility for the sake of responsibility, and recognize cares and business as ours – losing the thought of God.

The Sufis, considering their life as a journey toward the spiritual goal, recite in order to awaken their group to this idea, "*Hosh bar dam, nazr bar gadam, khilwat dar anjuman*" which means: let the breath be God-conscious at each swing; watch thy steps and realize who walks, keeping thine eyes lowered that the tempting world may not attract them; realize thyself amid this crowd of the world of variety.

CHAPTER XI

Self-Mastery

THERE ARE three things which we must master during our everyday life and three ways of achieving them.

Consider the power of half an hour concentration compared with the weakness of giving in all day. We must use concentration during the whole day. Then we can control ourselves in all the requirements of the body and of our senses, and the mind must give permission to every demand on their part without being confused in the matter. There is the beginning of the act, there is the act itself, and there is the result of the act. These three stages in the life of self-mastery or self-control bring increasing happiness and satisfaction. There is satisfaction in the thought of granting some particular desire, there is satisfaction during the time it is being granted, and there is satisfaction after it has been granted. When there is no confusion, or depression, or despair, or remorse, or repentance, then the happiness increases. There is no other proper way of directing one's life.

The various practices recommended by the mystics all have the same purpose, whether it be fasting, or stretching out the hands, or clasping the fingers, whatever it be. The mystic holds a posture for a moment, perhaps for half a minute or for fifteen minutes. Nature wants to set in motion; so, when we stop that desire and sit straight and erect, the mind at once sets a grasp on the whole body, because the whole body is now under discipline. When the body obeys the mind – that is discipline. That is why all through life our mind should be in control of all things.

The next thing to consider is the character. We must take care never to do anything that we consider a mistake, or undesirable, or actually foolish when we see another person doing it. If it is something of which we do not approve, something we cannot tolerate if another person does it, we must resist the inclination to do such an undesirable thing ourselves. This resistance to impulses is the way to control ourselves.

A more perfect way of behaving is the religious way. We must realize that the essence of every religion is to regard the God whom we are worshipping as our goal. He whom we seek is nowhere else than in the human heart. Reflecting on this thought, we come to recognize that whatever kind of person we meet – be he foolish or wise, weak or strong, poor or rich, wicked or virtuous – we are in the presence of the Lord, before whom we all bow; for if He is anywhere it is in the human heart, even in the heart of a wicked person.

Say to yourself, "My ideal, my religion, my desire is to please my Lord before whom I bow my head. So when I am before anyone I am before my Lord, my God. I must take care always to be considerate and thoughtful, lest I hurt my God". That is the real religion. If you take care not to hurt a loved one, a friend, but do not mind hurting a servant, or a wicked or foolish person, that will not be real religion. Love will recognize the ideal of love, the divine ideal, in every heart, and will refrain from using words which will make another unhappy: words expressing pride, thoughtless words, sarcastic words, any word which will disturb a person's peace of mind, or hurt his sensibilities.

Therefore, when developing fineness of character, we learn to consider another person's feelings. You may consider yourself very sensitive and so you do not wish that another person should hurt or insult you, or be rough with you. You think, "That person talks too much, he annoys me", or you think, "How badly he dresses". There is a person whom you know to be sensible and understanding, whereas of another person you think that he is not so. But you must forget what you yourself think, and bethink yourself of what another person thinks. It shows a great fineness of character not to give grounds for offence to another person, but it is very difficult to attain this state.

There is no benefit in making your own life so regular and orderly that it offends every other person. It is in the consideration of another's feelings that lies the real religion.

CHAPTER XII

Self-Discipline (6)

WHAT COUNTS most in the path of truth is self-discipline, and without this our studies and practices cannot produce great results. This self-discipline can be distinguished in many different aspects. By studying the lives of the ascetics who lived in mountains and forests, in the wilderness, we learn that those who have really searched after truth have done their utmost to practise self-discipline; without it no soul in the world has ever arrived at the realization of truth. No doubt it frightens people accustomed to the life of the world even to think of self-discipline and, when they think of it, they imagine it in its extreme forms. It is not necessary for us to go to the caves in the mountains, the forest, or the wilderness in order to practise self-discipline. In our everyday life we can do so.

The different ways in which self-discipline is practised are chiefly four. One way is the physical way: the practice of standing in the same position, of sitting in the same posture for a certain time. When one begins to do it one will find that it is not so easy as it appears to be. A person may sit in a same posture or stand in a same position without knowing it, but as soon as he begins to practise it, he finds great difficulty in doing so. When this is achieved then there are different positions of holding hands or legs or eyes or head; these practices develop the power of self-discipline.

Then there is another aspect of self-discipline which is connected with eating and drinking: to avoid certain things in one's everyday food or drink, and to make a practice of being able to live without them, especially things that one feels one cannot live without. So you will see that there are adepts who live on a fruitarian or vegetarian diet without certain things that one is accustomed to drink, and are without these for days or weeks or months.

Another aspect of self-discipline is the habit of thinking and forgetting: to be able to think of the same thing of which one wishes to think, to continue to think of it, to hold that thought – and to practise to forget things, that the thoughts may not get a hold over one's mind. By doing so one becomes the master of one's mind, in the same way trying to check thoughts of agitation, anger, depression, prejudice, hatred. This gives moral discipline.

After one has practised these three aspects of discipline, one is able to arrive at the fourth aspect which is greater; it is greater, because in this way one arrives at spiritual experience. That discipline intends to free one's consciousness from one's environment. This is the experience of the adepts who have worked at it for a long time in order to achieve it. In the old schools of the Sufis, and even to-day, there is the custom that, when they arrive in the room of meditation, or when they go out of it, one of them is there to suggest this idea in words. He says, "Solitude in the crowd", which means: when you are in the midst of the crowd, even then you can hold your tranquillity, your peace; you are not disturbed by the environments. It is this which enables one to live in the midst of the world and yet progress spiritually. It takes away that necessity which compelled many souls in ancient times to go to the wilderness in order to develop spiritually.

It is difficult no doubt, yet at the same time it is simple and in a small way everyone experiences it, but automatically. A person engaged in something that interests him most or that occupies his mind altogether, often is not conscious of his environment. A poet, a writer, a composer, a thinker, when he is entirely absorbed in something he does, is for that moment not conscious of his environment. It happens very often that one is so absorbed in something one is doing or thinking about, that one is not conscious of one's own body or one's own self. Only that which a person is conscious of, that alone, exists, not even his self. This is the stage which is termed by Sufis *fana*. The word *nirvana*, of which so much has been spoken, is simply to be understood in this manner: it is only an experience of consciousness. In other words it is freedom of the soul, it is being able to arrive at a stage where one is not thinking about oneself, where one is not thinking about environments that surround one.

One might ask: is this not dangerous in any way? And many may think so. But I should say: everything is dangerous in this world. If we think of it, there could be a danger every moment: in eating, in drinking, in going out and coming in. It is dangerous to go into the water, but when you can swim, that acts against it. It is even dangerous to walk in the street, but if you can walk and run, that acts against it. It is in being able to meditate and to raise the consciousness above environments that lies the secret of spiritual development. (7)

The practice of self-discipline no doubt will seem difficult in the beginning, but later it becomes easier and, once a person is accustomed to it, it does not take long to experience its beautiful results. It is a complaint of everyone that the person who stands by his side does not listen to him. Every soul complains, "The others do not listen to me". One rises above this complaint, because one begins to realize that "it is myself who does not listen to me". Then the thief is caught, one finds the mischief-maker; it was not the other person, it was the self. As one begins to get power over the self one begins to feel a great mastery, a mastery over one's kingdom. It is a feeling of kingship. Then, naturally, one begins to experience in life this phenomenon that little by little all things begin to be easy.

CHAPTER XIII

A Question about Fasting

Question: Do you advocate a long fast from 30 till 90 days in order to purify the body for spiritual attainment?
Answer: I am not an advocate of asceticism, but at the same time I see the good work that many ascetics have done and I do not wish to depreciate it.

Coming to the question of fasting, I think that fasting is one of the ways by which the denseness of the body can be diminished. And when one knows the right way of fasting, when one is under the direction of someone who really knows when a person should fast, and why and how he should do so, and how he could gain the benefit of his fasting, then great benefit can be obtained by it. Surgeons keep a person without food for so many hours or days knowing that it will help them to heal quicker. In the same way spiritual teachers may prescribe a fast to their pupils: sometimes being without cereals, sometimes without eating meat, sometimes without bread, sometimes living on milk, on fruits, and sometimes, for a certain limit of time, without anything. They see the capacity of the pupil: what he can endure and how he can be benefited by a particular fast.

But, to tell the truth, I am the last person to prescribe fasting. I only give some advice if persons themselves wish to fast, for I know a story of a disciple who went to a teacher and was told, "In order to begin the practices you must start with a three days' fast". One day he felt so hungry that he ran away from the city in order never to see the teacher again!

There is always a meaning if a teacher prescribes a fast; he has a reason for it. There is an amusing story of a great Sufi who lived in Bagdad. There are many stories of his wonderful achievements. He had told a young pupil of his to live on a vegetarian diet. The mother of this young man, having heard that since the boy went to the teacher he had grown pale and thin, came to give the teacher a little talking to. He was at table when she came and there was a chicken dish on the table. So the mother said, "You are teaching your pupils to live on a vegetarian diet, and you yourself are enjoying chicken!" The teacher opened the dish and the chicken flew away. The teacher said, "The day your son can do this too, he can also eat chicken"!

CHAPTER XIV

Self-Control

1

SELF-CONTROL is the most necessary thing to be learned; a person may have great spirituality, illumination and piety, but in the absence of self-control this is nothing. Self-control also is the only way of happiness and peace. Often we hear or read that persons of great repute in the world for their spirituality and mysticism do something that astonishes us very much, or make a quite childish mistake. It is want of self-control that makes them commit a mistake, against which they themselves have spoken and written many times.

The spiritual student learns self-control in three ways: by postures, by *tasawwur* -visualization- which is concentration, and by *amal*, which is the highest practice. After this there is *samadhi*, which is meditation and which is called by the dervishes *masti*; it means illumination, to halt in illumination. The difference between meditation and concentration is that concentration is done on a form, on an object, and meditation without form or object.

Repose and control of the body are taught by postures and positions. When a person has been still for some time, he will begin to move. There is no need for him to move but he moves his foot or his arm, or he drums on the table with his fingers, or he chews his lips, or he blinks his eyes. The activity increases more and more until at last a person jumps in his sleep; when the first sleep comes, he starts and jumps. To control the activity of the body, to sit quiet in the postures and positions is the first lesson.

However, there must not be stillness only. If a person has kept his hands still for a long time and then wishes to play the piano, he will not be able to. He must make his fingers active enough to be able to play the piano well. As much stillness there is, so much activity there must be.

Sleep and do not sleep; eat and do not eat; walk and do not walk; speak and do not speak. This means: if you sleep every night, sometimes do not sleep; if you eat every day, one day in seven do not eat; or if you eat all month long, one or two days in the month do not eat. This gives a mastery that you cannot gain by renunciation alone. It does not mean that you should starve. The body must be given good food, fresh food, and all its needs must be satisfied. This is better than that it should always long for what it sees before it. You must give the body what it needs, but you must control its needs, and not be controlled by them.

After this comes control of the thoughts, which is the second step, control of the body coming first. Thousands of people have found that they can sit in the postures for hours, but cannot keep their mind still. This has to be learned by degrees. A person cannot control his mind by willing to think of nothing; that will never be possible. First let the mind hold whatever thought interests it, any thought of love, of goodwill – whatever interests it. Check its tendency to jump from one thing to another. When you catch the mind jumping from one thing to another, bring it back and hold it. You must say: I am greater than my mind, my will is greater than my mind, and I will make my mind obey my will.

Then comes mastery of the feelings, of the heart. There must be no feeling of revenge, of unkindness, of bitterness against anyone in the heart. When such a feeling comes, one must say: this is rust coming into my heart. When all such feelings are cleared off the heart, it becomes like a mirror. A mirror without rust reflects all that is before it; then everything divine is reflected in the heart, then all inspirations, intuitions, impressions come, and what we call clairvoyance. There is no need to go after such things; they come of themselves.

After this there is only one thing more to be done: to keep from the soul all the thoughts that come from others and all the thoughts and feelings that arise within the self. Keep away even all feelings of love and goodwill whilst you are in this meditation; then, as a matter of course, come ecstasy, rapture, and peace.

2

Many people ask: How can we control our thoughts? What can we do, if our thoughts do not obey us, if our mind does not obey us, if our body does not obey us? How can we like a thing, if we dislike it, or dislike it, if we do like it? It seems to us impossible! To a person who has gone beyond likes and dislikes this sounds like a child's question, because he does not know of opposites.

The way to gain self-control is first of all to do the reverse of what your inclination would lead you to do. If you feel inclined to eat, sometimes do not eat, control the hunger. If you feel inclined to drink, do not drink, control the thirst. If you are inclined to sleep, do not sleep; at another time, when you are not inclined to sleep, sleep. There are a thousand inclinations, each sense has its inclinations. Do not give way to these inclinations, rule them, that they may not govern you. This is called by the Yogis *hatha yoga*, and the Sufis call it *nafskushi*.

I have seen the Nizam of Hyderabad stand for seven or eight hours, if he wished to stand, although he was a king and had all things ready in his house. If he wished not to sleep, he did not sleep for seven, eight, nine and ten days. By this he became such a master that he mastered the secret of curing snake bites. In India there are many snakes; while the Nizam lived he advertised all over India, and if anyone was bitten by a snake, people wired to him. When the Nizam said, "He is well", the person was healed.

When one has learned to control one's inclinations, the second lesson is to govern the inclination in the act. Do not eat whilst you are eating, do not drink whilst you are drinking. When a person has learned this, he is master of the solitude and the crowd. He does not need solitude to be spiritual; he is spiritual in the crowd too.

3

Question: How to gain self-control?
Answer: By doing the reverse of that which one's inclination
would lead one to do. If you are inclined to eat, do not eat;
if you are inclined to drink, do not drink; if you are inclined
to be active, be still; if you are inclined to be still, be active; if
you are inclined to speak, be silent. Eating is not a sin, but if
you sometimes try how long you could do without eating, it
would be good. Drinking is not a sin, but if you sometimes try
how long you could do without drinking, it would be good.
Sleeping is not a sin, but if you sometimes try how long you
could do without sleeping, it would be good.

Faqirs take the opposite way. They like what they dislike.
That is the reason why you may read that Mahadeva, Shiva,
drank poison and wore skulls and bones around his neck,
because no one would like to be in a grave among the dead.
A snake is always pictured around his neck; by this the conceit,
the ego, the *nafs*, is crushed. To every little man, to every boy
faqirs say "father", thinking, "He is the father and I am the
son". To every little woman they say "mother", thinking,
"She is much greater than I am". To all they say, "I am your
servant, I am your humble servant, your obedient servant".

Develop the will by slowness of movement, by slowness of
speech, by slowness and control of thought, for activity tends
to make us move faster and faster.

No thought or feeling should arise without our will. When
we have gained mastery over the self, we have mastery over all
things. The saints and sages have commanded a withered tree
to become green. How was it done? By their mastery over the
self.

4

The self-controlled ones are the only possessors of divine
wisdom; those who have not mastered this in life are imperfect. Though they may have all riches, comfort and power,
yet all this is as dross when the self is not under control. This

can be learned by noticing how many virtuous people are at times drawn into sin, and how foolishly the wise sometimes act. Dominant natures often become enslaved, and even the healthy become diseased through lack of self-control.

Self-control is an attribute which distinguishes man from the animal; both have their appetites and passions, but it is man alone who can control them. It is therefore not surprising if Sufis are sometimes seen submitting themselves to most awkward and uncomfortable practices. At first sight it may appear strange, yet on closer observation it becomes obvious that they prescribe this for themselves in order to gain self-control, which alone gives the assurance of a dependable and lasting happiness.

Self-control is mainly achieved by abstinence, which acts against the constant demands of the mind, the senses and the body. The control over each plane is won gradually by special practices of pose, posture and movement, adapted to this purpose. Every motion and action, even each organ and muscle of the body must work under the control of the will. All the powers of the body, whether in absorption or rejection, should be mastered by self-control. For both absorption and rejection control of the breath is necessary, and by the same power all things are controlled.

Control of the mind consists of control of imaginations, thoughts, emotions and feelings. Emotions are the outcome of thoughts and feelings, the vibrations of which are always ringing in the sphere of the astral plane. The scattered clouds in the sky join and separate, at every moment forming various distinct pictures. In like manner the will- as a magnet – gathers these vibrations in the astral sphere from different directions, forming them accidentally or intentionally into a picture which is either a thought, an imagination, an emotion or a feeling. Just as clouds do not remain unscattered in the sky, so the pictures formed in the astral world are liable quickly to be dispersed, except when the sky is overcast, or when the atmosphere is overwhelmed with depression or joy.

Vibrations of the same element will group themselves together, for they are naturally attracted to each other. Pictures are often impressed upon the mind and are reflected

from the mental plane upon the astral. The vibrations ringing
through the astral sphere may be called, in other words, the
atoms of the mental plane which are singly or collectively
impressed by the names and forms of the external spheres.

The same vibrations appear as different names, forms,
things and beings in the dream plane. They seem much
more real there when the senses are at rest, but in the waking
state they become mere imaginations. What is considered as
imagination in the waking state becomes a world of reality
in the dream state. All the things and all the beings seen in
the dream are a world within ourselves, reflected from the
external world and produced by the power of our will.

So the Judgement Day in reality is not the resurrection
of the whole creation, but of the world produced in each
individual for his trial. The power of the will gathers and
controls the desired vibrations through concentration, and
it is when control is lacking that, instead of the wished
for imaginations, various other pictures are formed, either
agreeable or disagreeable – whatever the vibrations may
happen to form through their contact with each other. In other
words, through self-control man governs his fate, otherwise
he is governed by it.

Lack of will-power causes involuntary happiness and sadness. The disturbing thoughts which crowd into the mind
during concentration can only be dispersed by the power
of the will; otherwise the mind will become occupied with
agreeable or disagreeable impressions from the external world
against our desire.

The way of strengthening the will is knowing how
to group and to scatter mental vibrations at will. This
can only be done by forming a mental picture of the
grouped vibrations, making every possible effort to hold
this picture steady, keeping the mental plane so occupied
with its reflection that no impression from the external
world can enter. Only those who by will-power can scatter
the mental vibrations find the way towards the Universal
Spirit, and to them the divine light is disclosed which is
hidden behind the mind.(8) This light can be found in every
creature.

Uncontrolled imaginations form the veil covering the divine light and cause darkness which produces delusion. When the will is able to scatter the clouds and allows the inner light to spread forth its rays, then there is still one more step to be taken. That is the absorption in the light: to become so lost in it that the false ego may become unconscious of itself, which in other words may be called the state of Eternal Consciousness.

The astral plane, the seat of which is the heart, which is situated in the midst of the body and the soul, can only be controlled by a strong love or devotion. Just as the horse is controlled by the will of the driver, in the same way a man whose will controls both driver and horse can hold the rein over his action, speech, thought and feeling. The mind is prone to different temptations and, uncontrolled, it wanders about like a wild horse in a jungle. The will produces an object of love and directs the heart to follow the right path, the path of love, along which one journeys resisting all temptations met with on the way.

The Sufi idealizes the pangs of love by which the heart is warmed. The fire of love melts the heart, no matter how cold and hard it may be; when once it is warmed it can be moulded in whichever way desired. Ice, the frozen condition of water, cannot reproduce the reflections of which it is capable in its melted state.

The resisting of temptations during the period of love helps to expand love, till the object of worship becomes the whole universe. Then self-control could be gained by even resisting the idea of the lover and the beloved. In other words, "I and you" finally becomes love in its pure essence.

The Control of the Spirit

A complete realization of the spiritual plane is difficult for everybody, and only an earnest mureed arrives at this stage through perseverance in the control of breath under the guidance of a Murshid, when all the senses can be opened or closed at will. The vision he sees and the phenomena he experiences there are unknown to the average man. This state is incredible to those who have received a worldly knowledge, but have not followed the mystic way.

Only he can control the self, making it rise above the physical plane, who loses himself in the phenomenon of the abstract plane. The mureed, holding this phenomenon in his meditation, becomes so absorbed in it that in the end neither he nor the phenomenon remain, but only the consciousness of being.

The Control of the Consciousness

This is the control which liberates the consciousness from its attachment to the lower planes. That attachment keeps the consciousness deluded and confined to the earth; by self-control it can be liberated. Self-consciousness grows through lack of self-control. Man attaches such importance to his life that his slightest joy or sorrow becomes of world-wide importance to him, and thus he becomes a prey to every form of weakness; for it is a natural law that a single atom of depression gathers clouds of gloom, and a slight pain reflected in the consciousness grows into a mountain.

Self-control is the way by which the Sufi makes the consciousness free from all worldly reflections, hereby attaining the blankness out of which the whole world was manifested. This perfection can only be attained by absolute self-control.

CHAPTER XV

Physical Control

LIFE MAY be recognized in two aspects: the known and the unknown. What is generally called life is its known aspect as its other aspect is unknown to many. The unknown aspect may be called the immortal, the eternal life, and the known aspect may be called mortal life. What we generally know of life is its mortal part; the experience we have through our physical being gives us the evidence of life, and therefore the life we know is the mortal life. The immortal life exists, but we do not know it; it is our knowledge which is absent, not the immortal life.

In this life known to us everything we have, whether an object, a living being, a thought, a condition, a deed, or an experience – all break and die away. Each of these things has birth and death; sooner or later what is composed must be decomposed, and what is visible now will disappear.

This shows that there is a struggle between what we call life and the life which is behind it. In Sufi terms we call these two aspects of life *qadha* (Kaza) and *qadr* (Kadr): *qadha* the unlimited aspect of life, *qadr* the limited aspect. *Qadr* draws upon the life of *qadha* for its existence, and *qadha* wakes with its mouth open to swallow what comes into it. Therefore the thinkers and the wise men, those who are called mystics or Sufis, have discovered the science of how to withhold the experience of life – which alone gives us the evidence of life – from the mouth of *qadha*, the ever assimilating aspect of life. If we do not know how to withhold it, it will fall into the mouth of *qadha*; for *qadha* is always waiting with open mouth. As an illness awaits the moment when a person is lacking in energy, so in all different forms *qadha* is waiting to assimilate all that comes to it, and which then is merged in it.

The question arises: how can we withhold, how can we keep something from falling into the mouth of *qadha*? And the answer is: by controlling our body and our mind. Much is known about physical culture, but what is known is what can be obtained by action, by gymnastics, by movements. Very little is known about what can be obtained by repose, by poise and posture.

I have seen in the East a man lifting a heavy stone on one finger. One might think: how can a man's little finger – these fine bones – stand such a heavy weight? It is the power of will alone which sustains the heavy stone, the finger is only an excuse. I have seen myself those who experiment in the field of spirit and matter jumping into a raging fire and coming out safely, cutting the muscles of their body and healing them instantly. It is not a story that mystics know how to levitate; the demonstration of this has been seen by thousands of people in India. I do not mean to say that this is something worth learning or following, I only wish to tell you what can be accomplished by the power of will. And in order to obtain the reign of will over the physical body the first thing necessary is physical control.

Among the different kinds of physical culture known to the modern world there is nothing that teaches the method, the way, the secret of sustaining an action. For instance, to be able to sit in the same posture without moving, to be able to look at the same spot without moving the eyes, to be able to listen to something without being disturbed by something else, to be able to experience hardness, softness, heat, or cold, keeping even vibrations, or to be able to retain the taste of salt, sweet and sour. Since all these experiences come and go, man has no control over his means of pleasure or joy. He cannot enjoy any experience through any sense as long as he wishes to enjoy it. So he depends upon all outer things, and has no control sustaining the experience he has. If there is any way of sustaining experience, it is through control.

There is another side to this question. Being unconsciously aware that every experience which is pleasing and joyous will soon pass away, man is over-anxious and, instead of trying to retain the experience, he hurries it and loses it; so for instance his habit of eating hastily, or of laughing before the mirthful sentence is finished. He is over-anxious that his joy will pass away, but so his joy is finished even before the mirthful sentence ends. In every experience man loses the power to sustain it because of his anxiety about losing the pleasure it gives.

The great joy of watching a tragedy in the theatre lies in experiencing it to its fullness, but some people are so thrilled that they have already shed their tears in the beginning, and then nothing is left for afterwards. Once the zenith is reached, there is no more experience to be had and so, instead of keeping it away from the mouth of eternal life, man throws every experience he makes, without knowing the secret of it, into the life behind.

The mystics, therefore, by sitting in different postures and by standing in different poses, have gained control over their muscles and nervous system, and this has an effect on the mind. A person who lacks control over his nervous and muscular systems has no control over his mind; he eventually loses it. But by having control over one's muscular and nervous systems one gets control over the mind also.

The means by which life draws its power is breath. With every breath one draws in, one draws life and power and intelligence from the unseen and unknown life. And when one knows the secret of posture, and draws from the unseen world energy and power and inspiration, one gets the power of sustaining one's thought, one's word, one's experience, one's pleasure, one's joy. Thought-power is necessary with both posture and breath in order to gain physical control.

One must rise above one's likes and dislikes, for they cause much weakness in life. When one says, "I cannot stand this, I cannot eat this, I cannot drink this, I cannot bear this, I cannot tolerate, I cannot endure" – all those things show man's weakness. The greater the will-power the more man is able to stand all that comes along. It does not mean that one has no choice; one can have one's choice, but when one gives in to one's choice then life becomes difficult. There is a false ego in man, called *nafs* by the Sufis, and this ego feeds on weakness. This ego feels vain when one says, "I cannot bear it, I do not like it, I do not look at it". All this feeds the ego and its vanity. It then thinks, "I am better than others", and thereby this ego becomes strong, and so man's weakness becomes strong. But the one who has discrimination, distinction, choice, while at the same time having these all under his control, the one who enjoys sweet but can drink a bowl of something bitter, – that person has reached mastery.

Someone asked a wise man what was the cause of every tragedy in life. The wise man answered, "Limitation; all miseries come from this one thing, limitation". Therefore the mystics have tried by exercises, by practices, by studies to overcome limitation as much as possible. There is no worse enemy of man than helplessness. When a person feels, "I am helpless, I cannot help it", it is the end of his joy and happiness.

Impulses also weaken a person, when he helplessly gives in to them. For instance, when he has an impulse to go to the park, instead of waiting till it is the right time to go to the park, he quickly puts on his hat and goes along. He follows his impulse immediately and loses power over himself. The one who subordinates his impulses, controlling them, utilizing them for the best purpose, attains mastery.

Besides, indulgence into every comfort, seeking convenience, always looking for the path of least resistance, also brings weakness. However small the work may be, if a person takes it seriously and finishes it with patience, he gains much power over himself. Patience is the principal thing in life, although patience is as bitter, as hard, as unbearable as death. Sometimes one prefers death to patience.

It is a great difficulty that the people in this land of America are losing this quality of patience more and more every day, because Providence has blessed them so much*. They have conveniences, they have comforts, they are the spoilt children of Providence, and when it comes to having patience, it is very hard for them. Individuals have to practise this spirit, for we do not know what may come to follow. We live in this world of uncertainty, and we do not know in what condition we may be placed to-morrow; if we have no strength of resistance we may easily break down. Therefore it is most necessary for the human race to develop patience in all conditions of life, in all walks of life, in all positions

---

*This lecture took place in San Francisco, on April 5th, 1926.

in life. Whether we are rich or poor, high or low, this is the one quality that must be developed. It is patience that gives endurance, it is patience that is all-powerful, and by lack of patience one loses so much. Very often the answer to one's prayer is within one's reach, the hand of Providence not very far off – but one has lost one's patience and so lost the opportunity.

All such things as mastery and patience are acquired by physical culture. Physical control can build a foundation for character and personality, a foundation to be built in order to bring about spiritual attainment.

Question: Would you, please, explain something more about posture?

Answer: The fantasy of the whole creation lies in the direction of every movement; it is in accordance with this direction that its fantasy takes form. Where do all the opposites such as sun and moon, man and woman, pain and joy, negative and positive, come from? Since the source is one and the goal is one, why such differences? They belong to the direction; the secret of every difference is direction. It is an activity, an energy working in a certain direction which makes a certain form. So it makes a difference whether you sit this way or that way, whether you sleep on the right side or on the left; whether you stand on your feet or on your head makes a difference.

Mystics, therefore, have practised for many, many years, and have found out different postures of sitting while doing certain breathing exercises. They have made a great science out of this. There is a warrior's posture, an artist's posture, a thinker's posture, an aristocratic posture, a lover's posture, a healer's posture: different postures in order to attain different objects. By those postures it becomes easy for man to attain these objects, for then he has arrived at the science of direction. Posture does not denote anything but direction.

CHAPTER XVI

Questions about Vaccination and Inoculation

Question: Will you, please, tell us if vaccination is desirable?
Answer: All things are desirable if properly used, and all are undesirable if abused. In fact, the idea of vaccination comes from the same theory which is taught by Shiva – or Mahadeva – as *Hatha Yoga*.

It is said of Mahadeva that he used to drink poison, and by drinking it he got over the effect of poison. Mahadeva was the most venturous among the ascetics; one can see this by his wearing a serpent around his neck – now, would you like to do that? If one can be such friends with a serpent as to keep it round one's neck, one can no doubt sit comfortably in the presence of someone one does not like. That hatred, prejudice and nervousness, felt in the presence of someone one does not like, will not arise if one can wear a serpent around one's neck, if one can take a bowl of bitter poison and drink it – which is against nature. Once the soul has fought its battle with all that makes it fear and tremble, shrink back and run away, then that soul has conquered life. It has become the master of life, it has attained its kingdom.

No doubt the methods which Mahadeva adopted are extreme methods. No one could recommend them to his pupils and be thought sane in this modern world!

Vaccination is related to fear; fear of germs which might come and enter our body: we might breathe them in or take them in with our water or food. Vaccination is partaking of this poison which we fear and which might come to us some day in some form. Such a method may meet with a great deal of opposition and prejudice, but there is a very strong reason for the principle behind it. This brings us to a higher realization and to a great conception of life. It makes us think that even that which we call death, if it were put into a cup and given us to drink, would bring us to life.

Question: Would you, please, tell us something more of the Shiva aspect in life?

Answer: This is a very vast subject and difficult to explain in two words. However, the aspect of destruction can be easily understood by something we see in science, by the method of inoculation. By putting that destructive element one fears in one's body one makes the body disease-proof. That particular disease is no longer a disease but the nature of that person. This is the method of the mystic, it is destruction from a spiritual point of view.

Death is death as long as man is unacquainted with it. When man eats it up, then he has eaten death, and death cannot eat him; then he is master of death. This is the mystery of the message of Jesus Christ who, from beginning to end, spoke of eternal life. And the mystery of eternal life is that once a person has eaten death, he has eternal life.

In little things one person says, "I do not like to touch vinegar, it harms my health"; another says, "I cannot bear eating cream, I cannot digest it"; yet another says, "I cannot stand sugar in my tea, I do not like it". For the latter sugar is poison. If he took poison and made it part of his nature, the same poison would become sugar. But by making things foreign to his nature a man makes his nature exclusive, and by becoming exclusive he subjects himself to them in a way. There comes a time when they rule him, a situation in which he is in their power may occur. A person may say for instance, "Quinine is too bitter, I cannot stand it". But when he is in a fever the doctor says that he must take it. The patient dreads it, but his condition forces him to take it.

It is for this reason that the way of Shiva was always to work against his weaknesses. He counted these tendencies as weaknesses, he did not count them as his nature. What is nature? All is in our nature. But what we cannot stand we make foreign to our nature when we separate it, and a time may come when we become so weak that we cannot help becoming subjected to our weaknesses. There are snake charmers who, by making snakes bite them a little at a time,

have gradually become inured to the poison. They catch the
snake in their hand, and if it bites it does not hurt them. It
was the same with Shiva who is pictured with a cobra around
his neck. Out of death he had made a necklace. There was no
more death for him.

One can go to extremes in this way, but still it is a law
which should be studied and known. The only mystery it
teaches is not to consider anything foreign to our nature: if it
was not in us we would not know about it. That is the way to
overcome all the destruction which is the source of fear, pain
and disappointment.

Question: If nothing is poison, does that mean that there is no
good and bad, no moral?
Answer: No, it does not mean that. Good is good and bad is
bad. But one can rise above badness or one can be submitted
to badness. One can become weak before evil or become
strong. The idea is to become strong before evil instead of
weak.

Question: How to understand the sentence from the Gayan*:
The only thing that is made through life is one's own nature?
Answer: One makes one's nature by one's likes and dislikes,
by one's favour and disfavour. When a person has said that
he does not like a certain edible thing, he has built a nature
in himself. If afterwards he would eat such a thing it would
disagree with his nature. It is not because it was not meant
to agree with him, but because he has built up the idea that
it would not agree. It is the same when one says, "I cannot
endure it, I cannot stand it".

One makes one's nature either agreeable or disagreeable.
Either one makes one's nature so hard as a rock which will
not allow anything to enter; or one makes one's nature so
pliable as water, through which all boats and ships can pass
without hurting it. Water gives way for all to pass, and it is
there just the same.

* A book of aphorisms, poems and prayers by Hazrat Inayat Khan.

Man, by his thoughts, makes his nature. When he says, "I cannot agree with this", he will not agree with it; he has made a wall before himself. When he says, "I cannot bear that person", once he has said it, he has created something in himself which makes him sick when that person comes to him. That person becomes his master. The man wants to run away from him; wherever that person comes, he makes him ill. It is not because that person brings him illness: the man has brought that illness upon himself.

CHAPTER XVII

Breath (9)

1 Questions about Breathing

Question: Should we observe a certain form of breathing?
Answer: There are five different things to consider in connection with breath: the far reach of breath, the depth of breath, the volume of breath, the centralizing of breath, and the rhythm of breathing. If the breath is not far-reaching it causes weakness; if it is not deep enough it is a cause of weakness too; if it is not centralized it creates uncertainty in life; if it has no proper rhythm it causes lack of balance; if it has no volume it takes away vitality. Therefore breath must be trained in these five different ways: it must be rhythmic, centralized, deepened, it must reach far, and its volume must be spreading.

Breath must have the quality of covering a large ground. The atmosphere of one person is felt, of another person it is not felt. A person may have so much atmosphere that it may fill a large horizon; it is the breath which gives that atmosphere. Besides, in the atmosphere of some person you may feel uneasy, restless, out of rhythm, because he has no rhythm in his breath, his breathing is not right.(10)

Question: How is rhythmic breathing acquired?
Answer: This is a science in itself. We are far away from a natural life. We have to run after tram-cars and taxi-cabs, we have to catch our trains; a thousand things like these disturb our rhythm. Do you think that in the East a sage, or an adept who practises meditation will run after a tram-car and spoil his rhythm? All these things disturb the rhythm of breathing. What we think natural is not natural; from morning to evening our life has no rhythm.

Question: Do you recognize a system which includes positive and negative breathing?
Answer: Yes, it is just like the two wires in the electric lamp a negative and a positive one; if one wire is absent there will be no light. In order to have light there must be two currents, and these two currents make positive and negative energy. They have a relation with the rising and setting of the sun: the current of the breath changes. And if it does not change in accordance with the time, if it is not in consonance with the rising and setting of the sun, then either a person is ill, or unbalanced; something is wrong with him.

Question: What means centralizing of breath?
Answer: In music we have many notes, but we call one note the key-note. Really speaking, every note can be a key-note, and there must be a central point for everything. For a plant it is the root which is the centre, and for the breath there is a seat in the body. If the breath is properly seated there, it is just like a plant which is well-rooted into the ground and will grow nicely and bear fruit. If the plant is not rooted well there is always a chance of its being destroyed. So in the life of man, if the breath is not centralized in its centre, in the seat where it ought to be, then it is doubtful whether the person will live long and be happy.

In the East sages know for six months or a year before their death that their time has come, and they know it from this one secret: they find that their breath no longer centralizes in the place where it ought to centralize. My spiritual teacher told his family a year beforehand that he was to leave the earth. Sages know this, because they practise every day. Therefore breath for them is an object they feel, see and know.

Not every person can feel whether he is breathing from the left or the right nostril, but those who practise know it instantly. There are times when one breathes through one nostril, and there are times when one breathes through two nostrils. Breathing through the two nostrils is a passing moment, and then the breath goes from one nostril to the other; it is a critical moment.

Question: Does the position of the body during sleep control the breath?
Answer: Yes, this also concerns posture. Whichever side you lean or lie upon, every direction towards which you strike with force, all bear upon the rhythm and the direction of the breath. But the subject of breath is a deep one, and it is not only related with health but with the affairs in life.(11)

Question: Can everyone have the power of far-reaching breath?
Answer: A certain condition is necessary for far-reaching breath; it is just like the wireless. Far-reaching breath is the most wonderful thing there is. As far as your breath reaches, so wide is your kingdom.

Question: Do you mean by breath: as far as one can blow?
Answer: What we call breath is not all the breath that is there. For instance, what we call voice is only the voice that reaches so far and is not heard any farther. At the same time, on the wireless it travels farther. This shows us that the voice which reaches as far as it is audible to the ears, is limited; in reality it reaches far beyond. And so the breath is far-reaching; if only we experimented with it we would be surprised. Others cannot readily believe it, it should be experienced by ourselves, and we should keep quiet about it. To speak about it will create difficulties. Many disbelieve, or have wrongly experimented; therefore mystics have kept this for the initiated. That is why initiation is given.

2 The Mystery of Breath

Breath seems to be the sign of the beginning and the end of life. With the first breath that is drawn the body is said to be alive, and when the breath departs, the body is spoken of as dead. It is for this reason that the Yogis have called breath *prana*, meaning the very life. Besides this, all slight changes that take place in man's body come from an alteration in the mechanism of breath. That is why physicians in all ages have observed the signs of a person's condition in different illnesses from the beat of his pulse, which is caused by the breath.

Mental changes are also caused by breath. For instance, there are people with whom it is better not to talk when they first rise from sleep; they are excitable and irritable at that time. Again there are others who listen better at that moment than at any other time. Some people coming home from their work or their office in the evening are irritable and difficult; if one lets them rest for an hour or so they gradually change. All this shows that the condition of the breath changes the mental condition of that moment. Immediately after concentration upon work the rhythm of the breath is very rapid and exercises its influence on the mind. After a while this rhythm changes and becomes normal; so the condition of the mind changes also. In sleep some people work up the rhythm of breath and the condition of mind becomes unsettled and disturbed, but as a rule sleep helps the breath to be normal and its influence produces tranquillity of mind.

It can be seen how various emotions, passions and sentiments change the rhythm of breath. Sometimes breath goes out of man's control in emotions such as anger, passion or fear; he then has no control over his words or actions. When man loses control over himself, the first thing he loses is control over breath.

It is the basis of this philosophy that by gaining control of breath man can gain control over himself; the one who controls his breath is the ruler over his mind and body. How few really know how to breathe aright and what are the methods of keeping the channels of the breath clear and in order ! Breath, uncontrolled, is dangerous.

In mystical terms the two different directions of the breath have been called by different names, and have been considered to be like the sun and the moon, representing the positive and negative aspects of the power and influence of breath. How few really know how many times in the day and night the breath changes its direction, and how it works through different parts of mind and body producing different effects and results. How often mans's ignorance of the science of breath makes him act or think or speak against its influence

– which is like swimming against the tide. We often notice in life that at one time success is achieved by the least little effort, and at another the greatest effort produces nothing but failure. Shiva, the great Lord of the Yogis, said, "He who has the knowledge of breath knows the secret of the whole universe".

What we generally know as breath is that little inhaling and exhaling which we feel through the nostrils. We think that is breath and attach little importance to it, while in reality breath is a life-current running through the innermost part of man's being towards the surface.(12) It would be no exaggeration, according to the mystical point of view, to say that breath connects heaven and earth. It is the mystery of breath which shows the mystic that life is not the material part of man's being, but consists of the part of his being which is unseen. Breath is the bridge beween soul and body keeping the two connected, and the medium of their action and reaction upon each other.

In the Qur'an it is said, "We have made man to be king of Our creation", which in other words means that man himself is the dominion as well as the king of that dominion: that dominion being man's body and mind, and the king being his spirit, his soul. As a horse can be controlled and directed by getting the rein in hands, so life can be controlled and directed by gaining control over breath. Every school of mystics has, as its most important and sacred teaching in the way of attainment, the control and understanding of the mystery of breath. Modern science has discovered the importance of physical culture and correct breathing, and for all diseases of the lungs there is no greater or more beneficial remedy than sending the patient to a place suitable for breathing freely. Psychologists will some day come to realize that for all illnesses and disorders of the mind the way of breathing also is the best remedy.

For the mystic breath is not only a science, but the knowledge of breath is mysticism, and mysticism to the thinker is both science and religion. The mystery of breath is not a thing that can be comprehended by the brain only. The principles of mysticism rise from the heart of man. They are learned by intuition and proved by reason. This is not only faith, though it is born of faith: it is faith with proof.

Therefore study and practice of breath have been kept a mystery – not in order to monopolize them for a certain school, for no true mystic can be without generosity. The first sign of a mystic is that he is ready to give to everyone. The first and last lesson is to give – to give to the end, to give everything one possesses. There is no end to the giving of the mystic, as there is no end to the inspiration he receives. If breath has been made a mystery, it is only as one would keep an object of glass from a little child, fearing that he might break it, hurting himself and others.

Think what an intoxication life is in this world! Realize what are man's needs, temptations and desires! What would he not do to attain them? Man is so absorbed in striving after all these things that he does not know what he really wants or how rightly to obtain it. He does not know what harm he may cause to himself or others; he uses power not knowing what will be the result. Therefore, to give mysticism to all is like giving a sword, unsheathed, to a drunken man. One does not know whom he will kill, or how he may wound himself. But apart from mysticism, it is necessary that everyone should know how to live a balanced life, a life of power and tranquility, and how to use and control the power of breath that he may be better fitted to manage his life.

If we consider the conditions of life to-day, we see that, however much man thinks he has progressed, certain aspects of life are neglected in the way of health, repose, balanced thinking, and in the way of kindness and love to one another. All these things are lacking, and the spirit of the present time seems to be going in quite the opposite direction. Selfishness seems to be so much on the increase; real religion, the spirit of forgiveness, generous giving, regard for old age, refinement, culture – all seem to be disappearing. Man in general does not know even if there is a God or Truth. If this is the spirit, how can we expect to find that harmony, peace and love which make heaven upon earth?

It is useless to discuss the peace of the world. What is necessary just now is to create peace in ourselves that we

ourselves become examples of love, harmony and peace.
That is the only way of saving ourselves and the world. Let
man try to become more considerate of others; let him ask
himself, "Of what use am I in the world? Am I born for a
certain purpose?", and then try to train himself to self-control
by the mystery of breath, the best means for accomplishing
that purpose.

3 The Science of Breath

The nature of every creature can be known by his breath.
Animals such as the lion, tiger, or bear, who kill and eat
other animals, show from their breath strength, power, and
yet an upset condition which gives them upsetting of mind,
temper, jealousy, a fighting nature, greed and a tendency to
bloodshed. Other creatures like the cow, sheep and goat have
a settled breath which keeps them thoughtful, considerate and
sociable to their own kind, which is proved by their living
together in herds. They content themselves with feeding on
grass, avoiding the presence of cruel animals.

Among all creatures a change of breath can be found
through their spells of passion, anger and fear. The breath
of man likewise shows his nature. A man who works and
is always busy with material things has a noisy breath,
similar to that of the animals, and the irregularity of his
breath shows the unsettled condition of his life; the breath
of a thoughtful person is much more rhythmic and fine.
Of course more physical energy makes breath grosser, and
a person becomes thoughtless. When his breath is normal,
man becomes thoughtful. When the energy is less, a person
becomes still wiser, but incapable of making a right use of his
wisdom, owing to the weakness of the means: his physical
body.

The value of breath is more than all wealth and power one
can have in life, for every breath gone has lessened that much
life. Suppose a person is made with the energy of a hundred
breaths – he may take them in one hour and die, or by
controlling them through rhythm he may finish a hundred
breaths in a day. It is just like a clock: if its tick goes slower

it will last much longer than the hours of its limitation, and when the beat is quicker it will stop long before its winding hour.

When lying down the breath is least strained, by sitting it is more strained, by standing still more, and by walking and running still more again. The influence of passions quickens it most; for this reason the life of celibacy has been practised by ancient mystics, and that is why the Sufi finds it necessary at times to lead a secluded life, which settles his external self as well as his mind. This does not only help to create peace and harmony in man, but even to prolong life much longer than the alotted time.

There is a vast distance between the finer plane and the grosser; they are linked by only one source and that is the breath. The nature of breath is just like the air; when the air is farther away from the earth it becomes finer, and in the same way it becomes heavy when nearer to the earth. Such is the case with the breath: when it enters the body, it materializes itself and becomes audible during sleep and even when awake, according to the fineness or grossness of a man's nature. But when breath approaches the spirit it loses its weight. That is why the average person feels his breath to a certain limit, beyond which he cannot even imagine that it could flow. Breath in its highest reach spreads all over, and in its lower flow it is confined to the least portion of time and space.

Breath is a chain which links the Infinite with His manifestation. In other words, it might be called a lift in which the Infinite descends to earth in order to experience life, and again through the same lift He makes His return journey to His origin. The speed of the journey depends upon the power of the breath and its control. Breath can reach every being, thing and atom of the universe, regardless of time and space. It is also the source of all inner and outer communication. In fact, as the length of breath joins the Infinite with the manifestation, so the width of breath connects the whole universe. Lack of consciousness keeps man in limitation; otherwise, through breath, he could expand his knowledge to the whole universe.

Breath is vouchsafed to the senses as far as their reach of perception goes. Breath makes a complete circle within the body, entering through the nose, passing through the brain and down the spine, ascending again through the abdomen and lungs, going out through the nose. When breath reaches the higher spheres, the senses, unless developed, cannot follow it there. Though one circuit of the breath takes a circle through earthly and heavenly planes (13), yet to an average person it seems as if some air goes out and comes in. But the mystics follow this chain of breath in the pursuit of the Infinite and, by holding on to it at the sacrifice of all earthly temptations which lead one on to death, they drive their lives towards immortality.

When this condition is brought about by a mystic of his own will in meditation, then he becomes the controller of his life, and death becomes his servant. By dying every day in meditation and again experiencing this momentary life the mystic becomes familiar with that state which every man fears and calls death. The greatest punishment that man can inflict on man is death – which to a mystic becomes his everyday playground. Thus he gets beyond the interest of this life and the fear of death. The difference between the mystic and another person is as that between the swimmer who would quite fearlessly swim and dive into the water and the non-swimmer who would die with fear even before sinking. That which is a comfort to the one becomes death to the other; so death, most alarming to the average person, is peace to the mystic. In all religions, directly or indirectly, this secret of mysticism is suggested,. Of course the truth cannot be revealed plainly before everybody; that is why the study of breath is kept secret and is termed mysticism.(14)

4 The Philosophy of Breath

As the books, the precepts and doctrines of a religion are important to the follower of that religion, so the study of breath is important to the mystic. People ordinarily think of breath as that little air they feel coming and going through the nostrils, but they do not think of it as that vast current which goes through everything, that current which comes from the Consciousness and goes as far as the external being, the physical world.

In the Bible it is written that first was the word, and from the word all things came. But before the word was the breath which made the word. We see that a word can make us happy, and a word can make us sorry. It is told that once a Sufi was healing a child. He repeated a few words and then gave the child to the parents saying, "Now he will be well". Someone who was antagonistic said to him, "How can it be possible that by a few spoken words anyone can be healed?" From a mild Sufi an angry answer is never expected, but this time the Sufi turned to the man and said, "You understand nothing about it, you are a fool!" The man was very much offended; his face was red, he was hot. The Sufi said, "When a word has the power to make you hot and angry, why should not a word have the power to heal?"

Behind the word is a much greater power: breath. If a person wishes to study the self, to know the self, what is important is not the study of mind, thought, and imagination, nor of the body, but the study of breath. The breath has made the mind and the body for its expression. It has made all, from the vibration to the physical atom, from the finest to the grossest. The breath, a change of breath, can make us sad in the midst of happiness, it can make us joyful in the saddest, the most miserable surroundings. That is why without reason in some places we feel glad, in other places a melancholy comes over us. It is the air that makes us so. One may say, "How can breath do all this? How can it make the body?" I have seen people in the course of years become as their breath is. What exists in the breath is expressed in the form: as the breath is, so the child becomes.

There are three sorts of breath: there is the stronger breath, *jalal*, and the weaker one *jamal*, and there is the breath that unites the *jalal* and *jamal*, and by uniting them destroys, annihilates both: this is *kamal*. By uniting *jalal* and *jamal* the breath forms a circle. This explain the circular form of guns, shells and cannons: the circle is the form of destruction.

All elements – earth, water, fire, air and ether – are in the breath, according to the direction it takes. We can taste them in the breath. There are five directions, four outward and one inward. You may ask, "What influence can the direction have?" I shall answer that if you take a ball and throw it in every direction, the ball will not go equally far at every throw; it will sometimes go farther, sometimes not so far. Even in our words the direction of the breath has its effect. Sometimes we say, "Yes, I see", directly. Sometimes we say, "Yes", sarcastically, "I see", and our head is thrown back, the breath comes obliquely; the effect is quite different. If you say, "We cannot feel, we cannot perceive the elements in the breath, we do not know where they are", I shall say that this is a science. It cannot be understood in a moment; it is a study.

You may ask, "Is the direction the only thing that has influence upon the breath?" There are two other forces that influence it: *uruj* and *nuzul*, the rise and the fall. In the jets of water in a fountain some of the jets rise very high, others less high, others rise only a few inches, according to the force by which they are predestined. So it is with the breath.

5 The Control of the Breath (1)

Reading books cannot give anyone control of the breath: practice is needed. Reading the theory of music cannot make anyone a composer, a singer, a piano player. Ask composers, singers, violinists how much they have to practise. The practice of breath is very difficult and arduous. We see Yogis sitting or standing for hours in the same position, practising for hours in the night or before dawn. Through control of the breath all things are gained. If a man is a great writer, it is because his breath holds the thoughts that are in his mind. Sandow*, through control of the breath, developed ideal muscles. Before control of breath is learned, control of the body must be gained by the practice of postures and positions. For instance, if a small child is trained once a day to sit still for four or five minutes, not to run about, if it is

* Sandow – famous as a "strong man" early in the century

trained not to begin to eat at dinner until everybody eats –
that will give it control.

The ways of control of the breath are many. It must be done
by realization of the self. But as long as we think that this body
is our self, we cannot realize our self. And often we not only
think that our body is our self, but we think that our overcoat
is our self ! If it is miserable we think that we are miserable; if
it is very grand we think that we are very grand. It is natural
to think that what is before our view is our self. We always
remember the words of our great poetess Zeb-un-Nisa, "If
thou thinkest of the rose thou wilst become the rose; if thou
thinkest of the nightingale thou wilst become the nightingale.
Thou art a drop, and the divine Being is the whole. Whilst
thou art alive, hold the thought of the whole before thee, and
thou wilst be the whole".

The mystic always consults his breath in the evening and
in the morning in order to know whether it is harmonious
with the sun, with the moon and with the planets. He is
always conscious of the breath. This is achieved through
concentration; the Sufi gives a lesson to teach it, which is
called *fikr*. My spiritual teacher, my Murshid, once said,
"People say that there are many sins and virtues, but I
think there is only one sin". I asked him what it was, and
he said, "To let one breath go without being conscious of
it".

6 The Control of the Breath (2)

We say that the hand is in control, when it can grasp
something and hold it in its grasp. The fingers we say are
in control, when they move up and down the piano, when
they strike B when B is wanted – not striking E. Control is
both in repose and in activity. Sometimes we find that we
have become angry, we have become impatient, we have lost
control over our mind, but before losing control of the mind
we had lost control of the breath.

Since I have been in the West, people have said to me more
than a thousand times, "We cannot control our mind, we
cannot keep our mind fixed on one point". The first step is

to lessen the activity of the mind; then thoughts come more slowly. One should first control the breath, and make it slow and regular. By this the health of the body is improved as well as the health of the mind.

People have invented a fan to purify the air by fanning it very rapidly. By the practises of *qasb* and *shaghl* breath also is fanned, and this rapid fanning changes it from one element into another and purifies it.

In the Qur'an it is said, "Surely, We revealed it on the night of power". What was the night of power to the Prophet whose whole life was revelation? It was the sending of the breath within. It is natural that we always look outward. The breath is directed outward. We see what is outward, we hear what is outward, we taste what is outward, we are touched by what is outward. When the breath is sent within, then a person sees what is within, he hears what is within, he tastes within, he is touched by what is within. When this is done and the breath is purified, the mystics see forms and colours in it which reveal past, present and future to them. They know the past, present and future of every person whom they see. But if the control of breath tells them past, present and future, it is too little, it is not worthwhile. It must tell them more: from this limited being it must bring them to that unlimited existence, from this mortal being to that immortality.

In the account of the *miraj* (15) it is said that a *buraq* was brought for Muhammad to ride, an animal like a horse with a human face. This *buraq* was the breath: the horse whose rein is in the rider's hand.

If a person exercises the breath and practises concentration with a scientific idea only, he soon becomes tired. He thinks, "Why take so much trouble? For what result?" If it is done with the thought of God, with the repetition of the names of God, then – by the thought of the idealized God in whom is all perfection, all beauty, who is the Friend to whom we can tell our sorrows, all our sorrows, all our troubles – a happiness comes, a bliss. Sa'adi says, "In the thought of God is the blessing that it draws us every moment nearer to Him.

CHAPTER XVIII

The Power of Silence

FROM A scientific point of view I shall say that speech is the breath of breath. In the Vedanta breath is called *prana*, which is life. It may be said that breath is the chain that links body, heart and soul together, and is so important that the body – so loved and cared for, kept in palaces, its slightest cold or cough treated by doctors and medicines – is of no more use and cannot be kept anymore when the breath is gone. Speaking being the breach of breath means that, when one is speaking, one takes ten breaths in the time which would be normal for one breath. One says, "Where are you going?", and for these four words one takes three breaths.(16)

Breath is like the hoop with which a child plays. According to the force of the blow from the stick, so many turns the hoop makes, and when the force is spent the hoop falls down. It is like the ticking of the watch. The watch goes on for the time for which it is wound; it may be for three days or for twenty-four hours, or for a week or a month. Longer than that period it cannot work, because it was not wound for it. Breath is like a child's top. According to the strength with which it is spun so many turns the top makes, each turn helping the other, and when the force is expended the top falls down. In accordance with the first breath, so long will life last: so many breaths.

By speaking we take away so much of our life. A day's silence means a week longer of life and more, and a day's speech means a week less of life. From ancient times there have been mystics in India who are called *muni*; they never speak. They have, of course other characteristics as well, but they are called *muni* because of their abstinence from speech. They often have lived very much longer than we live in the present time: three hundred, five hundred years and more.

By not speaking the breath is not interrupted, it is regular and even. Mystics have always attached great importance to breath, and have made its study their first object. Those who have mastered the breath have mastery over their lives; those who have not mastered it are the ones who have consumption, paralysis and all kinds of diseases. There are some who have mastered it unconsciously, such as boxers and wrestlers, and also the people of a righteous life.

In the present age we have become so fond of speech that, when a person is alone in the house, he likes to go out if only to find someone to talk to. Often, if a person is alone, he speaks to things. Many people speak to themselves, if they have no other person to speak to. If it were explained to them, they would understand how much energy they really lose by each word spoken. There are other great benefits that are gained by silence but, if it were only for the energy and vitality one gains, its power is very important.

Now speaking from a moral point of view, I shall say that many benefits are obtained by silence. Most of our follies are follies of speech. In one week, if we commit one folly of action, we commit a thousand follies of speech. Often we offend someone, we hurt someone, only by speaking too much; if we had refrained from speech we would not have hurt him. There are families where always some quarrel is going on, only because they speak too much.

A story is told about a woman who went to a healer and said to him, "My husband is very bad tempered. Every evening when he comes home he scolds me and there is a quarrel that ends in a very disgraceful manner. Can you give me a remedy for it?" The healer said, "Certainly", and gave her seven pieces of candy, explaining, "These are charmed pieces of candy. When your husband comes home, put one of these in your mouth". She did so, and that evening there was no quarrel: such a miracle, after ten years of continual quarrelling! The next day the woman went to the healer, thanked him a thousand times and told him that he had done such a miracle. She said, "I do not know what to do to thank you. I want you to give me a big box of that candy which might last for some time". The healer answered, "The candy is not necessary, silence is needed". This teaches us that often we quarrel only because of our speech. Silence is a great peacemaker. "Blessed are the peacemakers".

Then there is exaggeration; idealists, admirers, exaggerate everything. If such a person has gone out and has seen on a poster that a Zeppelin* is coming, he wants to frighten his friends. At once he says that twenty Zeppelins are coming. His friends are alarmed, and he feels satisfaction. Idealists, if they take a fancy to a person, tell him that he is the sun and the moon and the heavens. There is no need to say all this.

By speaking a person develops a tendency to contradiction. Whatever is said, he wants to take the opposite side to it. He becomes like a boxer or a wrestler: when there is no one to box or wrestle with, he is disappointed; he has such an intense inclination to speech. I have many times had this experience, and will tell you about one.

I was at a reception at a friend's house and someone was there who disputed with everybody, so that all were tired. I avoided him, but my friend put me forward to speak with him, so I had to go and meet him. When he heard that I was a speaker and a teacher of philosophy he thought, "This is the person I want", and said, "I do not believe in God". As it is the work of the Sufi to harmonize, to unite, I said, "Do you not? But you believe in this manifestation and in the beauty of this world of variety, and that there is some power behind it which produces it." He said, "I believe all that, but I do not call it God". I said to him, "You believe that every effect has a cause, and that for all these causes there must be an original cause. You call it cause, I call it God; it is the same". "I believe in that", he said, "but why should I worship this personality, why should I call it God?" I replied, "There is some officer whom you salute, some superior before whom you bow, there are your father and mother for whom you have a feeling of respect, there is some fair one whom you love and adore, some power before which you are helpless. How great must be that Person who has produced and who controls all these, and how much worthy of worship!". He answered, "But I do not call that divinity, I call it a universal power, an affinity working mechanically, harmonizing all". When I tried to fix him on one point, he ran to another corner,

---

* Hazrat Inayat Khan lived in London during World War I

and when I followed him there, he ran to another until at last I ceased, thinking of the words of Shankaracharya, "All impossible things can be made possible save the bringing of a fool's mind to the point of truth".

The tendency to contradiction grows so much that, when a person hears even his own idea expressed before him, he will take the contrary point in order to prepare a position for discussion. There is a Persian saying, "O silence, thou art an inestimable bliss. Thou coverest the follies of the foolish and givest inspiration to the wise!"

How many foolish things we say only through the habit of speech! How many useless words we have to speak! If we are introduced to someone, we must speak, if not we are thought impolite. Then come such conversations as, "It is a fine day", "It is cold", and one tells how the season is: speech without reason which in time turns into a disease, so that a person cannot get on without emptying the head of others by saying useless things; he cannot live one moment without speaking owing to his self-interest. A person becomes so fond of speech that sometimes he will tell the whole story of his life to a stranger, preventing him from speaking himself, and boring him so much that he would like to say, "What do I care about all that!"

Also people give out secrets that they afterwards repent of having told. Yet during the spell of this passion for speech they say things which they may never have wanted another person to know; yet at that time they do not care. Under the same spell a person shows impertinence in his words, pride and prejudice, for which afterwards he repents. Lack of power over speech causes all that.

A word is sometimes prized more than the whole world's treasure, and again it sometimes is a word which puts a person to the sword. And there is a saying, "Sweet tongue is a sword which conquers the whole world".

There are different ways of receiving inspiration, but the best is silence. All the mystics have kept silence. All the great people I saw during my travels through India and other different places kept silence for two or three hours a day, or at least for one hour.

In Hyderabad there was a mystic called Shah Khamosh. He was called so because of his silence. When he was young he was a very clever and energetic boy. One day he went to his Murshid and as usual had some question to ask, as is natural in an intelligent person. The Murshid was sitting in ecstasy and did not wish to speak, so he said to him, "Be quiet" (*Khamosh!*) The boy was much struck; he had never before heard such a word from his Murshid who was always so kind and merciful and willing to answer his questions. This lesson was enough for him for his wole life, for he was an intelligent person. He went home and did not speak to his family, not even to his parents. His Murshid seeing him quiet did not speak to him. For many years Shah Khamosh never spoke and his psychic powers became so great that only to look at him was enough to be inspired. Wherever he cast his glance he healed. This happened not very long ago, perhaps twenty-five years ago.

Nowadays activity has increased so much that from morning till night there is never any repose owing to our daily occupations which keep us continually in movement. At night we are so tired that we only wish to sleep, and the next morning activity begins again. In this way life is much destroyed. Man does not think of life; he is so eager for his enjoyments that he does not think of the life that is there for him to enjoy. Every person should have at least one hour in the day in which to be quiet, to be silent.

After silence of speech comes silence of thought. Sometimes a person is sitting still without speaking, but all the time his thoughts are jumping up and down. The mind may not want the thoughts, but they come. The mind is let out to them like a dancing-room, and they dance around in it. One thought then must be made so interesting, so important, that all other thoughts are driven away by it.

When thoughts have been silenced, comes silence of feelings. You may not speak against some person, there may be no thought against him in your mind, but if there is a bitter feeling against him in your heart, he will feel it; he will feel there is bitterness for him in that heart. Such is also the case with love and affection.

The abstract is that existence beyond this world where all existence commingles, where it all meets. The sound of the abstract is there, and when that sound is silenced too and a person goes beyond it he reaches the highest state, *Najat*, the eternal Consciousness. Of course a great effort is needed to attain this state.

Silence is surely the remedy for much, but a person living in the world cannot practise it continually. He must keep watch over his words and remember that for every word he will be awarded heaven or hell.

CHAPTER XIX

A Question about Feelings

Question: Is there need of explaining things in words to one's Murshid, or is it sufficient to keep all one's thoughts and feelings in silence?

Answer: The truth need not be spoken; the existence speaks louder than words. Still the law of life in the world is such that words give a fuller expression to one's thoughts and feelings, resulting in a greater satisfaction. Therefore the best thing is to say what can be said, and not to try to put into words what can never be expressed in words, trusting in one's own sincere devotion and in the sympathy of your Murshid that nothing will remain not understood.

I think that, by expressing a thought or a feeling in words, one makes a clear picture of them which, in an abstract form, can be perceived only by one who is greatly evolved. But it must be remembered that there are certain sentiments, unexpressed and yet solid and living. Such sentiments in time become personalities, and they live as human beings, filling their place in life. For instance, a thoroughly sympathetic person not only has sympathy as his attribute, but he has sympathy as a living spirit, moving and walking about with him, and going with him wherever he goes.

Life is far more productive than man can think, productive of good and evil, of right and wrong, of joy and sorrow. It depends upon the person what he wishes to produce. Life for me is a place where every person is given a piece of ground – one person a larger piece, one person a smaller – and he is told, "Now you have the ground, and here are seeds: grass, weeds, corn and good fruit, flowers and poisonous fruits. Sow what you like, sow all that interests you and produce, or do not sow at all – but still the ground belongs to you".

So is the life of an individual in this world: every person has his farm. There are some who sow thorns, and when the thorns have sprung up and become painful, they say, "Why did we do this", or they say, "I am so tired of this farm, I wish I were not here". They wish they could be taken away from that farm and placed in a farm where flowers and fruits are already growing, without having to take the trouble of sowing. But that is against the law. Man is intended to live on his farm, and all through life he is sowing what will be his hereafter.

Heaven and hell are not made ready for a person after his life on earth. The same farm that is given to man is hereafter turned into his heaven or hell. So man must build heaven now on the farm that is already his possession. He must put into it all that he likes and loves, and remove from it all that is hurtful, harmful, or disagreeable, making now, while on earth, his farm of the nature of heaven – which in the hereafter will culminate into a perfect heaven.

CHAPTER XX

The Control of the Mind (17)

1

IN SANSKRIT the mind is called *mana* and from this word comes *manu* which means man. Also the word man is much the same as *manu*, and from that we gather that man is his mind. Man is not his body, nor is he his soul; for the soul is divine, it has no distinction, and the body is a cover. Man, therefore, is his mind.

Once we begin to look into the minds of men we begin to see such a phenomenon that no wonder in the world can be compared with it: looking in the eyes when they are afraid, when they doubt, when they are sad and want to hide it, when they are glad; seeing how men from lions turn into rabbits, when they have a guilty conscience. As flowers emit fragrance so minds produce atmosphere. Apart from seeing it in the aura, even in the expression of man we can clearly see the record of his mind. Nothing can show man's mind better than his own expression. Mind therefore is the principal thing. We distinguish men as individualities, and it is the culture of the mind which develops individuality into personality.

The difference between mind and heart is that the mind is the surface of the heart, and the heart the depth of the mind: they are the two different aspects of one and the same thing. The mind thinks, the heart feels. What the heart feels the mind wants to interpret in thought; what the mind thinks the heart assimilates expressing it in feeling. Neither is the mind the brain, nor is the heart a piece of flesh hidden under the breast. Those who do not believe in such a thing as the mind think that thoughts and impressions are in the brain, that a person thinks with his brain. It is not true. The brain only helps to make impressions clear to man's material vision.

The mind does not belong to the same element as the body; the body belongs to the physical, the mind to the mental element; the latter cannot be measured or weighed or made intelligible by physical instruments. Those in the world of science who are trying and hoping one day to produce machines which make thoughts and impressions clear, if ever they are successful, will only be so in the sense that the impressions of thoughts affecting the physical body will be felt by their instruments, but not the thoughts from the mental sphere; for the mind alone is the instrument that can take reflections from the mind.

The mind can be seen as five different faculties working together: in thinking, remembering, reasoning, identifying and feeling.*

Thinking is of two kinds: imagination and thought. When the mind works under the direction of the will there is thought, when the mind works automatically without the power of the will there is imagination. The thoughtful person is he who has a rein over the activity of the mind; an imaginative person is the one who indulges in the automatic action of the mind. Both thought and imagination have their place in life. The automatic working of the mind produces a picture, a plan, which is sometimes more beautiful than a plan or an idea carefully thought out under the control of the will. Therefore artists, poets, musicians are very often imaginative, and the beauty they produce in their art is the outcome of their imagination.

The secret that is to be understood about imagination is this: everything that works automatically must be prepared first, then it works; just like a watch must be prepared to work automatically. We must wind it up, then it can go on; we need trouble no more about it. This shows that we need prepare the mind to work automatically to the best advantage in life. If people become imaginative without having prepared their mind, it leads them at least to an unbalanced condition, and maybe to insanity; for when an imaginative person becomes unbalanced, and has no control over his mind, it may lead him to insanity.

---

* The identifying faculty is the ego. This, as well as the faculties of remembering and reasoning, are dealt with in the second lecture.

Now the question arises: how to prepare the mind? The mind is just like a film taking all the photographs to make a moving picture, and it produces the same that was once taken in. The one who is critical, who looks at the ugly side of human nature, who has love for evil, love for gossip, who has the desire to see the bad side of things, who wishes to find the bad points of people, prepares a film in his mind. That film projected on the curtain produces undesirable impressions in the form of imagination.

The great poets who gave us beautiful teachings in moral, in truth, where did they get them from? This life here is the school in which they learned, this life is the stage on which they saw and gathered. They are the worshippers of beauty in nature and in art. In all conditions of life they meditate upon beauty and find good points in all those they see. They gather all that is beautiful, from the good and the wicked both. Just like the bee takes the best from every flower and makes honey from it, so they gather all that is beautiful and express it through their imagination in the form of music, poetry and art, as well as in their thoughts and deeds in everyday life.

I began in my early life a pilgrimage in India – not to holy shrines, but to holy men, going from one place to another and seeing sages of different natures and characters. What I gathered from them all was their great love-nature, their outgoing tendency, their deep sympathy and their inclination to find some good. In every person they see they are looking for some good, and therefore they find it in the most wicked person. By doing so they themselves become goodness because they have gathered it: we become what we gather. In their presence there is nothing but love, compassion and understanding – of which so little is found in this world.

In our domestic life, in our social or political life, in business, in commerce, in national activities – if we had that one tendency, it would make life different for us, more worth living than it is to-day for so many souls. The condition to-day is that people are rich, they have all convenience and comfort – but what is lacking is understanding. Home is full of comfort, but there is no understanding, there is no happiness. It is such a little thing, and yet so difficult

to obtain. No intellectuality can give understanding. This is
where man makes a mistake: he wants to understand through
his head. Understanding comes from the heart; the heart must
be glowing, living. When the heart becomes feeling then there
is understanding, then you are ready to see from the point of
view of another as much as you can see from your own point
of view.

The other aspect of thinking is thought, which is heavier,
more solid, more vital than imagination, because it has a
back-bone which is will-power. Therefore, when we say,
"This is a thoughtful person", we make a distinction between
the imaginative and the thoughtful person. The latter has a
weight about him, something substantial; one can rely upon
him. The imaginative person one day may come saying, "I
love you so much; you are so good, so high, so true, so great",
but it is just like a cloud of imagination which has arisen.
The next day it is scattered away, and the same imaginative
person, who yesterday followed this cloud, would try to find
some fault, and nothing is left in his hands. How very often
this happens! Those are angelic people perhaps, but they
ride on the clouds. For this dense earth they are of no use,
one cannot rely upon them; they are as changeable as the
weather. The thoughtful person, on the contrary, takes his
time to express both his praise or his blame. The mind of the
thoughtful is anchored and under control.

The one who learns how to make the best of imagination
and how to control his thought shows great balance in life.
How is this to be achieved? By concentration. In India there
is a sacred Hindu legend relating that two sons of God* were
in a country where the younger one saw a horse which was
set out free by the government. The one who would catch
the horse would become king of that country. This youth
was so attracted to the horse, and to the idea that was behind
it, that he ran after it. He could not catch it, for the horse
would sometimes slow down, but run away as soon as the
youth nearly reached it. His mother was worried and asked
the elder brother to go and find him. Then the elder brother

_____
* The two sons of Rama, who was an incarnation of the God Vishnu

came and saw that his brother was pursuing the horse. So he said to him, "That is a wrong method. You will never be able to catch the horse in that way. The best way of catching it is not to follow, but to meet it". Instead of following the horse the youth met the horse, and so caught it. The mother was very pleased and proud that her son had been able to catch the horse, and he became entitled to the throne and crown of his father.

The horse in this story is the mind. When the mind is controlled then mastery is gained and God's kingdom attained. The younger brother is the pupil, the elder brother the guru, the teacher. The way of controlling the mind is not by following it, but it is by concentrating: by concentrating one meets it.

It is also told that a Sufi had a pupil who said to him, "Teacher, I cannot concentrate on one thing. If I try to concentrate on one object, other objects appear; then they become so muddled that I do not know which is which. It is difficult to hold the mind on one object". The teacher said, "Your difficulty is your anxiety. The moment you begin to concentrate, you are anxious that your mind might wander away. If you were not anxious about it, your mind would have poise; your anxiety makes it more active. If you just take what it gives you, instead of looking behind it in order to see where it goes, if you change this tendency and meet the mind face to face, seeing how it comes to you and with what it comes, you will be able to concentrate better".

From this story a great lesson is to be learned, for this is always the case! The moment one sits down to concentrate the mind changes its rhythm for the very reason that the person is anxious to keep it under control. The mind does not wish it; it wants its freedom. As you stand for your right, so the mind stands for its right. The best way is to greet the mind as it comes to meet you. Let it bring what it brings when you stand face to face with your mind, and be not annoyed with what it brings. Just take it, then you have the mind under control, for when it comes to you, it will not go further; let it bring what it brings. In this way you make a connection with your mind, and as soon as you begin to look at it, you have your mind in hand. The photographer has his subject in hand when he has focused the camera on his subject. It is the same thing with a person and his mind: as soon as he has focused himself on the mind he has got it under control.

Concentrations can be considered as different stages of evolution. The first concentration is on a certain designed object and is divided into two actions. One action is making the object and then holding it in the mind. It is just like a child who takes little bricks, pillars and different things making a little house out of them. The first action is this making of the house, the second action is looking at it. This is one kind of concentration, and another kind is that there already is an object which the mind must reflect by focusing itself on that object.

The next stage of concentration is improving on the object. For instance one imagines a tiger, and then one also imagines the background of the tiger: rocks behind it, a mountain, trees, a forest, a river. That is improvement: holding at the same time the background and changing it according to the activity of the mind. Even if the tiger changes, it does not matter as long as one has that particular kind of concentration.

The third concentration is on an idea. The idea has some form which is inexpressible – but the mind makes it.

Now coming to the realm of feeling – feeling is such an important thing in our lives that our whole life depends upon it. A person, once disheartened, sometimes loses enthusiasm for his whole life. A person, once disappointed, loses trust for his whole life. A person, heart-broken, loses self-confidence for all his life. A person, once afraid, sustains fear in his heart for ever. A person, who has once failed, keeps all through life the impression of his failure.

In the East they love bird fights. Two men bring their birds to fight, and as soon as a man sees that the bird of the other man will win in the end, he takes his bird away while it is in the action of fighting – before it has accepted defeat. The man admits defeat while the two birds are fighting, but he does not allow his bird to go as far as to be impressed by defeat. Once impressed by it the bird will never fight again. This is the secret of our mind, and once we learn to take care of our mind – just as the man took care of his bird – going to any sacrifice but not giving the mind a bad impression, we will make the best of our life.

Besides this, we read of the lives of great heroes and great personalities, how they went through all difficulties and sorrows and troubles, and yet always tried to keep their heart from being humbled. This gave them all their strength; they always escaped humiliation. They were prepared for death, wars, suffering and poverty, but not for humiliation.

I will tell you an amusing anecdote. I once was in Nepal, near the Himalayas, and I wanted a servant; so I sent for one. He was of the warriors caste, Kshatriyas, of a fighters'tribe in the mountains. I asked him what work he wanted to do, and he said: "Any work you like, anything you like". I asked: "What about the pay?" "Anything you will give", he answered. I was amused to find that he wanted to do any work I would give him and to accept any pay. "Well", I said, "then there is no condition to be made?" He said: "One. You will not speak a cross word to me". Imagine! He was ready to accept any money, willing to do any work, but no humiliation. I appreciated that spirit of the warrior beyond words; this was what made him a warrior.

Friends, our failure and our success all depend upon the condition of our mind. If the mind fails, failure is sure, if the mind is successful, conditions do not matter: we shall succeed in the end.

Question: Is it possible, when humiliated, to spare our mind the injury of humiliation by seeing that the person who humiliates us is beneath us?
Answer: That is not the way, because as soon as we accept humiliation we are humiliated, whether we think it or not. It does not depend upon the other person, it depends upon ourselves. No sooner do we admit humiliation, there is humiliation. If the whole world does not accept our humiliation, it does not matter as long as our mind feels humiliated, and if our mind does not accept humiliation, it does not matter if the whole world takes it as such. If a thousand persons come and say to a man, "You are

wicked", he will not believe it as long as his heart says, "I am not wicked". But when his heart says, "I am wicked", if a thousand persons say, "You are good", his heart will continue to say, "No, no, I am wicked". The heart keeps him down just the same. If we ourselves give up, then nobody can sustain us.

Question: Is it possible then to develop a state of mind that lifts us out of humiliation?
Answer: Well, the best thing would be to avoid humiliation, but if a person cannot avoid it, then he must be as a patient who must be treated by a physician, then he needs a person powerful enough to help him, a master-mind, a spiritual person. He then can be doctored, attended to, and get over that condition. When a person is a patient he cannot very well help himself. He can do much, but then there is the necessity of a doctor.

Question: Can that condition be treated by counter-irritation?
Answer: Yes, it can be met with that.

Question: What to do when the feeling of humiliation has entered the mind?
Answer: To take it as a lesson, to take poison as something that must be. However, poison is poison. What is put in the mind will grow. It must be taken out. Every impression, if it remains, will grow: humiliation, fear, doubt. When it is there it remains; there will come a time when the person will be conscious of it. It will grow, and because it is growing in the subconscious mind it will bear fruits and flowers.

Question: Would the study of mathematics be good for an imaginative person?
Answer: Yes, it can bring about a balance. I have seen this in the case of one of my pupils who was extremely imaginative; he could not stay on the earth. But later on he got into a business where he was obliged to count figures, and after some time he obtained a great deal of balance.

2

I have given this as a title in order to make my idea intelligible, but when explaining the subject, instead of using the word mind, I shall use the word spirit. The word mind comes from a Sanskrit root which means mind and also man. In this way the name itself explains that man is his mind. Since the word mind is not understood in the same way by all those who use it in their everyday language, I think it best to use the word spirit instead.

The spirit can be defined as consisting of five different aspects: mind, memory, reason, feeling and ego, and each of these five aspects is of two kinds.

The mind is creative of thought and of imagination. Out of the work of the mind, directed by the will, comes thought, and out of the automatic working of the mind comes imagination. So the thoughtful person is different from the imaginative. Thought is concrete because it is constructed, it is made by will power. The thoughtful person therefore is dependable and more balanced, because he stands on his own feet. The imaginative person, on the contrary, floats in the air; he rises and falls with his imaginations. He may touch the heights of heaven, and he may fall deep down on to the bottom of the earth; he may float to the north, the south, the east or the west. However, both thought and imagination have their proper places.

The automatic working of the mind which produces imagination has its power, inspiration and beauty peculiar to itself. Poets, musicians, painters, sculptors create out of their imagination, and they reach further than the ordinary man. This only shows that the power of the automatic working of the mind is very great, although there is always a danger of being unbalanced. So often one sees a great genius, a composer, a poet, a great artist with a wonderful skill, and yet unbalanced, because the imagination makes the spirit float in space. The one who by floating takes the risk of falling, also has the chance of rising further than anybody else. To a practical and thoughtful man of common sense an artist or a composer, seems to be very unpractical, sometimes he seems to be very ignorant and childish. And looking at them from this point of view he is right, for however large a balloon may be, it is a balloon, it stays in the air. It is not a waggon one can rely upon to stay safely where one has put it. A balloon will fly, one does not know where it will take one. Nevertheless, the waggon remains on the earth, it never touches space; it does not belong in the air. Being a waggon, it misses the joy of rising upwards.

Thought has its place; it is solid, it is concrete, it is distinct. A thoughtful man seldom goes astray, for he has rhythm, he has balance. Maybe he cannot fly, but he walks and you can depend upon him.

Now as to the spiritual aspect in connection with thought and imagination, there are two kinds of seekers after spiritual truth: the thoughtful and the imaginative. The imaginative at once jumps into religion; he does not walk, he jumps into it. He revels in superstitions, he cherishes dogmas and beliefs, he interests himself in amusing and bewildering stories and legends connected with religion, he maintains beliefs that are impressed upon him. And yet, with all faults and weaknesses, the imaginative person is the one who is ever able to make a conception of God and of the hereafter. The one who has no imagination is not able to reach the zenith of the spiritual and religious ideal. Often an intellectual or materialistic person without imagination stands on the earth like an animal compared with a bird: when the bird flies up the animal looks at it and wishes to fly, but it cannot, it has no wings. The imagination therefore is as two wings attached to the heart in order to enable it to soar upwards.

The thoughtful seeker after the spiritual ideal has his importance too, because he is not led by superficial beliefs and dogmas. One cannot fool him, he is thoughtful and every step he takes may be slow, but it is sure. He may not reach the spiritual ideal as quickly as the imaginative, but if he wishes to reach it he will arrive there, slowly and surely.

The second aspect of the spirit is memory, which again has two sides. There are certain things we need not look for; they are always clear in our memory, such as figures, and the names and faces of those we know. We just have to stretch out our hand and touch them; we can recall them at any moment we wish, they are always living in our memory. But then there is a second side to the memory which is called by some the subconscious mind. In reality this is the depth of the memory. In this part of the memory a photograph is made of everything we have seen or known or heard, even just once in a flash. This photograph remains located there, and some time or other, maybe with difficulty, we can find it.

Apart from these two sides of our memory there is still a deeper sphere to which it is joined. That sphere is the universal memory, in other words the divine Mind, where we do not only recollect what we have seen, or heard, or known, but where we can even touch something that we have never learned, or heard, or known, or seen. All that can be found there also; only for that the doors of our memory should be laid open.

The third aspect of the spirit is reason, of which there are two kinds. One kind is affirmation, and the other is both affirmative and negative. Affirmative reason is the one we all know. When a person is bankrupt we have reason to think that he has no money for the very fact that he is bankrupt. When a person shows his bad side we know that he is wicked, because people call him bad. Every apparent reason makes us reach conclusions that things and conditions are so and so. This is one kind of reason.

The other kind is the inner reason which both contradicts and affirms at the same time. This means that, if a person has become poor, we say, "Yes, he has become poor – and rich". If a person has failed we say, "Yes, he has both failed – and gained". Here is a higher reason which one touches. The higher reason weighs two things at the same time. One says, "This is living", and at the same time one says, "This is dead", or one says, "This is dead and at the same time living". Everything one sees gives a reason to deny its existence and at the same time to affirm its opposite – even to such an extent that when one has a reason to say, "This is dark", by that higher reason one may say that it is light.

When one arrives at this higher reason one begins to unlearn – as it is called by the mystics – all that one has once learned to recognize as such and such, or as so and so. One unlearns and one begins to see quite the opposite. In other words, there is no good which has not a bad side to it, and nothing bad which has not a good side to it. There is no one who rises without a fall, and no one who falls without the promise of a rise. One sees death in birth, and birth in death. It sounds very strange and it is a peculiar idea, but all the same it is a stage. When one climbs above what is called reason one reaches that reason which is at the same time contradictory. This explains the attitude of Christ. When a criminal was taken to him he had no other attitude towards him than that of the forgiver; he saw no evil there. That is looking from a higher reason.

Feeling is the fourth aspect of the spirit. Feeling is different from thought and imagination; it has its own vibrations and its own sphere. Thought and imagination are on the surface, feeling is at the depth of the spirit. Feeling also has two sides: one is likened to the glow, and the other to the flame. Whether one loves or whether one suffers, there is intense feeling, a feeling which cannot be compared with the experience of thought and imagination. A feeling person has a different consciousness, he lives in a different sphere. A person who is feeling has a different world of his own. He may move among the crowds and live in the midst of the world, and yet he does not belong to the world. The moment feeling is awakened in man, his consciousness becomes different. He is raised up, he touches the depth, he penetrates the horizon, and he removes what stands between man and the deeper side of life.

Is there anyone in this world who will own that he has no feeling? And yet there are hearts of rock and of iron, of earth and of diamond, of silver and of gold, of wax and of paper. As many objects as there are in this world, so many kinds of hearts there are; one heart is not like the other. There are some objects that hold fire longer, there are others which burn instantly. There are objects which will become warm and cold in a moment; others, as soon as the fire touches them, will melt, and others again one can mould and turn into ornaments. So is the heart-quality. Different people have different qualities of heart, and by the knower of hearts each is treated differently. But since we do not think about this aspect of feeling, we take every man to be the same. Although every note is a sound, all notes are not the same, they differ in pitch, in vibrations; so every man differs in pitch, in the vibrations of his heart. According to the vibrations of his heart he is either spiritual or material, noble or common. It is not because of what he does, nor because of what he possesses in this world – he is small or great according to how his heart vibrates.

All my life I have had a great respect for those who have toiled in the world, who have striven all through life, and reached a certain greatness, even in a worldly sense, and I always have considered it a most sacred thing to touch their presence. This being my great interest, I began to make a pilgrimage to great people in the East, and among these wonderful visits to writers, sages, philosophers, and saints I came in contact with a great wrestler, a giant man. Since I had this admiration for great toil, I thought that I should go and see this man too. And would you believe it: this in appearance giantlike man, with that monstrous muscular body, had such a sympathetic outgoing nature, such simplicity and gentleness connected with it, that I was surprised and thought, "It is not his giantlike look that has made him great. What has made him great is that which has melted him and made him lenient".(18)

Feeling is vibration. The heart which is a vehicle, an instrument of feeling, creates a phenomenon, if one only watches life keenly. If one causes anyone pain, that pain returns; if one causes anyone pleasure, that pleasure returns. If you give love to someone, loves comes back, and if you give hatred, that hatred comes back to you in some form or other. Maybe in the form of pain, illness, health, success, joy, or happiness – in some form or other it comes back, it never fails. Generally one does not think about it, and when a person has got a certain position where he can order people about and where he can speak harshly to them, he never thinks about those things. Every little feeling that rises in a man's heart, and directs his action, word and movement, causes a certain reaction and rebounds; only it sometimes takes time. But do not think that you can ever hate a person – even have the slightest thought of it – and that it does not come

back; it surely comes back some time. Besides, if you have
sympathy, love, affection, a kind feeling for a person, even
without telling him so, it returns in some form or other.

The fifth aspect of the spirit is the ego, and again there are
two sides to the ego: the false and the real. They are just like
the two ends of one line. If we look at the line in the centre, it
is one line; if we look at the line on the ends, it is two ends. So
the ego has its two sides: the first is the one we know, and the
next the one we must discover. The side we know is the false
ego which makes us say "I". What is it in us that we call "I"?
We say, "This is my body, my mind, these are my thoughts,
my feelings, my impressions, this is my position in life". We
identify our self with all that concerns us and the sum-total of
all these we call "I". In the light of truth this conception is
false, it is a false identity. If the hand is broken off, or a finger
is separated from this body, we do not call the separate part
"I", but as long as it is connected with the body we call it so.
This shows that all that the false ego imagines to be its own
self is not really its self.

Besides, it must be remembered that all that is composed,
all that is constructed, all that is made, all that is born,
all that has grown, will be decomposed and destroyed,
will die and will vanish. If we identify our ego with all
these things which are subject to destruction, death and
decomposition, we make a conception of mortality, and
we identify our soul which is immortal, we identify our
self, with all that is mortal. Therefore that is the false ego.

Now coming to the most important truth about spiritual
attainment: those who are thoughtful and wise, those who
go into the spiritual path, do not take this path in order to
perform wonders or to know curious things, to perform
miracles or other wonderful things. That is not their motive;
their motive is to rise above the false ego and to discover the
real. That is the principal motive of spiritual attainment; for
no one will consider it wise to be under a false impression, to
be under the impression that "I exist", when one has nothing
to depend upon in one's existence. Therefore striving in the
spiritual path is breaking away from the false conception that
we have made of ourselves, coming out of it, it is realizing

our true being and becoming conscious of it. No sooner do we become conscious of our true being and break the fetters of the false ego, than we enter into a sphere where our soul begins to realize a much greater expansion of its own being. It finds great inspiration and power, and the knowledge, happiness and peace which are latent in the spirit.

CHAPTER XXI

The Mystery of Sleep

1

WE SEE in our daily life that the greatest friend of the child is the one who helps him to go to sleep. However many toys we may give him, however many dolls and candy, it is when the child is helped to go to sleep, that he is most grateful. When the mother with her blessed hands puts him to sleep, it is of the greatest benefit for the child; it is then that he is happiest.

Those who are sick and in pain, are happy if they can sleep; then all their pain is gone. If only they can sleep, they say they can endure all else. They ask the doctor, "Give us something, anything to make us sleep". If you were offered a king's palace and every enjoyment, every luxury, the best surroundings, the best dishes, on the condition that you should not sleep, you would say: "I do not want it, I prefer my sleep".

What is the difference between the happy and the unhappy one? The unhappy one cannot sleep. His sorrow, care, anxiety, and worry at once take sleep away from him. Why do people take to alcoholic drinks and drugs of all sorts? Only for this: when a man has drunk alcohol, because of the intensity of the stimulant, a light sleep comes over him. His feet and hands are asleep, his tongue is asleep; he cannot speak plainly; he cannot walk straight, and falls down. The joy of this sleep is so great that, when he has drunk once, he wants to drink again. A thousand times he decides that he will not drink any more, but he does it all the same.

There is a poem of our great poet Rumi where he says, "O sleep, every night thou freest the prisoner from his bonds!" The prisoner, when he is asleep, does not know that he is in prison, he is free. The wretched is not wretched, he is contented; the sufferer is no more in pain or misery. This shows us that the soul is not in pain or in misery. If it were, it would also be so when the body is asleep. The soul does not feel the misery of the body and the mind, but when a person awakes then the soul thinks that it is in pain and wretched. All this shows us the great bliss of sleep.

This great bliss is given to us without a price, like all that is best: we do not pay to sleep. We pay thousands of pounds for jewels, for gems that are of no use to our life – bread we can buy for pennies. Man does not know how great the value of sleep is, because the benefit it gives cannot be seen or touched. If he is very busy, if he has some business that brings him money, he will rather be busy in that and take from his sleep, because he sees, "I have gained so many pounds, so many shillings"; he does not see what he gains by sleep.

When we are asleep we generally experience two conditions: dream and deep sleep. The dream is the uncontrolled activity of the mind. When we are awake and our mind works without control, it shows us pictures that come from its store of impressions, and we call this imagination; when we control the activity of the mind, we call it thought. The imaginations that come during sleep we call dreams. We do not call them real, because our waking state shows us something different, but as long as we are not in the waking state the dream is real.

During the deep sleep a person is usually conscious of nothing. When he wakes up, he feels refreshed and renewed. What are we doing while we are fast asleep? The soul then is released from the hold of body and mind. It is free, it goes to its own element, to the highest spheres, and it enjoys being there. It is happy, it experiences all the happiness, all the wisdom of those spheres, it enjoys all bliss, and peace.

Besides the dream and the deep sleep there are visions. These are seen when the soul, during sleep, is active in the higher spheres. What it sees there the mind interprets in allegorical pictures. The soul sees the actual thing plainly, and the mind takes from its store of impressions whatever is like that which the soul sees. Therefore it is seen as a picture, as an allegory, a parable which the wise one can interpret, because he knows the language of those spheres. If he sees himself going downstairs or walking up a mountain, he knows what it means; if he sees himself in rags or very richly dressed, in a ship, or in the desert, he knows what it

means. The ignorant one does not know what it means, he
thinks it is merely a dream, it is nothing.

In a vision a person sees either what concerns himself, or
what concerns others in whom he is interested. If he is
interested in his nation or in the whole of humanity, he will
see what concerns his nation or the whole of humanity.

In a dream a voice may be heard, or a message given in
letters. This is the higher vision. Sages and saints see in the
vision exactly what will happen or what the present condition
is, because their mind is controlled by their will; even in sleep
it does not for one moment think that it can act independently
of their will. And so, whatever the soul sees, the mind shows
it exactly as it is seen. Sages and saints see visions even while
awake, because their consciousness is not bound to this earthly
plane; it is awake and acts freely upon the higher planes.

Besides the dream, the vision and the deep sleep, the mystics
experience two other conditions: the self-produced dream and
the self-produced deep sleep. To accomplish this is the aim of
mysticism. It is so easy that I can explain it to you in these
few words, and it is so difficult that I should like to bow my
head before him who has achieved it. It is accomplished by
concentration and meditation.

Can you hold one thought in your mind, keeping all other
thoughts away? Can you keep your mind free from all
thoughts, from all pictures? We cannot: a thousand thoughts,
a thousand pictures come and go. By mastering this the
mystic masters all. He is awake upon this plane and upon
the higher plane; then the one becomes sleep and the other
the wakeful state.

People may say that mystics, Sufis, are great occultists,
very psychic people. That is not their aim; their aim is the
true consciousness, the real life, the Consciousness which lies
beyond: Allah. When this Consciousness is open to them, then
all wisdom is open to the soul and all the books, all the learning
in the world become to them mere intellectual knowledge.

You might say, "Then lazy people who are always sleeping
are all saints". No, the soul also must have experience on
the earth. It must learn what virtue is, it must learn to be
virtuous.

2

By sleep we understand the covering of ourselves from the world of which we are conscious, but we do not realize that, when we are awake, we are covering ourselves from another world which, in fact, is more real; it is the self which is covered. The difference between the sleeping and the waking state is that, when we cover ourselves from what, in fact, is real, we say, "I am awake" and, when we cover ourselves from what is unreal and illusion, we say we are asleep.

The reason for this is that in the state in which we are conscious of all things around us we are able to point to things about which we have no doubt. We recognize the objects around us, therefore we say that we are awake, and during the time of sleep we think we are dreaming, we do not know where we are or what we are doing. In reality that is the very time when we are experiencing our real life.

What does our real life consist of? Our real life consists of natural happiness, peace and purity. By purity I mean that our heart, our mind, our intelligence are pure from all worries, anxieties, pains and tortures, from bitterness or sweetness, such as we experience in the world. Otherwise our heart reflects on these things all the time and accordingly brings us suffering.

How valuable is the peace we obtain in sleep! We cannot realize this until we long for sleep which will not come. At such a time we shall realize that everything we possess in the world is worth sacrificing for the peace which sleep brings and the happiness we experience then. All the pleasures in the world afford only a glimpse of that happiness which is within us, in our innermost being. In our everyday external life that happiness is as buried. If there is a time when happiness is experienced by the soul, it is the time during which we are asleep. The little happiness we experience in this world is not real, but only a shadow which we call pleasure, whereas the true happiness which we experience by our natural life we do not call happiness, for we do not know what it is. Only its after-effects remain with us, and we feel happy when we come to the wakeful state after having had a good sleep.

The peace we experience during sleep cannot be compared with the peace we experience in the form of rest in a comfortable chair or on a couch, in the form of material comfort at home or elsewhere. The life we experience during sleep is outside a wall, a prison-wall; the pains and diseases of this world are within the prison during this time. In the waking state we are in the prison, our life is unhappy; when fast asleep we are free. The moment sleep comes to a person who is in pain and suffering all his disease is left behind; at that moment he is above all suffering and pain. This shows that during sleep we experience a life which is beyond this mortal existence.

Although man experiences sleep every day, he never realizes it as the greatest blessing of his existence, until he suffers from lack of it. Man disregards all natural blessings, and not regarding them as blessings he remains discontented. A person who can see the blessing which is in life itself will be so thankful that whatever may be lacking in his outward life will seem insignificant. The inner blessing is so much greater, compared with what is lacking in the outer world, that, indeed, there is no comparison between them.

All this shows that what develops a person and helps him to advance along the spiritual path, should be sought no further than along the natural lines of the mystery of sleep. Once this mystery is solved, the deeper question of the inner cult is solved as well. The explanation of things is so near to us and yet, at the same time, it is so far beyond our reach!

In Sufi terms there are five stages of consciousness: *Nasut, Malakut, Jabarut, Lahut* and *Hahut.*

Nasut is the consciousness which depends upon our senses. Whatever we see by means of the eyes, or hear by means of the ears, whatever we smell and taste, all these experiences which we gain by the help of the material body, prove to us that this is a particular plane of consciousness, or a particular kind of experience of the consciousness.

Malakut is a further stage of consciousness working through our mental plane. By means of this higher consciousness we experience thought and imagination – which are beyond our senses. Very often it happens that a person does not notice a passer-by, so deeply is he thinking upon some subject. You may speak to him, but he will not listen, so deeply is he absorbed in his subject. Though his ears are open he cannot hear, though his eyes are open he cannot see. What does this mean? It means that at that moment his consciousness is experiencing life on a different plane. Though he is sitting before you with open eyes and ears, his consciousness is on another plane, working through a different body.

The plane of *Malakut* is experienced by every person not only when absorbed in thought, but also in dreams. While the different sense-organs are resting, the mind is free to work, and it works with the aid of the same mechanism* which it has collected during the experience of the *Nasut* condition. In other words, all the experiences which a man gathers during the day are assembled during the night, and the mind works with that mechanism; whatever has been collected during the day is at work during the night. Therefore, if a person has acquired an impression of fear, fear will manifest itself in the dream in different forms; if a person has acquired an impression of love, love will appear in the dream in various forms; if of success the dream will show success in different forms. So the mind prepares a cover for every impression it receives, it prepares an outward appearance for it: that is what accounts for the meaning of dreams.

Suppose that a person goes to a wise man saying, "I have seen flowers in my dream. What will be the result of it?" The wise man will answer, "Love, happiness, success". Why? Because the wise one knows that the mind disguises itself and the impression it receives into something beautiful, when something beautiful is going to happen, and into something ugly, when something bad is going to happen.

It is, however, not only so that the mind adorns itself with a certain form in order to tell you that you are going to have a good or a bad experience. There also is the natural outcome of things, there is action and reaction: what we take from the outer world is prepared in the mind, and it reacts again in another form. This gives us a sort of key by which we

* formed by the assembled experiences and impressions of the senses

can understand what the next step will be. In that form the dream is a warning.

There is no need to take it as a warning in a spiritualistic form, and claim that a spirit, a ghost or an angel came to tell you the future. It is your own mind which disguises itself as a spirit, a ghost or an angel, in whatever form you wish it to come to you, or in whatever form you are accustomed to. It will never come in a form strange to you, such as you have never known; it will only come in a form to which you are accustomed. For instance, if you were to see a dog with wings, it would still be the form of a dog with which you are familiar; only the mixture or combination of forms is curious. Although wings are attached to the dog, the form is not actually new; you are seeing something which you recognize.

In the dream the state of the mind has two different aspects. When the mind is not expressive but responsive and is not acting in a positive but in a negative rhythm, then it becomes visionary. That mind is visionary which is apt to catch the reflection of whatever other mind falls upon it. Thus it may catch the reflection of a living person's mind, or of a deceased person's mind, of a spiritually advanced person, or of a very ordinary person. That mind lies open like a piece of uncultivated ground which a person may turn into a farm or into a garden; in that soil he may sow seeds of flowers or only seeds of thorns.

This accounts for people having different experiences in their dreams from those they had in their waking life. When people say, "I learn something from my dreams, I am inspired by them, I have received new ideas, new lessons in my dreams", it is because their mind was exposed to the given impressions. However, a mind open to impressions in this way may reflect a satanic as well as an angelic impression, a wrong one as easily as a right one: it is open to whatever comes into it. Such a person is as likely to be led astray as to be helped. The result, therefore, is only good as long as the impressions to which the mind responds are good ones.

What then is the way in which one can be sure to have the mind focused upon good things, and so to receive only good impressions? There are three considerations.

First, one must be able to keep all the ever-moving thoughts away which come into one's mind. One must develop that mental strength, that will-power which will keep all thoughts away which come into one's mind during concentration and take one's mind away from the object on which one focuses it.

Secondly, the mind will always focus itself upon the object which it loves. If one does not have love for the divine Being, for God, if one does not have that ideal, then it will certainly be difficult, for it cannot be done by the intellect. The person who only uses his intellect keeps asking, "Where shall I direct my mind, on what object shall I focus it? Please, picture it for me, and point out where it is". It is the lover of God whose mind cannot wander anywhither, save always directly to God.

Then, purity of mind is necessary. The mind must be pure from all fear, worry and anxiety, and from every kind of falsehood, for all this covers the mind from the vision of God. When the mind, full of faith, love, purity and strength, is focused upon the ideal of God, man will receive teaching, inspiration and advice directly and for every case he meets with in life.

The simple teaching of all the religions during every age, the essence of all religion and philosophy, is contained in these words: Go and stand before God in simple faith, being as a little child before God. At that moment you will say, "I know nothing, I have not learned anything, I am only an empty cup waiting to be filled. I have only love to offer You, and because my love is too insufficient, I ask to be given more. I have only faith, and yet that is insufficient; so I ask that it be strengthened and developed so that it will be strong enough to hold me before You. Purity I need, but I do not have it, or at least, if I have it, it is only Your own essence which is within my being, and I wish to keep it as clean as possible. With these three things I come, as a simple child, with no knowledge of my own, leaving aside all doubts and questions or whatever can come between us". Here is the essence of religion.

It is so simple that even a child could do it, should he wish so. He does not need much learning to be able to do it; once it is explained to him he will understand it. We need not have learning or great intellectual knowledge to be able to do it.

The next stage, beyond the plane of *Malakut*, brings us to *Jabarut*, the plane of consciousness where the experience is like that of a person in deep, dreamless sleep – who is said to be sound asleep. The blessing here is greater still. In this higher experience there is God's own Being through whom we experience the life, peace and purity which are within us. Moreover, whilst anyone may experience this blessing during sleep, the person who follows the path of spiritual development will experience it while awake. Yogis call this state *Sushupti*. This joy of life, peace and purity the mystic experiences with wide open eyes, wide awake; others can only touch it during deep sleep.

A still further experience of consciousness is *Lahut*. This raises a person from the material to the immaterial plane. In this plane the state of being fast asleep is not necessary. There is greater peace and joy, and nearness to the essence which is called divine. In Christian terms this stage is called communion. In Vedantic terms it is called *Turiyavastha*, and the further step to this is called *Samadhi* which may no doubt be described as merging in God. In other words, in this stage we dive into our deepest selfhood; God is in our deepest self. In this state we have the ability to dive so deep as to touch our deepest being, which is the home of all intelligence, life, peace and joy, and where worry, fear, disease or death do not enter.

Hahut is the experience which is the object of every mystic who follows the inner cult. In Vedantic terms this stage is called *Manan*; the equivalent in Christian terminology is at-one-ment.

From these considerations it may be seen that the work of the Sufi is to aim at ennobling the soul. When initiated into the Order we take the path of ennobling the soul – there is no wonder-working, no communication with spirits, no performing of miracles, no developing of magnetic or psychic powers, no clairvoyance or clairaudience, nor anything of the kind. The one single aim is to become humane, to live a healthy life, to try and better the moral conditions of our life, to ennoble our character, and to meet not only our own needs, but also those of our neighbours and friends. Our work is to try and develop that spark which is in every soul, whose only satisfaction lies in the love of God and in approaching towards God, with the intention of one day having a glimpse of that truth that cannot be spoken of in words.

CHAPTER XXII

Dreams

1 The Nature of the Dream

THERE IS a Hindustani saying calling this world the dream of life. In the Vedanta this world is called the dream of Brahma, the dream of God. It makes a person afraid to think that all our affairs, to which we give so much importance, should be unreal, should be a dream. When people came to talk to me, I have several times experienced their great disappointment when they said, "Do you mean to say that all this is a dream, that it is not real? Now here you are standing, I am sitting, you are speaking. Is it all a dream?" They meant, "What a foolish idea to call this life a dream". To him who has experienced only materially through his five senses, without even a glimpse of an idea of something else, this life seems real and we cannot blame him for thinking it real. It is only when he awakens from this life that he sees that it is unreal. If, while you are dreaming, someone comes and tells you, "Do not believe it, it is a dream", you will never believe him, you will think it is real.

The dream is recognized as a dream because of its contrast to physical life, as everything is recognized by its contrast. We recognize woman because there is man; day is recognized because there is night, but to find the contrast to the dream of life is very hard. Let us see what makes a dream to be called a dream. There are three things: its changing character, its momentariness, and its deluding nature. Life in this world has the same attributes. If we consider ourselves – our body, the body of another – we see that at every moment we are changing. At one moment we find ourselves so angelic, so good, so mild, at another we find ourselves so rebellious that we would fight with Satan. As to the momentariness, the transitory nature – where are those who were so great as Dara and Sikandar* whose glory promised to last always?

* Dara and Sikandar – Darius and Alexander the Great

Nothing is left. Then, as to its deluding nature, how jealous are we if our rival gets what we hoped for. It may be a passing joy; to-morrow the joy and the rival may not be, but whilst they last how jealous we are! If great riches come into our hands, we think it so great a thing; it promises us all. It all passes away, but while it is there we are so happy or so sad. This is life's deluding nature.

Why is this world called the dream of Brahma, the dream of God? Because each of us experiences only a part of the dream, and only God, the Whole Being, experiences all the time the whole of the dream.

God lost in the manifestation is the state which we call waking. The manifestation lost in God is realization. In my language I would call the latter awakening and the former a dream.

In the physical world you are here, everything else is outside of you, and you are contained in space. In the dream all you see is contained within you. You may dream that you are in Paris, but if you really were in Paris, the Parisians would know that you were there. If they knew nothing of it, then you were not in Paris. Paris and everything else in the dream is within you. In that state you are so great – but you call it a dream, an imagination, and you think that imagination is nothing.

Question: Is it better to be always in a dream or always awake?
Answer: This is a very interesting question and one that should be asked of great people. If a person wishes to be always in a dream, he should go to the caves of the mountains, to the wilderness, because in the world people will not only take all he has, but they will eat his bones, his skin, his flesh. We see at what point people have come by being always awake! If such a person wishes to eat, the thought comes, "What can I gain, what business can I do", and will not let him eat. If he wishes to sleep, the thought, "What benefit can I have", will not let him sleep. The politician who is always thinking, "What office can we take, what territory can we gain, how can we get more than others", can never have any rest.

The best course for those who are seeking the truth – not for everybody, but for those who are on the way of truth – is to be just so much awake as is needed to carry out their responsibilities in life, not allowing themselves to be quite trodden upon, and to be so much in the dream as they can without neglecting their life's responsibilities.

2 How Dreams are formed

Let us now consider how the dreams that we dream every night are formed. Our mind is made of vibrations, or let us call them atoms. These have the property of receiving impressions; they are just like a photographic plate. They are continually receiving impressions: impressions of heat or cold, of friends or enemies. These are stocked in the storehouse of the mind – so many thousands, so many millions of impressions, more than can be counted. When you are asleep, when your body is resting but your mind is active, these pictures appear before you, just like a moving picture on a screen. Then, when your mind is fully exhausted, deep sleep comes.

Some pictures we develop very much by keeping them often before us; the pictures of enemies, for instance, or of friends of whom we often think. Other pictures are very little developed, they just come and go. That is why sometimes in the dream we see the faces of our friends just as they are, sometimes we see forms that seem familiar but whom we do not recognize, and sometimes we see pictures that seem quite strange. Two or three of the pictures that are little developed join and form one picture which seems familiar.

If asked whether we can dream of what we have never seen, I would say: No, all that we dream we have seen. The *Jinn*, who have never manifested themselves on earth, cannot form a picture of things of this world. The imagination is just the same as the dream.

Dreams go by affinity, which means that like attracts like. If at the beginning of the night we have a sad dream, all night sad dreams come. If at the beginning of the night we have a joyful dream, all night pleasant dreams come. If there is one tragic dream, then all night tragedy goes on. If there is one comic dream, then all night comedy goes on.

Question: Is there any means of keeping an undesirable dream away?
Answer: There are a thousand ways of keeping an undesirable dream away, but if it is a warning then it will be very difficult to keep it away, or if one particular dream is kept away, another unpleasant dream will come.

3 Dreams are of Three Kinds

The dreams we dream every night are of three kinds; there is a fourth sort of dream, but that is more a vision.

There is a dream in which a person sees during the night what he has been doing during the day; when his mind has been very much engaged in all thoughts, occupations, and cares of the day, these appear before him in the dream. This dream is called *Khwab-i khayali*. It does not have much effect upon the mind, because it is not very deep.

The second kind of dream is *Khwab-i ghalti*, in which one sees the opposite of what really happens: when one sees someone dead that person recovers from his illness, or one sees someone as one's enemy who in reality is one's friend. When the mirror of the mind is distorted, then the image falling upon it is distorted too, just as in some mirrors everything appears reversed: if you are thin, you appear as fat and round as a ball, and a short person appears as tall and thin as a column.

The third kind of dream is *Khwab-i ruhi*, in which events are shown exactly as they are. This dream comes to the upright, pure mind, to the righteous, pious person. It is seen either in a dreaming or half-waking condition. If something is lacking in the person's piety, he may see something reversed in the dream. He may see the death of the father when it is the death of the mother, or the illness of the daughter when it is the illness of the son, but if he is absolutely pious he sees the exact event. This dream comes only to the few, to the chosen ones, but we should remember that in all of us the

soul is the same; it is only its cover that is different. So we
may all dream this dream at times.

Many years before the Prophet Muhammad came forward
as a master, as a prophet, his wife knew he was a prophet,
because every morning he used to tell her what he had dreamt
in the night, and it was always that which happened the next
day. Whilst he himself was not yet sure of his message, she
believed that he was the chosen one, and she encouraged him.
If there was a first disciple of Prophet Muhammad, it was his
wife.

The three kinds of dream are the most wonderful subject
of study in life. The kind of dream, which is the exact picture
of a reality which a person may sooner or later experience in
his so-called real life, teaches us that the incidents which we
experience unexpectedly in life were pre-ordained for us. It
also teaches us that, although here in the physical plane we
appear to be separate one from the other, in the plane of
the dream the whole world exists upon the surface of the
individual's mind. He who is one single being on the physical
plane inverts into the whole world on the plane of the dream,
although even there where he is alone he still holds fast his
individuality.

The nature of the second kind of dream, in which everything appears to be the reverse of what may happen, is the
opposite of manifestation: a person seen dead in this dream
will have a long life, and the sickness of a friend seen in the
dream would, on the contrary, bring him good health. It is
because of their negative nature that things like the printer's
block, the photographic plate, and all other things of negative
character, will show their opposite before they produce the
right image.

The kind of dream produced before the view of man, in
which he sees what he has been doing during the day, is of
little consequence. It is either caused by unbalanced activity
of the mind, or by physical disorder. Such dreams as a rule
have no importance and, although they create before man a
moving picture, they are surely a waste.

This kind of dream, caused by the activity of his mind, is
given to each person in his everyday life. The second kind

generally manifests itself before the view of those who possess the attribute of humanity, who first think of the world and its responsibilities, together with the thought of God. The third kind of dream generally is vouchsafed to the spiritual person; it is, of course, seldom seen by the average man.

The first thing that happens in the spiritual development of a person is that his dreams change. First he dreams a thing and the contrary happens. Then he dreams a thing and that thing happens exactly as he dreamed it. Then God gives him warnings in pictures, just as the first writings were picture-writings. Then, when his soul discloses itself more, he hears a voice and he sees angelic beings. Then, when his soul opens still more, he realizes the true being of God. When the true being of God is realized in the waking condition, then he is a saint.

CHAPTER XXIII

Spiritual Healing

ALL THROUGH the long history of the human race there are records of the practice of healing by magnetic, mental and spiritual methods. The great messengers have practised the art themselves and have enjoined it upon their disciples. Even among the most primitive races we find traces of such ministration.

It is true that there was a time, when to be ill and weak was accounted a sign of saintliness, when those who were seeking to tread the spiritual path neglected and ill-treated their bodies, starved and ill-used them until they were living skeletons, reduced to the lowest possible state of misery and distress, and quite incapable of constructive thought and action. These days are past, wiser counsels now prevail, the mind of man has come to a saner and wiser opinion. He realizes that the body, which is the temple of God, should be a fitting habitation for its heavenly Guest, and that the instrument through which man functions should be as perfect a machine as possible.

The engineer in charge of a delicate piece of machinery sees to it that it is kept clean, well oiled and free from dust in order that it may fulfil his will and carry out his commands. He well knows there is danger unless these conditions are fulfilled; yet man, who is using as his instrument the human body, the most delicate piece of machinery that has come from the hands of the great Engineer, often neglects and misuses it and fails to keep it in good working order.

It is often asked why people are ill. Many answers might be given; probably none of them will satisfy the engineer wholly, until he can hear within his heart the "still small voice" telling him in no uncertain language the cause of the trouble in his own case. It is certainly true that at the back of every apparent cause there is lack of harmony; some part of man's being is out of tune, and the jarring note sets up vibrations which affect the whole system. It may be that there is some habit or weakness in his life which is poisoning the springs of his being. No one who is holding in his consciousness anything which falls below his own ideal can be in a state of harmony, for all the time – whether he is aware of it or not – the struggle for mastery between the higher and the lower self is going on.

But then it may be asked why people, who are quite frankly living a life devoted to material pleasures, are so often well and happy, while they deny themselves nothing that will minister to their own physical and emotional satisfaction. May not the answer be: because in their case there is no struggle, the soul is not yet awake, the higher consciousness is sleeping. They are travelling along the line of least resistance, there is no conflict as yet for them.

Then again it is asked why so often good people are ill, and we may perhaps answer that question by asking another: What is goodness? Some people who are called good are very negative; they allow their minds and bodies to be open to every sort of influence that comes to them from without. The garden of their soul is not guarded and tended by the wise gardener, and the winds blowing from north and south, from east and west, carry all sorts of seeds: seeds of weeds and thistles and thorns which fall upon the soil, take root and spring up very quickly; often they choke the flowers that are also growing in that garden, and then, in a sensitive personality, there is struggle for mastery. Disharmony results from it and consequently weakness and illness.

Let us strive for wisdom, that we may know what to take in and what to cast out; for when wisdom guards the threshold we shall become strong and steady like the waterwheel which revolves at such a rapid rate that it resists and throws off any object, however heavy, that is thrown against it.

Above the portal of a small convalescent home in an English country village these words are written, so large that all who enter may read them and take heed:

> For good may ever conquer ill
> Health walks where pain has trod
> As a man thinketh so is he
> Rise then and think with God.

We read in the Christian scriptures: "Whatsoever things are good, whatsoever things are pure, whatsoever things are holy, whatsoever things are of good report – think on these things". Thought is creative, thought has a dynamic power: "as a man thinketh so is he". We are taught that every thought has its birth and death, and that the life of every thought is far longer and more enduring than the life of the human being.

Hundreds of wireless messages are passing by us during every hour of the day, but only the instrument that is tuned to the right note can receive them. The discovery of wireless telegraphy has been to the thinker a most illuminating example on the physical plane of what is always happening in the spiritual spheres. Distance is no longer any obstruction, and just as in the physical world a receiver is necessary, so also in the spiritual world; for the law is universal both in the spiritual realm, the realm of reality, and in the physical world, which is only the shadow of the real one.

Let us see to it that our hearts and minds are tuned to the higher vibrations, so that only those things that are good, pure, holy and of good report can enter and dwell there. Let us keep out the idle thoughts, the unkind thoughts, the envious thoughts that come knocking at the door of the heart and which, if we admit them, will result in speech and action, and produce in our bodies illness, weakness, weariness. Then when this happens, man in his ignorance of the true cause goes to the doctor or surgeon who perhaps performs an operation, and often the patient may be no better but rather worse, for the real cause of the trouble is untouched.

One may ask: is pain always an evil thing? – and I would answer: far from it. Sometimes pain comes to us as a kindly warning. It is the moving finger pointing to us and bidding us to give heed to our ways, to take account of our doings. There are different kinds of pain: pain of the body which is often hard to bear, pain of the mind which is far worse, and pain of the heart, the deepest part of man's being, which may be agony. Yet the cry of agony which comes from the depth of the heart may be a sound of the greatest beauty, for pain has its beautiful aspect. Think of the pain expressed in the most perfect music, the finest poetry. There are moments of intense feeling when pain and joy meet, and one cannot distinguish where one ends and the other begins; they have their meeting place in the heart of man. Pain is like the herb in the hands of the great Transmuter, the divine Alchemist; falling on the melted silver of the heart it turns it into the purest gold, and renders the heart of man more fitting to be the altar of God.

Who are those to whom people go for sympathy when they are in trouble? Surely to those who have suffered much, those who, having gone through great tribulation, have overcome and have learned by experience that true happiness comes from within and is independent of outward circumstances. They can feel not only for others but with others, and out of the depth of their own experience teach them how to find courage and faith and hope. They can help them to bind up their wounds, and heal their broken hearts. If suffering can develop in us the blessed gift of sympathy, then surely we have not suffered in vain; we may well thank God for every pang which we have endured.

What of the pain endured by all the great Saviours and Masters of humanity? We feel here that we are touching a most sacred mystery which words cannot express – but may we not reverently believe that, by taking to themselves the burden of pain of all the world, they transmuted it by the process of alchemy, and sent it out as a fountain of love and power springing up into everlasting life?

However, while pain is one thing, disease is quite another thing. Disease must always be contrary to the divine Will, and it is our duty to combat it by every means in our power and to order our lives along the lines of sane, healthy living, obeying the laws of health in matters of diet, sanitation and clothing. Disease is largely the product of over-civilization. People of less highly evolved civilization know how to keep themselves in health by simple nature remedies, such as herbs. It is said that the North-American Indian, when he comes home tired after a long day's hunting, will fling himself down upon the ground, relax every sinew and muscle, and draw into himself fresh stores of energy from the magnetic currents of the earth, so that after an hour's rest he is ready to rise up and to go forth again, if necessary, with renewed strength and vigour.

Among wild animals in their natural state there is very little disease. They die of old age, of accidents, or of the attacks of enemies stronger than themselves.

We in the West have lost the knowledge of the use of simple nature remedies, and there is scarcely one who really knows how to relax. We should do well to try to get back this lost knowledge, for health is more likely to be gained in this way than by the use of drugs or the surgeon's knife. Man is the microcosm of the macrocosm; every substance in the earth is to be found in the body of man, even to the lately discovered radium. Therefore it is in a very true sense that we speak of Mother Earth, and the closer we live to nature, our great mother, and the simpler we make our manner of living, the healthier shall we surely become.

What is health? Health is surely wholeness of body, heart and mind, complete harmony of the whole being. Wholeness is also holiness. Nothing short of this should content us, if as Sufis we are endeavouring to tread the path which leads to the culmination of love, harmony and beauty – that perfect trinity which is the goal of all life. God alone is the Healer; those who minister will only truly heal when they keep this truth always before them, for it is not the solid wood that makes the flute, it is the empty reed. The healer is only the instrument which God Himself is using and, only in so far as he can put aside his own lower personality and dedicate and consecrate his life to the great service, will he be successful in the work he has undertaken. He should endeavour to cultivate an attitude of calmness, serenity and poise, of harmony within and without; for just as the waters of a lake, when tossed to and fro and broken up by the winds of a great storm, cannot reflect the clear blue sky, neither can the heart of the one who is disturbed and distracted by the turmoil of the world and confused by the sound of earth's many voices, reflect the will of the God and Father of us all.

It has been said that we grow into the likeness of that which we habitually contemplate. Therefore constant and habitual contemplation of the perfect ideal, dwelling in thought upon the attributes of divine beauty, keeping the heart tuned to the note of love and harmony, and making this the practice of daily life, the mind still and calm, the heart pure and open so that it can reflect the perfect Will – this should be the aim of life of the one who aspires to serve humanity as a spiritual healer.

We are told that one of the properties of radium is that, if for a time you shut up certain substances in an appropriate receptacle with even a tiny portion of radium, these substances will acquire some of the properties of the radium and will show its power. After some time they lose these properties and have to be replaced close to the radium in order to be recharged. We read of the great masters that, when exhausted after days of teaching and ministering to the sick, they retired into the mountains and forests to commune with Almighty God, and came forth again charged with fresh power to resume their work of healing and inspiring. If even for the great ones these times of quiet were necessary, how much more for us. The action of the radium is a parallel of the Almighty Father's power, it speaks to us of the refreshment which comes from quiet communing with the Supreme.

What should be the attitude of the patient? He must have a living faith, he must do his part in the work. We read of Jesus Christ that in one place even he could do no mighty works because of the unbelief of the people, and again in another place people came to him with all manner of diseases and he healed them all. The patient must believe in the power of God to heal and he must have confidence and trust in his healer. God holds His blessings out to us, but we must take them from His hands. If we refuse to co-operate in the work of healing, we cannot receive the blessing; if we set up obstacles, we can obstruct even the river of life itself.

So the patient must have confidence and trust in the healer; he must open himself to receive the healing currents for the conveyance of which the healer is only the channel, for life and health are the gifts of God Himself.

THE PRIVILEGE OF BEING HUMAN

CHAPTER I

Man the Purpose of Creation

IN EVERY SCRIPTURE it is mentioned that man is the ideal of creation. In the Qur'an it is said, "We have made man the Caliph of the whole creation", in other words, the master of creation. The deeper we study life the clearer we see that life, under all its aspects, under all its names and forms, is constantly working towards the plane of the human being, helping the human being in his life's purpose which is to become God's instrument. One can see that camels, elephants and horses yield to the will of man. One sees that animals like dogs and cats, that birds like parrots and many singing birds, such as canaries, in time become satisfied even when imprisoned in a cage; in their captivity they can enjoy the companionship of man.

It is said that saints and sages in ancient times knew the language of animals. That was not only true in the ancient days, it is true in all times. One can hear what the animals say, one can understand their language. It is a matter of opening the heart, it is the ears of the heart that can hear their language, which cannot be understood in any other way. What one hears is a word, coming from the heart of the animals, which is expressed most in their glance that says not only, "I love you", or, "I adore you", but, "I would like to be like you". When the dog and the cat look at man, they do not only say, "I love you", it is more than that; it is, really speaking, the perfect desire. Desire has its stages, there is a stage of desire where one wishes to be like another. That desire reaches its highest stage when one wants to become another, and herein lies the secret of the mystics and the mystery of life.

When a sculptor wishes to create an object he needs clay, and with it he makes different models in order to produce, to bring forth the perfect object he desires. So all God's creation, in all its stages from animal and bird to man, and in all the different aspects of names and forms which we see before us, is a preparation to fulfil the desire of God which is man. God's words in the Qu'ran are, "We have made man that he may enjoy the creation". If there is any form of life that pleases God it is man.

No doubt man, through his ignorance, has exaggerated this ideal and has gone a little astray*. He does not recognize divinity in man, he wants to separate the divine from man. Christ did not. He did not say, "My Father in heaven"; he said, "Our Father in heaven". But when man in his ignorance separates Christ from God and Christ from man, man from Christ and man from God, he misinterprets that most beautiful idea of God given by Christ: the Fatherhood of God and the blessed sonship of man.

Through all the different processes of life evolution has progressed and man, as the ideal of creation, has risen higher than all, which shows that man represents divinity to the whole universe. For instance, the mineral is in man, the vegetable kingdom is in man, the angel is in man, and there is no being of the heavens and of the earth that man does not reflect. No one has ever pictured an angel as different from man; whenever man's imagination produces an angel it sees the angel which is in man – as it also finds a devil in man. Man embraces in himself all the different classes of beings, and at every step he develops and becomes greater than those. If he develops the animal nature, he is more animal than the animals, if he develops devilishness he becomes greater than the devils, and in developing the angelic nature he becomes greater than the angels, for after all angels have bowed at the feet of man.(1) Thus every spirit, every element throughout the whole world, is to be found in man – and yet man is puzzled as to the purpose of his life.

The moment man realizes this, the soul begins to open its eyes to truth, but until then man is asleep, his soul is not yet born. No doubt the answer to man's questions comes in time. Perhaps a thousand answers will come one after another. Every answer will explain something and yet something will be left unexplained. Every veil we lift gives

* i.e. wanting enjoyment for his own pleasure – not for the sake of God.

an answer, and yet not the answer. Another answer is still waiting to come in time.

When we observe the purpose of the lives of the different beings in this world we shall surely find a distinct purpose in the life of the human being. For instance, man is very much inclined to pleasure, food, drink and play. Now if he was born for that, how is it that the animals also have those tastes? They also are fond of food and play, but gaining those necessities of life – those animal necessities – causes great disturbance in the case of man, whereas with animals they cause very little of it. If food and sleep and free dwelling can give happiness, then the animal is much happier than man. Man, after the toil of the day, thinks, "How can I find the means to satisfy my desire for pleasure?". He can never be so peaceful, so contented as the animals. If food, drink and play were the purpose of his life, man would be the most miserable of beings.

Then arises the question: is man born to cause all the falsehood, deceit, treachery and harshness that he inflicts upon others? The answer is that, no doubt, he makes life easy for himself by falsehood and by doing harm to others, but at the same time he often is very miserable and cannot avoid the result of everything he does. All the hurt and harm he causes to others must return to him some time or other a thousandfold.

If it were purposed that man should be an angel and lead a pious, good and retired life in the wilderness, in the forest, or in the caves of the mountains, there would have been no necessity to create him. The angels would have been sufficient, for through the very nature of his being a man cannot live as pure, pious and spiritual a life as the angels who are not burdened with the material world. This shows that man was born neither to become an angel (2) nor to be an animal, living the life of an animal. The whole universe is for man.

How can we find out the qualities which may be considered human qualities? They will be apart from the angelic, devilish and animal qualities, and there chiefly is one which can be called a distinct quality of man: sympathy. A great poet has said in Hindi, "Sympathy is the root of religion, and so long

as the spirit of sympathy is living in your heart it is illuminated
with the light of religion". This means that religion and
morals can be summed up in one thing and that is sympathy,
which in the words of Christ, as interpreted in the Bible,
is charity. All beautiful qualities as tolerance, forgiveness,
gentleness, consideration, reverence and the desire to serve
– all these come from sympathy. Another poet has said in
Urdu that it was for sympathy that man was created, and the
day when man discovers this special attribute in himself, he is
shown his first lesson of how life should be lived.

First we find how many things there are in life that we
should be grateful for, but in our troubles and in the miseries
around us the things for which we should be grateful
are forgotten, and instead of thankfulness we develop an
ungrateful nature. The more complaining a person, the less
gratitude he shows in his nature, and the more his gratitude
develops, the more he will begin to understand. Sa'adi says,
"The sun, the moon, the planets, the air, the water and the
earth are all serving you, aiding life's purpose and preparing
for your food. Yet you regard all this unthankfully, absorbed
in your own little troubles which are as nothing before the
great forces of nature, always working, night and day".
Our little troubles overwhelm and disorder our life, and by
our absorption we are robbed of the knowledge of God's
perfection and greatness.

The first lesson given to man was to be grateful for his daily
bread, because that was the greatest necessity of his life. Now
that has become so simple and life has changed so much that
man forgets to be thankful. He even thinks, "Why should I
give thanks?" He forgets that behind his own personality he
covers God. His own toil seems more to him than the toil of
every atom of nature that is preparing blessings for him.

Self-pity is the worst poverty; it is the source of all
unhappiness and blinds man to all he should be thankful for.
The constantly complaining habit and the tendency to demand
sympathy from others bring the greatest thorn into man's life:
he becomes dependent upon the sympathy of others. The best
thing is to give sympathy. The food of which every soul is in
need is the understanding and sympathy of another.

Man's greatest enemy is his ego which manifests itself in selfishness. Even in his doing good, in his kind actions, selfishness is sometimes at work. When he does good with the thought that one day it may return to him and that he may share in the good, he sells his pearls for a price. A kind action, a thought of sympathy, of generosity, is too precious to trade with. One should give and, while giving, close the eyes. Man should remember to do every little good action, every little kindness, every act of generosity with his whole heart, without the desire of getting anything in return making a trade out of it. The satisfaction must be in doing it and in nothing else.

Every step in evolution makes life more valuable. The more evolved you are, the more priceless is every moment; it becomes an opportunity for you to do good to others, to serve others, to give love to others, to be gentle to others, to give your sympathy to souls who are longing and hungering for it. Life is miserable when a person is absorbed in himself; as soon as he forgets himself he is happy. The more he thinks of himself, his own affairs, work and interests, the less he knows the meaning of life. When a person looks at another he cannot at the same time look at himself. Illness, disappointments and hardships matter very little when one can look at them from a higher standpoint.

Besides this moral point of view there is the mystical aspect, and when looking from the mystical point of view one sees that God's greatest purpose is accomplished by man. In explaining this philosophy I should like to give you the simile of an artist who has produced a beautiful picture. The dogs have looked at it and the cats have looked at it, but that is not enough. When a man who has not understood the idea of the picture, the art, the feeling of it, comes, looks at it and says, "There is nothing in it", then the purpose for which the artist painted the picture is not attained. At last some one else comes, looks at the picture and says, "Oh, what a beautiful idea! It suggests something to me, I can read something from it, it tells me something, it is living". It means that his man has not only understood the picture, but has understood the soul of the artist.

The whole beauty of creation – the dogs have seen it, the cats have seen it, the peacocks and other birds have seen it and in their way they have been delighted, they have enjoyed it, they have danced and rejoiced over it. They have admired it in their own way, but man – besides admiring – sees beyond, his sight penetrates all he sees, and he touches God, the Creator. It is not only praising God, but it is knowing and understanding God which gives the greatest satisfaction to the Deity, because that is the purpose of the creation of man: that he may understand and know. And it is only by seeing the sublimity of nature's beauty, by being impressed by it, by understanding it, by knowing its language, by hearing its voice, that this can be done. The man who is living, who can hear and see and whose heart can feel, has risen above ordinary humanity. It does not mean that man has to become an angel: he needs to live a fuller life, a really human life.

What a great thing is understanding! It is priceless. No man can give greater pleasure to his fellowman than by understanding him. The closest friend in life is the one who understands most. It is not your wife, brother or sister, it is the one who understands you most who is your greatest friend in the world. You can be the greatest friend of God if you can understand God. Imagine how man lives in the world – with closed eyes and closed ears! Every name and every form speaks constantly, constantly makes signs for you to hear, for you to respond to, for you to interpret, that you may become a friend of God. The whole purpose of your life is to make yourself ready to understand what God is, what your fellowman is, what the nature of man is, what life is.

Now coming to a still greater secret of life I want to answer the question: how can we grow to read and understand the message that life speaks through all its names and forms? The answer is that, as by the opening of the eyes you can see things, so by the opening of the heart you can understand things. As long as the heart is closed you cannot understand. The secret is that, when the ears and eyes of the heart are open, all planes of the world are open, all names are open, all secrets, all mysteries are unfolded.

The question arises: what is the manner of opening the heart? The way to it is a natural life, the life of the child, smiling with the smiling one, praying with the praying one, ready to learn from everyone, ready to love. The child has enmity against no one, he has no hatred, no malice, his heart is open. It is in the child that you can see the smiles of angels; he can see through life.

When the grown-up person is made ready, when he has acquired the attributes of the child, then he creates heaven within himself, he understands. The child with his innocence does not understand, but when a man with understanding develops the childlike loving tendency, the purity of heart of the child with the desire to be friendly to all – that is the opening of the heart, and it is by that blessing that he can receive all the privileges of human life.

CHAPTER II

Character-Building

1

WHAT IS character? Character is, so to speak, a picture with lines and colours which we make within ourselves. It is wonderful to see how the tendency of character-building springs up from childhood, just as one sees in a bird the instinct of building a nest. A little child begins to notice all kinds of things in grown-up persons and to adopt all that seems best to it: words, manners, movements, ideas. Everything that it grasps from the grown-up it attracts and gathers, and builds, so to speak, a building with it which is its character. It is being built all through life.

By this we understand that, when a person is absorbed in himself, he has no time for character-building, because he has no time to think of others: then there is no other. But when he forgets himself, he has time to look here and there, to collect what is good and beautiful, and to add it naturally to his character. So the character is built. One need not make an effort to build it, one has only to forget oneself. For instance, actors and actresses with great qualifications cannot act if they do not forget themselves. If the musician cannot forget himself when he is playing, he cannot perform music satisfactorily; the singer's voice will not come out. And so it is with the poet and all other artists.

Think then how the whole work of building oneself, and everything else, depends on how much one is able to forget oneself! That is the key to the whole life, material and spiritual, and to worldly and spiritual success. It seems such a simple thing, and yet it is so difficult.

During my travels, whenever I met with people great in art, science, thought, religion or philosophy, I found that whatever was their work they had touched greatness through this quality, the quality of forgetting themselves. It was always the same everywhere. And again I have seen people with great qualifications, but who remembered themselves so much that they could not do the best with their lives.

I have known a vina-player, a very wonderful musician, who used to play his instrument for six and nine hours daily. But whenever he came into an assembly he became nervous, because the first thought that came to him was himself, and then all the impressions of the people present would fall upon him. Generally he would take his vina, cover it up and run away and with all his qualifications he never had a chance of being great. Self-confidence is a great thing, but forgetting oneself is greater still. I also have seen Sarah Bernhardt singing a simple song, the national anthem of France; that was all. But when she came on the stage and sang that song she would win every heart, for at that time she was France*, she was able to be France because of her concentration and her forgetting herself.

2

Character-building is much greater and more important than the building of a house, a city, a nation, an empire, a race. One might ask, "Why is it so important? It is only the building of our little self which is so small". I shall reply that many have built up an edifice, a nation, a race, and they are gone, no memory of them is left. The Taj Mahal is the most beautiful building in the world. Those who see it – artists, architects – have such a great admiration for it, but that is all. No one cares who made it, no one's heart is moved on account of the builder.

To this day Hindus repeat early in the morning, "Ram, Ram". The Buddhists call on the Lord Buddha, and the Christians on Christ. Why? Only because of their ideal personality, of their magnetism. The words of Christ spoken so many hundreds of years ago are remembered to-day because of his personality. It is not spirituality alone: there have been many *madzubs*; they were very spiritual, they were with God. They have gone and no one remembers them. It is

* After the outbreak of World War I

not piety: there are many pious people sitting in mosques and churches turning their rosaries; their piety is for themselves, they cannot move the world. So it is not spirituality, it is not piety. What is it then? It is the development of humanity in us, and this concerns our intelligence, our heart and our mind.

It concerns the intelligence because, if we have love but not the intelligence to know the pleasure of the beloved, then we may be a great lover, but we cannot express our love adequately. It concerns the heart because, if we have intelligence but no feeling, no sympathy, we may speak very politely, we may be very polished in manner, but if there is bitterness within, if within we do not feel what we say, it would be better if we had not spoken. It concerns the mind because, if we have intelligence and feeling but no thought, we have not the manner, we are ignorant. You may know all European manners and decorum very well, but if you are sent out to the court of an Eastern king, you will be at a loss. Or you may know all the etiquette of an Eastern court, but if you come to Europe you know nothing.

It is so great a privilege to be human that we should develop our humanity, and be human in reality as well as in form. It is man who is the ideal of God. It is not the rock which does not know whether a king or a beggar stands upon it, whether a holy man or a wicked person. It is not the angels who have no heart to feel sympathy for one another; they feel the praise of God, they praise God. It is man who has been given a heart.

A Hindustani poet says, "To become *nabi, ghawth, qutb* (3) is very difficult. What shall I tell you of the difficulties of life, since it is even difficult for man to become human?" To attain to spiritual grades is very difficult. We should first try to be human. To become an angel is not very difficult*. To be material is very easy. To live in the world, in all the difficulties and struggles of the world, and be human is very difficult. If we become that, then we become the miniature God on earth.

---

* i.e. to live as an angel without having passed through the stage of being human.

CHAPTER III

Human Nature

1

I HAVE seen in my life that it is not difficult to have occult or psychic powers; to be virtuous, to keep our life pure, is not very difficult. To be merciful, to be compassionate, is difficult: it is difficult to be human.

God has many names: the Great, the Powerful, the Mighty, the Sovereign, but he is always called Merciful and Compassionate. In these qualities we are never perfect, we shall never be perfect. As it has been said, "Go into your room at night and repent of what you have done, of all the thousand bad thoughts you have had of friends and enemies". A Persian poet has said, "The whole secret of the two worlds is in these two words: With friends be loving, with enemies courteous".

If you have understood that this world is nothing, if you have recognized that it is a passing thing, why not let others enjoy while you renounce? Why not let others put on the nice dress while you look at it? Why not let others eat the dinner while you be in the kitchen and cook it? Why not let others sit in the car while you drag it, instead of you sitting in the car and making others drag it?

Keep your life noble; that is: be merciful and compassionate. It is the tendency of everyone to take the best of another. Even in friendship there is this tendency. All are seeking their own enjoyment and leave the worst for another. If you are a seeker of God, take the opposite way. Let all the world go one way, while you go the contrary way.

2

Since the world always oppresses the good, tramples upon the meek, and robs the generous, what conduct of life would be best?

There are three courses. The first is renunciation. This is the way of the saints and sages: to follow the ideal and to accept whatever troubles and sorrows and ill-treatment. The second way is selfishness: to be more selfish than all the rest of the world. The third way is the greatest and the most difficult: it is to have all responsibilities, all the cares of life, to have friends and all, to be as unselfish, as good as possible, and just selfish enough not to be trampled upon.(4)

3

Life in the world can be pictured as everyone pushing away the other who stands in his way, thus making his way towards his object. Man generally does not mind when he pushes another away, he minds when he is pushed away. When he becomes somewhat considerate then he tries to refrain from pushing others away, and for that very reason he feels hurt when he is pushed away by another.

If a man who is gentle happens to be wise also, he – out of his gentleness – does not push anyone away, nor does he mind being pushed away; he goes on patiently in the pursuit of the object he wishes to accomplish. But when a man who is gentle and kind is void of wisdom, he stands still in life, blocking the way for others and putting himself in a place from where he will always be pushed away.

CHAPTER IV

Self-realization

1

THE FIRST thing is to be man. It is not enough to have the form of man, we must be man. If we think that we eat and therefore are men – the animals and birds also eat. If we think that we sleep and therefore are men – the animals and birds all sleep. If we give way to our anger and passions – the animals all have their anger and passions. All that is not enough to make man human.

It is told in India that there were two *madzubs* at Lahore. *Madzubs* are those whose interest in spirituality is so great that they quite forget their physical self and even their garb. We in India know them and pay them respect; if they pass, having forgotten their clothes, we just turn our eyes away. These two *madzubs* were a man and a woman; when they met in the street it was seen that the man tried to avoid the woman, and the woman tried to avoid the man, and they showed signs of confusion while usually they showed no consideration at all. A priest walking behind the man *madzub* followed him for three days thinking, "I must find out why he behaves thus". At last, after three days, the *madzub* said to him, "Why do you follow me? What is it you want from me?" The priest replied, "I saw that when you met the woman *madzub* you covered yourself. Why was it?" The *madzub* laid his hands upon the priests's head and said to him, "Now go and look at the world; then come back". The priest went into the city and, looking at every person, he saw upon the body of a man the head of a dog, or upon the body of a woman the head of a cat or of a camel or some other animal. Only the woman *madzub* had a human head. He went back to the *madzub* and told him what he had seen. The *madzub* said to the priest, "This must never be told, because the world would be offended. Now you have seen how the world is, and why it does not matter to me to appear as I am before the world. Do you wonder that

I cover myself before the *madzub* only?" This shows us how careful we should be to become at least human first.

If we cannot be trustworthy with our surroundings, with those who rely upon us, we are not human. If we cannot be self-sacrificing with our surroundings, our relations, we are not human. If we compare ourselves keenly with the animals we surely shall see what we must be in order to be human. We must have tolerance; the animal has no tolerance. We must be true; the animal has no truth. We must have shame; the animal has no shame. We must keep our promise; the animal cannot do it. We must share with others; the animal does not share, it sits beside its plate of food and, even if it has eaten enough, it will not let another come near. We must be accommodating; the animal does not accommodate others. We must have sympathy; the animal has no sympathy. We should give up those actions that give us a momentary joy, but of which we repent afterwards. Sometimes we do things of which for the moment we are glad, and then for years we repent. We should check the animal passions that carry us away. There is a great reward for it; for every little attempt to overcome, for every little check, there is a great reward.

How many times do we become troublesome to ourselves and others by our lack of human qualities? How many times are we annoyed with our own self? To become human is the most difficult thing. Hali, a great Indian poet, says, "What can there be easy when it is even difficult for man to become man?" How much do we have to learn before we can say that we are truly human!

It is by his quality of sympathy, by his kindness to others that man becomes human. When the animal-self, which is called *nafs* is before him, he wants to take everything for his own benefit. When he develops his sympathy, when he can sacrifice his self for the benefit of another, he realizes that moral which the cross symbolizes. Then he becomes *farishteh**, then he becomes God.

**farishteh* – an angel who is sent on earth

2

In order to reach the next stage, to become angel, we must become a soldier and make another our colonel: we must make God, our self within, our colonel and thereby learn discipline. We must please Him. If we have a need we must ask Him. We must not ask anyone else; we must not tell anyone else. If we have a sorrow we must tell Him; if we have a joy we must tell Him. A listener is there for our sorrow and joy. Why should we humiliate ourselves by bringing our joy and sorrow and want before others? If we feel an obligation, let us be obliged to Him. If we want to complain, let us complain to Him. Why should we complain to others who cannot help us?

We must become a lover and idealize God, our self within, as our Beloved, thinking of His mercy and compassion, admiring the sublimity of His nature, bowing most humbly before His almighty power, and considering Him at every move we make, lest He should be displeased with us. Then at every step astray we are warned from within, "This is not right for you". At every right step we are cheered from within.

The higher we rise, the more particular we should be, for if one goes into society a very small impoliteness disgraces a person, while a man from the slums may fight and box in his eating-house and the next day, when people meet, they say, "Hullo, good morning", and are ready to be as before.

The day we think, "I am good, I am perfect", our eyes are veiled. The day we think, "I am wise", darkness has come upon us, and all the progress we have made is lost. We must always be ready to learn: from a child, from a drunkard, from a foolish person, from everyone, from all those who act differently.

Perfection does not lie in the innocence of a child, nor does it lie in being a *jinn* or a fairy; it lies in going through all vibrations, from the highest plane to this one, in experiencing all. A child is friends with the enemy because it does not know that he is its enemy. To know that the enemy is an enemy and yet to be kind – that is to be truly kind. To know the badness of the world and then to become harmless – that is innocence.

In India there are many such holy persons. Their innocence is so great that it shines out from them – much more than from a child. Their presence is peace and joy. I knew a sage who was very much revered. His humility was so great that when little boys came to see him, before they could bow to his feet as is the custom or kiss his hand, his head was on their feet and he said, "I am your servant, I am your slave. You are much greater than me". Those sages always think that every other is much greater than they.

It is very difficult for a person of a certain evolution to like those of another evolution. If a person goes and sits in a café and always speaks of God or Christ, and says, "Christ was great, Christ said this or that", the other people will say, "Please, go to the church if you wish to speak of God and Christ". And if a person who wishes to drink goes to the church, they will say to him, "Go to the café if you wish to drink. Here it is not the place". I myself have sometimes been told, "Please, do not mention the name of God in our society, or the name of Christ. Say what you please about science, about the planes, but do not speak the name of God here".

That is why the Sufi takes the other way. He sees the good in every thing. He sees the face of God everywhere. He is in all companies. One Sufi always recognizes another, wherever he is, in whatever religious or social garb the other may be. That is the Sufi message of friendship. Unless each one of us bears this message into the world, peace can never come to the world.

3

Self-realization has been taught by all religions as it is their spirit. The underlying truth is the same in all, though their principles may differ. What is this self-realization, this knowledge of the self?

We all know the self that we see, we know: I am tall or short or of medium height, I am fat or thin. We know the name that has been given to us, whether John or Jacob or Henry. We know also: I have a temper, or: I have my

clever ways, I have these merits and these faults, I have
this work or this particular way of enjoyment in life, I have
responsibilities and cares and sorrows and joys, I have friends
and acquaintances and enemies. But all this is not enough.
We should consider whether that which we are doing from
morning till night, which we are striving after, to which we
give a great importance, will remain with us – be it money,
fame, name or whatever it may be. Does it make us happy?
Does it give us the knowledge of what we were and what we
shall be? We should know what we were before, whence we
came and whither we shall go, from what all this world has
come and into what it will turn.

If I were to explain from what all this manifestation has
come, how it has been produced and into what it will turn,
it would take a very long time. It is a long subject, but in a
few words I can say: How could there be room on this earth
for all the people that ever have been, if this matter remained
as we see it? Even for the people living on earth where they
are many, often famines come, diseases, plagues and wars.
If all that matter did not return by various processes to the
unseen from which it has come, there would be no room
left on earth, nor in the water, nor in space. Matter is all
destroyed, annihilated, and nothing can save it when the call
of annihilation comes.

If you think that fame and name can live, I will say: do you
suppose that Beethoven and Wagner were the only musicians
of their time? There have been many, many others who have
come and gone about whom no one knows anything, and a
day will come when those names which are known to-day
will also be wiped off from the world's memory.

The aim of all religions and philosophies is the understanding and the realization of unity. The Vedanta philosophy
teaches advaita: There is no such thing as "two"; the whole is
one and the same being. In the Bible it is said, "I and my
Father are one", which means unity, and then, "Be ye perfect
as your Father in heaven is perfect", which shows that in this
unity lies perfection, amplitude. When we come to the Hadith
we read, "By knowing himself man can know God", which
means that by realizing himself he realizes God.

Supposing that there are some people who believe this and ask, "If we ourselves are the Whole Being, why should we not do whatever we please? Whom should we fear? Before whom should we pray?" – I would say to such a person, "If I take all you possess, will you let me have it?" He at once will say, "No, it is mine". But then he is not the Whole Being, he is a limited being. He recognizes "you and I": separate beings. By learning this philosophy of "I am all" intellectually people have many times been led astray. It is not enough to have read a few books of philosophy and to think, "Now I know all". That is not mastery. By books one can learn intellectually that we are all, but books cannot give us realization, the realization by experience in which we are sure, in which no doubt can remain in the soul.

Self-realization can be learned only in one way, in three grades. For this one needs no books, no study; one can learn it only from life. If a least little insult makes one vexed, and a least little praise makes one feel so flattered – if that is one's condition – how can one call oneself God-conscious? The self-realized ones are those to whom insult or praise, rise or fall are indifferent. They will deserve to be called so whom neither sin nor virtue can touch. Heaven and hell are the playgrounds of their imagination. They are, although on earth, yet above the earth.

It is then that self-realization comes, *fana*. When does it come? When there is no thought, no idea at all anywhere touching the breath of one's existence as a limited being. When all idea of this external being is gone, then comes the consciousness of the unlimited Being, of God. This is annihilation, *fana*, which is shown by the cross. Christ's words have always taught renunciation, annihilation. This can be learned by the three grades of which I have spoken: first to be man, then to be angelic, then union with the Divinity.

CHAPTER V

The Art of Personality

THERE IS a difference between individuality and personality, just as there is a difference between nature and art. However much nature is near to man's soul, art is closer to his heart. If it were not so man would have preferred to live in the forest; he would have roamed about in nature and would have been quite satisfied in the wilderness; he would have found the greatest charm in what the wilderness can offer and in the beauty to be seen in the forest. Instead of all this man has created a world – a world which he has made for himself – and in that world he has made a nature of his own imagination, a nature which he calls art. If that is art then on this art much depends. People may say, "Is it not an imitation of nature?" Yes, it is an imitation of nature. You might say, "Then it is not as great as Nature", but I say: both nature and art are made by the same Artist. Nature is made directly by the Artist, and art is made indirectly through the pen of the Artist. Art is the finishing of that beauty which begins to manifest itself in nature. A person who has not come to this conception of art does not yet know the divinity of art.

Now as to the question what art has to do with personality, personality is art itself, and the greatest art. Once a lady told me, "My parents brought me up just like a plant grows in the wilderness". When I replied, "It is a great pity", she was surprised. What is education, what is culture, what is self-development? It is all art, it is the way for individuality to culminate into personality.

In ancient times the religious education and human culture in every form mainly had the culture of the personality as their central theme. To-day we are expected to learn mathematics, geography, history and other things, but never the art of personality which is of the greatest use in life. Apart from its spiritual significance, we see in our everyday life that a salesman who is pleasant, courteous and well-mannered is successful. If he lacks manner he will be repellent; he may have all kinds of beautiful things in his shop, he will have no success. If a clerk in an office, a secretary, an assistant, a supervisor has a charming personality, a kindly manner, a sympathetic attitude, he will win the affection of all; everything will be light, everything will go smoothly. If he lacks the art of personality, he may have all qualifications, he may be a most capable person, yet things will not run smoothly. A person, whether man or woman, may be a barrister, a solicitor, a doctor, a most qualified individual, but if the art of personality is not developed he will be disagreeable and unpleasant – in his own home and in all walks of life. The art of personality is the main thing to develop; if not, a person misses a great deal.

*(The ancient people lived on tradition, and especially in the East they regarded their ancestors not for their titles or their great works, but for the art of their personality. To-day in modern civilization people have become regardless of this art which considers the equality of all men. Equality to-day is working in quite another direction: instead of rising upward toward the level of the best, people want to go downward and join the level of the worst.

When you hear the word equality it seems a beautiful thing, it sounds very nice, it seems a religious, a philosophical idea. But what is life, if it is not a symphony? And is not every person a note in this symphony? Suppose that you want to hear music and that all the notes are the same. How would you enjoy that music? If all notes are equal, there is no music; if all persons are the same, there is no symphony. The way to understand equality is different: it is rising to the best, to the highest pitch. And everyone can rise to that pitch if he wants to rise. But since man takes the way of the least resistance, he falls to the level of the average person.)

It must be remembered that disregard of the principle, which is called the art of personality, may lead the present generation, the modern civilization, there where it can find nothing but disappointment, especially when materialism is prevailing all over and there is nothing to think about

* see the remark about this lecture in the List of Documents

but matter; this in itself keeps man away from the art of personality. If this art is not introduced, and if there is no love for it, what then happens is that the human being does not become any better than the lower creation.

Is a human being greater than an animal because he possesses wealth, or because he has read many books, or because he has learned much? Does that make him greater as a human being? No, man is greater when from an individual he has become a person. Very few of us distinguish between individuality and personality. Individuality is that which we have brought with our birth. We are born as a separate entity; that itself makes us an individuality. But personality is something that is acquired; it has not come with us, it is something we gain. If a tree grew in a garden in the same way as it grew in the forest, the gardener would say, "You are not welcome here; you should fit in with the surroundings. This is a garden, it is not a forest". Besides this, the art of personality is not only something one should learn in order to become pleasant to others: the art of personality fulfills the purpose of life.

Now arises the question: what is the art of personality? Is it mannerism, putting on different airs of expression, a special politeness, a society rhythm? Not at all; it is falsehood, which people adopt by being unnatural and acting unnaturally. Instead of giving a better impression of themselves, they give a worse impression. The art of personality expresses itself spontaneously. One need not act in a certain way, one need not put on something: it is the expression of oneself which shows the art of personality.

Expressing the art of personality is the sign of the great. Knowingly or unknowingly a person may develop that manner in himself and it is wonderful to watch it. When in India I was very fond of seeing the celebrities known in our country. One day I heard that a great wrestler was visiting our town. I had never approved of something which made one person win and the other fail, but because this man was a celebrity I wanted to see him. One would expect very little from the personality of a wrestler, but in this personality, in spite of all muscular and nervous strength, there was such a kindly manner, such a sympathetic look, such an outgoing attitude and such a serenity that I thought, even a wrestler, who does the most material and physical work, can show that it is his personality, and not something material, which has made him great.

One may ask: If we have a personality, why must we develop it? But even a diamond must be cut! It has light in it, yet cutting is required to awaken it. It cannot show its glow and brilliancy before it has been cut. It is the same with the personality.

Then one may ask: what are the different aspects of the art of personality? Its first aspect is action, or movement. Very often, before a person has spoken a word, he has achieved a movement which causes a jar upon the delicate sensibility of the one who sees it, and who may form an opinion about that person before he knows him – only because of that movement. In one movement a person can show his state of mind; unless he has the power to control it, he can show stubbornness, weakness, foolishness. All these things can be traced in a man when he walks, sits, or stands up. Those who can recognize a person in a twinkling of an eye need not study physiognomy: one movement shows them whether he is evolved or unevolved. When the science of movement has not been taught, has not been understood, and a person's movements are not directed, these may be such that they impress themselves upon his spirit and turn his whole being into a wrong personality. Education has given very little attention to this.

Another aspect of the art of personality belongs to the realm of speech. The more we understand about this, the more we shall know that for every word there is a time, and for every word there is a place. Everything we say, which is in its own place and which is fitting, will be good; it becomes wrong when it is said in a place which is not its own. People generally do not think about it. Often they are outspoken; they do not mind when to speak, what to say, where to speak. A person who has no control over his speech becomes a kind of machine that goes on and on and on without any will at the back of it. Remember that not only those persons do not

gain the affection, the approbation of others, but they repel
others. Being talkative they cannot keep any secret. They
have to tell it; they have the habit to speak, they have no
control over it(5). The art of personality is not so difficult to
learn; it is learning to be thoughtful. Those who speak much,
very often say so little; others who speak little say much. It
depends upon the way in which things are said.

In the Bible it is said, "First was the word and the word was
God". This shows what power the word has. If we control
our speech, if we know how to use a word, we know the
chemistry of life and how to utilize it to the best purpose.
Sometimes a person can change a situation by one word,
which another cannot change by using a hundred hammers.
One can hammer at a rock and break it – that is the way of
the hammer. And there is the way of the water. If the rock
is in the way the water will not hammer at it, will surround
it, will run smoothly over it and make its way over the top
of the rock, and so will its waves proceed.

If someone is upset, among ten people who want to console
him, there are nine who upset him more, and there is rarely
one person who consoles him. This also belongs to the art of
personality – if only one knew it!

Another aspect of the art of personality is sympathetic and
right thinking. By right thinking all one naturally says and
does becomes right, because the root of every speech and
action is in the mind. So by right thinking one naturally
speaks and acts rightly; one cannot do otherwise. But what
generally happens is that one never considers it in connection
with others: if there is any wrong it is in the other. And it
is very wonderful that the one who is most in the wrong,
is the one who sees most wrong in others. You will see that
the person who is full of wrong knows a thousand wrongs
about a thousand people. Besides, our experiences make us
so pessimistic that if anyone says, "I have seen someone who
is such a nice, kind and good person", we begin to doubt.
Unconsciously our first thought is, "Can it be true? No, it
cannot be true; there is no such thing as good in the world".
And as soon as someone says, "I have seen such a wicked
person", everybody is interested, because people believe that.

It shows that, as we always experience wrong things, we hardly expect that ever there can be something right.

The fourth aspect of the art of personality is feeling. The great drawback of modern civilization is that man to-day thinks that it is balanced and practical to think with the brain, to reason things out. But to feel with the heart he thinks is not practical, is not common sense. Therefore to-day is considered normal and balanced the person who lives in his brain, and the one whose heart is developed is called fanatic or unpractical. Imagine, after having read in the Bible the lesson that God is love, one comes to realize that he who has less God in him is more practical, and he who has more God in him is a good for nothing! When there is a discussion among intellectual persons, it is understood between them to keep sentiment apart: to discuss keeping to the point, just to recite facts, "that keeps reasoning clear". But this takes away the beauty of life! The art of personality is in the profound, the deep feeling which directs every thought, speech and action of man.

When Jesus Christ told the fishermen, "Come hither and I shall make you fishers of men", he said, in other words, to those who were absorbed in catching fishes at the sea-shore, "I shall teach you the art of personality". This is, therefore, not a subject which I bring before you, it is a subject which Christ taught. It is the art of personality which the prophets proved with their own lives to be of the greatest importance. The impression Buddha left upon millions of people in the East, who keep his statue in their temples, seeing the expression of God in Buddha – what is it? Is it the theories and dogmas and teachings he gave? No, it is his personality which made such a deep impression upon people that for centuries they held it sacred; it has proved to be more precious than anything else in the world. This is not a subject of which one can say that it is no better than any other. On the contrary, it is a subject of the greatest importance. There are millions of Muslims whose hearts are touched, whose eyes fill with tears on hearing the name of the Prophet. What is it that touches them? Is it the teaching that the Prophet gave? What touches them is the personality of the Prophet, his personality has made the deep impression which still remains, which never can be erased.

The art of personality, therefore, is a magic. The fishermen among whom Jesus Christ had to walk were incapable of knowing the greatness of the Master, and not ready to understand the message he brought. Yet they used to stand spell-bound in the presence of the Master; they used to be deeply impressed by the personality of the Teacher. What was it that impressed them? It was not the new teaching they received, it was the example before their eyes.

The Sufis of all ages considered the art of personality of the greatest importance. The Yogi principle of asceticism has nothing to do with it; it is another ideal. The wise ones of all ages thought that God manifested Himself in the form of man and, from an individual to a person, developed as a soul, and that herein lies the fulfilment of life's purpose. Therefore this was not only the main purpose of education, but also the central theme of religion and of life as a whole. What is religion taught for if not in order to make of man a personality? For every man is not a personality!

*(There is a metaphysical point to this subject, which distinguishes two aspects of man: the machine and the engineer. When man's machine part covers the spark which may be called the engineer, man is subjected to all outer influences such as cold and heat, wind and storm. These all condition his success or failure. The other part of man is a divine spark. It is that spark which makes him the engineer and gives him command over the machine. Instead of allowing the machine to be subjected to outer influences, the engineer part gradually gains his own influence over the instrument. Herein lies the secret of the art of personality. One condition is slavery, the other mastery. In the first condition one is placed by nature, to the next one is brought through development of the personality.)

Now you may ask: How does one learn the art of personality? In the same way as one learns the art of painting or drawing. First one learns how to draw a straight line, a horizontal line, a circle, a curve. In the same way, learning the art of personality, one learns how to say a thing and how not to say a thing, how to avoid saying a thing, and how to say a thing without saying it. Then one learns the art of light and shade. This art of light and shade is knowing how to hide a certain part in conversation and how to bring another part to prominence. Then there is the colouring. There is a great variety of colours. Every feeling, every thought, every idea has its particular colour, and when a person knows how many of these colours there are, and when he composes with them all he says and does in life, then this becomes an art: the art of personality.

If a person has collected diamonds, or if he has got pearls or rubies, what is it, if he has not developed in his personality that precious quality which makes a person precious? What is it all? All those things are nothing.

There are four grades through which one develops in the art of personality. The first grade is when a person becomes thoughtful, and so begins to observe his thoughts, to see his actions. The second grade is when he not only observes his thoughts and actions, but is able to control them. The third grade is when a spontaneous out-flow of sympathy comes from that person, when it is natural that his attitude is outgoing, that his personality attracts and becomes a blessing. And the fourth grade is a grade where no effort has to be made by the artist to realize the art of personality. In this grade the artist becomes art itself, and whatever he does – it all becomes a beautiful picture.

CHAPTER VI

Man is likened to the Light

MAN IS likened to the light: his soul the glow, his mind the flame, and his body the end of the flame. The heat that comes from the light is the atmosphere of man. The smoke that rises out of the light in reality does not belong to the light, it belongs to the fuel. As ignorance in man is troublesome, so the smoke rising out of the light disturbs.

As different lights differ in their degree of radiance, so do different souls. The substance of every man, however, is the same: it is light. We read in ancient scriptures that the angels were made of fire. It is not fire they were made of, it is light. But if we ask the question, "Were the angels made of light and no one else?", the answer will be that all, each and everyone, were created out of light.

The difference between our soul and our body, which sometimes we consider as great as between earth and heaven, is not so great. Soul and body are one light, and therefore the external part of man is expressive of his inner being, and the inner being of man also is dependent in many ways upon his external being. "Inner and outer part of man's being" is a term used for our convenience; in reality there is one being, there is one light. If a man lacks magnetism, if he lacks enthusiasm and courage, if he lacks power of accomplishment, it is all owing to the lack of that radiance which belongs to his being. The health of the body, the balance of the mind, the purity of the soul all depend upon the radiance of man's being. Health of the body therefore is spiritual, balance of the mind is spiritual, and so is the purity of the soul. A good atmosphere is a sign of spirituality; the power of the word, courage without fear, fearlessness, self-confidence also are signs of spirituality; the capability of accomplishing something and the strength of struggling along all through life – all these are the signs of spirituality.

The purpose of the life of an individual is to perfect the light in him, which is his very being. Whatever may be the

qualification of a person, whatever be his resources, position
and rank, if the light within him is not brilliant, he cannot
fulfil the purpose of his life. In the Bible, in the allegory of the
ten wise and foolish virgins, the same idea is explained. The
foolish ones did not keep oil in their lamps, the wise virgins
kept it. The wise ones, therefore, answered the purpose on the
day which was promised and the foolish ones repented. Ten
means one, zero meaning nothing: a wise soul and a foolish
soul. The wise soul collected all material in order to make
his light more brilliant for that day which was the day of the
promise. The foolish soul wasted it, and found it absent at the
time it was needed.

When we think of our life in the world, in our material
strife, in our spiritual struggle – what do we need? We need
that light the spark of which is within us, which is our being.
Every time when we are without it, when we lack it, it causes
us all failure and distress in life, since our health, our balance
and the clearness of our vision, all depend upon the light that
is within.

As every light needs fuel, so the light which is ours, which
is ourself, needs fuel also. The fuel for the physical part of our
life is what we call food, but for the life of the mind intellectual
sustenance is necessary. If the body is fed and the mind is not,
then naturally that light becomes less. The sustenance of the
soul is the divine ideal, which is both love and light. If the
soul does not receive that nourishment which is necessary for
it, then the soul is starved. The body may be nourished, but it
is not sufficient. That is why we see before our physical eyes
many famine-stricken souls, but if we saw with the spiritual
eyes we would see still more famine in humanity.

What do we learn in Sufism? We learn in Sufism that
mysticism which teaches us how to collect the fuel which
is necessary not only for the body, but for our mind and
soul. By concentration, by meditation, by all other ways
of contemplative practices, the purpose accomplished by the
Sufi is that purpose which is the longing of every soul.

Question: What are the means, except concentration and
meditation, to develop and strengthen that light in oneself?

Answer: Right living.

Question: What is right living? Is it doing what everyone thinks right?
Answer: If each person would have his way of right living there would be anarchy. I would consider right living that which is right for oneself and for others. If not, those who do good or who do wrong can all justify themselves by thinking that what they do is best. Reason is the slave of man, it always comes and sympathizes with him. One asks, "Have I not done right?", or "Have I not done wrong?", and the reason says, "Yes, you have".

Question: How can one live so that it is approved of by others?
Answer: It is impossible to live the life that one considers best and that others consider best. But one can do one's best.

Question: One sees people in whom the divine spark of light is more or less extinguished and who still live an apparent virtuous life.
Answer: An apparent virtuous life is something different. Right living in my sense is not only virtuous living. Right living has a still deeper meaning, for what I call a right life is the first step to that which may be called true life. The third step is truth itself. The mystics say that there are three steps to the goal: right life, true life and truth. A person who loves to live a right life and who tries to do it, even if he is not a contemplative or meditative or religious person, must certainly arrive at that high stage, at that goal which is the ideal goal; for within man there is truth, and the seeking of man is truth. Therefore right living helps him to realize truth.

If I were to interpret the words of Christ, "Strait is the gate and narrow is the way", I would say that there is a path in life, a path of going strait, and that path is like walking upon a wire. In the circus they make a show of it. It is exactly the picture: at every step one takes there is fear of falling either to one side or to the other. Jugglers in India even make a better picture of it. They take two very light bamboos and tie a rope on the top of them. The juggler stands on the rope in a brass tray and his task is to go from one point to the other. While he is travelling thus, his colleagues from below beat drums and sing horrible songs in order to distract his mind. He has to keep his concentration and secure his balance in spite of all the music calling him from below. That is the picture of right living.

Question: But once one is falling . . .?
Answer: Truth is merciful. One cannot fall but on truth; if one falls, one will only fall in the arms of truth. A seeker after truth has no loss. If apparently he loses something, it is not a loss in the end.

Question: What does it mean "to fall in the arms of truth"?
Answer: If a fall is caused in a certain struggle one has fallen in the arms of that particular struggle. If it is in the struggle for love, then it is in the arms of love that one falls. If it is in the struggle for righteousness, one falls in the arms of righteousness. Just as they say that in a holy war a person gives his life for a holy purpose, and is therefore in the arms of that holy object, so, if a person has fallen in the struggle for truth, he has fallen in the arms of truth.

Besides, the hopeful never falls: both his rise and fall mean success. Failure is the loss of hope. As long as there is hope there is no failure.

Question: And what of those who do not hope any longer?
Answer: Then that is the end of success.

Question: Is there nothing that can help them?
Answer: A miracle can do something; nothing is impossible. Nothing is more painful than the loss of hope. A hopeless person is a dead person. A person who is dead with hope is living, but a person walking on the earth without hope is as dead.

Question: How can one revivify a soul?
Answer: By imparting one's life to him, just as a lighted candle can light another candle which is put out. When the fire has

gone out in the stove one must bring some other fire to light it again. One has to give from one's own hope; therefore the one who gives must be powerful enough to give it.

Question: When can one consider oneself powerful enough to give?
Answer: One can judge it by one's own self-confidence, because that life one gives from one's own life to another comes from self-confidence. In the Sufi terminology it is called *iman*. It is the most sacred thing in the whole religion; self-confidence is the secret of all miracles.

Question: Is love for one's neighbour not sufficient to help?
Answer: Love is the substance, by self-confidence one makes that substance, and by the power of self-confidence one is able to impart it. For instance, if one sees a person who is very ill and one thinks, "What can I do, how can I do something?", then one can do nothing. For healing, it is all self-confidence that is needed, for healing oneself and for healing another. Not only for healing, but for all things – in business, in industry, in all work – self-confidence is necessary.

Question: How can self-confidence, confidence in oneself, in one's own affairs, help another person?
Answer: Self-confidence gives the power to manage one's affairs better and to help others too. Suppose a doctor comes to see a patient who is in a bad condition and says, "Oh, you have called me too late; this person has gone very far. Still, as you have called me here, I shall write a prescription". But another doctor may say, "It is never too late. I am sure that all will be well. I shall do my very best, and certainly the patient will recover". He may give the same prescription as the first doctor, but his prescription will be of much greater value. Why? Because besides the medicine, he has given his self-confidence which is a million times greater in healing-power than prescriptions.

It is the same in all things. A person may start a business, an enterprise, and someone may come along and take away all his strength by saying, "What a fool you are to have begun

this. Have you thought of this and that?" Then all the power
and radiance the man has can be lost in a moment's time.
Another person may say, "It is a noble undertaking; I am
sure you will succeed. Therefore my prayer, my thoughts are
with you; I shall do all I can to help you in your enterprise. I
wish you success."

Question: In order to be quite sure to be able to give to another
should one not have a great deal of vitality oneself?
Answer: Vitality also comes from self-confidence. Very often
one will see a person with no extraordinary strength and
vitality having more strength than a Sandow*.

Independence is the sign of self-confidence. It is just like a
wealthy person who has wealth enough for himself and who
always can give to others. A person with limited means, after
one day of generosity, the next day will be broken.

* see the foot-note at page 68

CHAPTER VII

Truth

WE GENERALLY confuse truth with fact, and we often use the word fact for truth. When we look at it from the mystic's point of view we find that words are too intricate ever to explain what is truth. All that is given to man as truth and that he has received as truth in all ages has been a kind of re-echo of the realization of truth, which language has always limited and made subtle. In reality everything is subtle and complex, but nothing is simpler than truth. Things are complex and difficult because man makes them so. Truth is simple and plain.

In the Sufi terminology there is one word, *Haqq*, which means God and also truth. This term itself explains that God is truth and truth is God. Truth is that which cannot be pointed out, because all things that can be compared have their opposite, but neither God nor truth has an opposite. Names are to point out forms, and words are to distinguish one thing from another, while definitions come from the pairs of opposites or at least from differences. That which is all-pervading and is in all things and beings, that which every word explains and yet no word can explain, is God and is truth.

Men have differed in all ages because they have called their Deity by different names. There have existed wars, fights and family feuds for ages, men dividing themselves merely for the difference of the names they gave to their Deity. Man always sees just what he sees; he cannot see beyond it. With the ideal of his Deity, with the separate names of man's Deities, with all the different attitudes of worshipping his Deity, man remains separate from God, for God is truth and truth is God.

In past ages people have founded new religions, formed in the name of God; they have built churches, founded in the name of God and truth; they held their scriptures in esteem and honour, and revered the names of their leaders, of the prophets and seers of the religion to which they belonged. And with all his progress man does not seem to have progressed any further than the religions as known to-day. Bias and bigotry exist in the followers of different creeds, in their temples and churches, in the houses of their prayers, in their congregations of particular communities. The consequence is that religion and the religious spirit has been enfeebled. This even has reacted upon the minds of others who stay away from religion and yet partake of that tendency towards difference, definition and separation which divides mankind into different sections called nations, races or communities. The reaction culminates into results still worse than the action. All wars, disasters and unhappy experiences that humanity has seen, are the outcome of this spirit of intolerance, division and separation, which naturally comes through lack of wisdom and understanding and through the ignorance of truth.

Then the question arises : what is the way to attain the truth? Can it be attained by study? The answer is that the source of realizing the truth is within man – but man is the object of his realization. There are words of Hazrat 'Ali, saying that the one who knows himself truly knows God.

Man, absorbed from morning till evening in his occupations which engage his every attention to the things of the earth and of self interest, remains intoxicated. Seldom there are moments in his life, brought about by pain or suffering, when he experiences a state of mind which can be called soberness. Hindus call this state of mind *sat*, which is a state of tranquillity. Man then begins to become conscious of some part of his being which he finds to have almost been covered from his eyes. When we look at life from this point of view we find that an individual who claims to be a living being is not necessarily living a full life. It is only a realization of inner life which at every moment unveils the soul, and brings before man another aspect of life in which he finds fullness, a greater satisfaction, and a rest which gives true peace.

Can he speak about this to his fellowmen? And if he does, what can he say? Can he say, "I am purer", or "more exalted than you", or "I understand life better than you"? As life unfolds itself to man the first lesson it teaches is humility; the first thing that comes to man's vision is his own limitedness. The vaster God appears to him, the smaller he finds himself. This goes on and on until the moment comes when he loses himself in the vision of God. In the terms of the Sufis this is called *fana*, and it is this process that was taught by Christ under the name of self-denial. Often man interprets this teaching wrongly and considers renunciation as self-denial. He thinks that the teaching is to renounce all that is in the world. But although that is a way and an important step which leads to the true self-denial, the self-denial meant is the losing of oneself in God.

Then the question arises: How can one lose oneself in God? The body is a person, the mind is active, there are feelings of joy, pleasure, love and hatred, and there is the existence with which we identify ourselves and which we call by a certain name and where we feel pain and pleasure. How can one deny oneself and lose oneself in God?

There also is another question which arises from the heart of the intellectual: "How can I even accept the idea that there exists a Deity? How can I lose myself in someone whom I do not know and cannot point out?" By reasoning with oneself and by trying to study oneself analytically it is possible to get nearer to the true knowledge of one's being. If we consider that every part that constitutes our being has its own name – the hand, the foot, every part of our being has a different name, quality and purpose, and even a separate form – what is it then in man which says "I", and identifies itself with what it sees? It is not our head, hand or foot which says "I", nor is it the brain. It is something that we cannot point out which identifies itself with all these different parts and says "I" and "mine" and knows itself to be the person who sees. This in itself is ignorance, and it is this which the Hindus have called *avidya*.

How can you be that which you possess? You cannot be horse and rider at the same time, nor can you be carpenter and tool at the same time. Herein lies the secret of mortality and immortality: it is the mortal being that, through illusion, claims immortality.

It is more important to find out the truth about oneself than to find out the truth about heaven and hell, or about many other things which are of less importance and are apart from oneself. However, every man's pursuit is according to his state of evolution, and so each soul is in pursuit of something – but he does not know where it leads him. The first sign of realization of truth is tolerance towards others. There are the words of Christ, "In the house of my Father are many mansions", and those of the Prophet, "Each soul has its own religion". This means that according to his evolution so man knows the truth and the more a man knows, the more he finds there is to learn.

The mystics have in all ages recognized the virtue of purity which is represented by innocence. A man filled with earthly knowledge – and what he calls learning is often only the knowledge of names and forms – has no capacity for the knowledge of truth, or of God. It is the innocent and pure soul who has a capacity for learning. When a person comes to take a lesson on any subject, and he brings his own knowledge with him, the teacher has little to teach him, for the doors of his heart are not open. His heart that should be empty in order to receive knowledge is occupied by the knowledge that he already had acquired. In order to know the truth or to know God earthly qualifications and earthly wisdom or learning are not necessary. What one has to learn is how to become a pupil.

We often start our lives as teachers, and then it is hard to become a pupil. From childhood on we start to teach our parents; there seldom are souls who have more inclination for pupilship than for teaching, and there are many whose only difficulty in life is that they are teachers already. Man thinks that perhaps his reading or study of different religions and doctrines has qualified him and made him capable to understand the truth and to have the knowledge of God, but he forgets that there is only one teacher, and that is God Himself. We all are pupils, and what we can do in life is to qualify ourselves to become true pupils.

It is the receptivity of our heart and the passivity of our mind, it is the eagerness, the thirst and hunger after truth, it is the direction of our whole life to that Ideal from who all light and truth come, that alone can bring to us truth and the knowledge of God. All knowledge of the earth is as clouds covering the sun. It is the breaking of these clouds and the clearness of the sky, or in other words the purity of heart, which give the capacity for the knowledge of God.

The question may be asked: Is any effort required for realizing the truth? The answer is: Yes, there is a work that one can do which is as the work of a farmer: it is to cultivate the heart. But where man makes a mistake is that, when he cultivates the heart, he wishes to sow the seed himself instead of leaving the sowing to God. As to the way how to cultivate the heart, the first condition is explained in a story. A young man went to a great seer in Persia and asked him for guidance on the spiritual path. The seer asked him, "Have you loved in your life?" "No", said he, "not yet". The seer answered, "Go and love, and know what love is. Then come to me".

According to the belief of a Sufi the heart is the shrine of God, and when the doors of the shrine are closed it is just like a light being hidden under a bushel. The pupil sees that God is love. If He is love He does not stay in the heavens; His earthly body is the heart of man. When that heart is frozen and when there is no love but bitterness, coldness, prejudice and contempt, unforgiving feelings and hatred – which all come from one source: want of tolerance, the feeling, "I am different and you are different" – then that spirit and that light of God, that divine essence that is in the heart of man, is buried as in a tomb. The work that one has to do is to dig it up, as one would dig the ground until one touched the water underneath.

What the Sufi calls *riyazat*, a process of achievement, is nothing else than digging constantly in that holy land which is the heart of man. Surely in the depth man will find the water of life. However, digging is not enough. Love and devotion, no doubt, help to bring out frequent merits hidden in the soul, as sincerity, thankfulness, gentleness and forgiving qualities, all things which make man a true man, all things which produce an harmonious atmosphere, and all things which bring men in tune with life, the saintly life and the outer life. All those merits come, no doubt, by kindling the fire of love in the heart. But it is possible that in this process of digging one may only reach mud and lose patience. So dismay, discontentment may follow and man may withdraw himself from further pursuit. It is patient pursuit which will bring the water from the depth of the ground; for until one reaches the water of life one meets with mud in digging. It is not love, but the pretence of love, that imposes the claim of self. The first and last lesson in love is, "I am not – Thou art", and unless man is moved to that selflessness he does not know justice, right or truth: his self stands above or between him and God.

There is a well known Eastern legend giving the idea of a soul who had found truth. There was a wall of laughter and of smiles. This wall existed for ages and many tried to climb it, but few succeeded. Those who had climbed upon it saw something beyond, and so interested were they that they smiled, climbed over the wall and never returned. The people of the town began to wonder what magic could be there and what attraction, that whoever climbed over the wall never returned. So they called it the wall of mystery. Then they said, "We must make an enquiry and send someone who can reach the top, but we must tie him with a rope to hold him back". When the man they had thus sent reached the top of the wall, he smiled and tried to jump over it, but they pulled him back. Still he smiled, and when the people eagerly asked, "What did you see there?", he did not answer, he only smiled. This is the condition of the seer. The man who in the shrine of his heart has seen the vision of God, the one who has the realization of truth, can only smile, for words can never really explain what truth means.

The nearest explanation one can give is that truth is realization. At every step of man's evolution his realization changes, but there is a stage where man arrives at the true realization, a realization which is a firm conviction that no reason or logic can change or alter. Nothing in the world can change it any more, and that conviction is called by the Sufis *iman*.

The realization which is attained is that there is nothing to realize any more. The process of this attainment is a sincere research into truth and life, and the understanding

of "what I am, and what the other one is", together with
the contemplation of God, a selfless consciousness, and a
continual pursuit after the receiving of the knowledge of God.

Question: Is suffering beneficial?
Answer: Suffering is always a blessing. If it is for higher ideas,
for God, for an ideal, it takes a person at once to the highest
heaven. If it is for lower ideas, for the ego, for pride, for
possessions, it takes a person to the lowest depth of hell.
But there, after much suffering, after a long, long time, he
loses these ideas and is purified. That is why the Christian
religion shows the symbol of the cross, of suffering. How
high our ideal may be, how low our ideal may be, in the end
each pain has its prize.

CHAPTER VIII

Selflessness – Inkisar

SELFLESSNESS DOES not only beautify one's personality, giving grace to one's word and manner, but it also gives a dignity and a power, together with a spirit of independence which is the real sign of a sage. It is selfishness which often produces humiliation in one's spirit, taking away the intoxication(6) which enriches the soul.

Independence and indifference, which are as the two wings which enable the soul to fly, spring from the spirit of selflessness. The moment the spirit of selflessness has begun to sparkle in the heart of man, he shows in his word and action a nobility which nothing earthly – neither power nor riches – can give.

There are many ideas which intoxicate man, many feelings there are which act upon the soul as wine, but there is no stronger wine than the wine of selflessness. It is a might and it is a pride that no worldly rank can give. To become something is a limitation, whatever one may become. Even if a person were to be called the king of the world, he would still not be the emperor of the universe; if he were the master of the earth, he would still be the slave of Heaven. It is the person who is no one, who is no one and yet all.

The Sufi, therefore, takes the path of being nothing instead of being something. It is this feeling of nothingness which turns the human heart into an empty cup into which the wine of immortality is poured. It is this state of bliss which every truth-seeking soul yearns to attain. It is easy to be a learned person, and it is not very difficult to be wise; it is within one's reach to become good, and it is not an impossible achievement to be pious or spiritual. But if there is an attainment which is greater and higher than all these things, it is to be nothing. It may seem frightening to many, the idea of becoming nothing, for human nature is such that it is eager to hold on to something, and to what man holds on most is his own person, his individuality. Once he has risen above this, he has climbed Mount Everest, he has arrived at the spot where earth ends and heaven begins.

The whole aim of the Sufi is, by the thought of God, to cover his imperfect self even from his own eyes, and that moment when God is before him and not his own self is the moment of perfect bliss to him. My Murshid, Abu Hashim Madani, once said that there is only one virtue and one sin for a soul on this path: virtue when he is conscious of God, and sin when he is not. No explanation can fully describe the truth of this except the experience of the contemplative to whom, when he is conscious of God, it is as if a window facing heaven were open, and to whom, when he is conscious of the self, the experience is the opposite; for all the tragedy of life is caused by being conscious of the self. All pain and depression is caused by this, and anything that can take away the thought of the self helps to a certain extent to relieve man from pain, but God- consciousness gives perfect relief.

CHAPTER IX

Indifference – Vairagya

THE WORD *vairagya* comes from the Sanskrit and means indifference. By Sufis it is called *fana*, and it is shown in the cross, the symbol of the Christian religion.

This indifference comes to every being and is the first step to his annihilation, because not one atom can have its evolution without annihilation. The lower beings, the mineral, vegetable and animal, evolve towards the higher beings, and as man is the highest creation, there is nothing for him to evolve to. But this indifference, when it comes, opens a way for him to God from whom he came.

This indifference comes to the child when she realizes that her doll is not so interesting as she had thought and that it would be more interesting to play with other children who at least are alive. So first the child takes the doll and loves it. She carries it about and if the dolly's hand is hurt the child wants some remedy; a bed is needed to put the dolly in and a carriage is needed to take the dolly out. But when the nature of the doll is understood it is thrown away, and the child realizes that to play with children of her own age is better than to play with dolls which never speak.

So it is with us, the children of the world. Our likes and infatuations have a certain limit; when their time has expired the period of indifference commences. When the water of indifference is drunk, then there is no more wish for anything in the world. The nature of the water one drinks in this world is that one's thirst is quenched for a certain time, and then comes again. When the water of divine knowledge is drunk, then thirst never comes again.

This indifference comes when the nature of the world is understood; it is the higher knowledge. Then it is understood that all those objects to which one attached so much importance, which one strove to attain, to achieve, are not important. Before reaching that stage a person attaches too much importance to his joys, to his sorrows. If he is sad the whole world is full of sadness; if he is a little joyful the whole world is full of joy – as if the sun would rise and set according to his joy and sadness.

Indifference, however, must be reached after interest has taken its course; before that moment it is a fault. A person without an interest in life becomes exclusive, he becomes disagreeable. Indifference must come after all experience – interest must end in indifference. Man must not take the endless path of interest: the taste of everything in the world becomes flat. Man must realize that all he seeks in the objects he runs after, that all beauty and strength, are in himself, and he must be content to feel them all in himself. This may be called the kiss of the cross: then man's only principle is love.

Vairagya means satisfaction, the feeling that no desire is to be satisfied any more, that nothing on earth is desired. This is a great moment, and then comes that which is the kingdom of God.

Why is God satisfied with the world whereas even man, when he reaches a certain grade of intelligence, is not satisfied? Or is God not satisfied? There are two sorts of dissatisfaction. The first is felt when a man has so much given in to the external self that the world can give him no more satisfaction. The other comes when the desire for more experience, for more enjoyment ceases. This is called *Vairagya*, this is indifference. Such a person is not unhappy, he is happier than others. He has only lost his intense interest in the world.

There is a story of a comedian who every day disguised himself in order to fool the king, the *Badishah*, at whose court he lived. But the king recognized him in all his disguises. The comedian then thought that he would disguise himself as an ascetic. He went to a cave in the mountains and lived there with two disciples, also comedians. He fasted for long periods thinking that in this way he disguised himself well. After forty days people, seeing his disciples, began to speak of the sage living in the cave of the mountain, They brought him presents: one hundred, two hundred dirhams. But he refused it all, saying, "Take it away. The sage does not want money or presents".

His fame spread more and more; the king heard of him and became anxious to see him. So he went to the cave, but for a long time the disciples would not let him enter. At last he was allowed to come into the presence of the "sage". The king said, "I have been kept waiting very long before I could see you". The "sage" replied, "The dogs of the world are not allowed to enter the house". The king was very much insulted. He thought, "This must be a very great person". He gave him a paper saying, "This is a *parvaneh* for the support of your disciples". A *parvaneh* means a grant of land, but the word has two meanings, it also means moth. The "sage" said, "If it is a *parvaneh* its place is in the fire", and he put the paper into the fire which was burning before him.

The king went away and the comedian got up thinking, "Now I must tell the king how well I have fooled him". Then a voice came, saying, "Your feigned indifference has brought the king before you. If it had been real indifference, We Ourselves would have come before you".

CHAPTER X

Independence and Indifference

DOES HAPPINESS depend upon the conditions of life or upon our outlook on life? It is a question that is often asked, and is most difficult to answer. Many who have some philosophical knowledge will say that this material world is an illusion and its conditions a dream; yet there are very few who can make themselves believe it. To know a thing in theory is different from practising it. It is most difficult in this world to rise above the effect that conditions produce. No doubt, there is only one thing that helps us to rise above conditions, and that is a change of outlook on life. This change is made practicable by a change of attitude.

In the language of the Hindus life in the world is called *sansara*. It is pictured as life in a mist; one thinks and says and does and feels, and yet one does not fully know why. If a person knows one reason for it, another reason is hidden behind it which he does not yet know. Very often conditions in life show a picture of captivity; often it seems as if one had to walk between water and a pit. To rise above conditions one needs wings: two wings attached to the soul, one independence, the other indifference – which not everyone has got. Independence needs a great deal of sacrifice before one can feel independent in life. Indifference is against one's nature of love and sympathy; it is like cutting one's heart asunder before one can practise indifference throughout life. No doubt once the soul is able to spread its wings, one sees the conditions of life as far removed; then one stands above all conditions that make man captive.

There is no difficulty which cannot be surmounted sooner or later. But even when a person has achieved something he desires in life, something else seems to be unfinished. So if he goes from one thing to another, achieving all he desires, the objects of his desire will multiply and there will never be an end to his desires. The more he has to do in life the more difficulties he must meet with. If he keeps away from the life of the world then his being here will be purposeless. The more important the task, the more difficult is its accomplishment. So evening follows every day, and this goes on till eternity.

For a Sufi, therefore, not only patience to bear all things is necessary, but to see all things from a certain point of view; that can relieve him for that moment from difficulty and pain. Very often it is his outlook which changes a person's whole life. It can turn hell into heaven, it can turn sorrow into joy. When a person looks from a certain point of view every little pin-prick feels like the point of a sword piercing his heart. If he looks at the same thing from a different point of view the heart becomes sting-proof, nothing can touch it. All things which are sent forth at that person as bullets drop down without having touched him.

What is the meaning of walking upon the water? Life is symbolized as water. There is one person who drowns in the water, there is another who swims in the water, but there is still another who walks upon it. The one who is so sensitive that, after one little pin-prick he is unhappy all through the day and night is the man of the first category. The one who takes and gives back and makes a game of life is the swimmer; he does not mind if he receives one knock, for he derives satisfaction from being able to give two knocks in return. But the one whom nothing can touch is in the world and yet is above the world. He is the one who walks upon the water; life is under his feet, both its joy and its sorrow.

Verily, independence and indifference are the two wings which enable the soul to fly.

CHAPTER XI

Overlooking – Darquza

THERE IS a tendency which manifests itself and grows in a person who is advancing spiritually, and that tendency is overlooking. At times this tendency might appear as negligence, but in reality negligence is not necessarily overlooking, negligence most often is not looking. Overlooking may be called in other words rising beyond things: one has to rise in order to overlook; the one who stands beneath life could not overlook, even if he wanted to. Overlooking is a manner of graciousness; it is looking and at the same time not looking; it is seeing and not taking notice of what is seen; it is being hurt or harmed or disturbed by something and yet not minding it. It is an attribute of nobleness of nature, it is the sign of souls who are tuned to a higher key.

One may ask: Is it practical? I may not be able to say that it is always practical, but I mean it all the same, for in the end the one who overlooks will also realize the practicality of it. Maybe he will realize it in the long run after he has met with a great many disadvantages of it. Nevertheless, all is well which ends well.

Very often overlooking costs less than taking notice of something that could well be overlooked. In life there are things which matter and there are things which do not matter. As one advances through life one finds there are many things that do not matter, and one could just as well overlook them. The one who, on a journey which takes all his life to accomplish, will take notice of everything that comes his way will waste his time. While climbing the mountain of life, the purpose of which is to reach the top, if a person troubles about everything that comes along, he will perhaps never be able to reach the top; he will always be troubling about things at the bottom. No soul, realizing that life on this earth is only four days long, will trouble about little things. He will trouble about things which really matter. In his strife with little things a person loses the opportunity of accomplishing great things in life. The one who troubles about small things is small, the soul who thinks of great things is great.

Overlooking is the first lesson of forgiveness. This tendency springs from love and sympathy; for of whom one hates one notices every little fault, but of whom one loves one naturally overlooks the faults, and very often one tries to turn the faults into merits. Life has endless things which suggest beauty, and numberless things which suggest ugliness. There is no end to the merits and no end to the faults, and according to one's evolution is one's outlook on life.

The higher a man has risen, the wider the horizon before his sight. It is the tendency to sympathize which brings the desire to overlook, and it is the analytical tendency which weighs and measures and takes good notice of everything. "Judge ye not", said Christ, "lest ye be judged". The more one thinks of this lesson, the deeper it goes into one's heart, and what one learns from it is to try and overlook all that does not fit in with one's own ideas as to how things ought to be in life, until one comes to a stage of realization where the whole of life becomes one sublime vision of the immanence of God.

CHAPTER XII

Graciousness – Khulq

NO SOONER does the soul touch the inner kingdom, which is the divine kingdom, than the true nobility of the soul becomes manifest in the form of graciousness. Kings and those belonging to aristocratic families were trained in the manner of graciousness, but it is born in the heart of man. This means that every soul shows the aristocratic manner from the moment it touches the inner kingdom, and it shows that true aristocracy is the nobility of the soul: when the soul begins to express in every feeling, thought, word and action that graciousness which belongs to God Himself.

Graciousness is quite different from that wrong manner which is termed patronizing in English. The gracious one, before expressing that noble attitude, tries to hide himself even from his own eyes. The reason why the great ones, the truly noble people, are gracious is because they are more sensitive to all the hurt and harm that comes to them from those who are unripe. Therefore, out of their kindness, they try to keep themselves from doing the same to another, however unimportant his position.

There is a story of a dervish who was standing in the royal road at the moment when the procession of the king was passing. Happy in his rags as he was, he did not at all mind who was coming, and did not move an inch at the warnings of the pages who were running ahead of the procession, until they pushed him away. Yet he did not move far, he only said, "That is why". Then came the bodyguards on horseback. They did not push him, but they said, "Away, away, dervish! Do you not see the procession coming?" The dervish did not move an inch, but only answered, "That is why". Then followed the noblemen. They saw the dervish standing there. They did not like to tell him to move, they moved their own horses instead. The dervish seeing this said, "That is why". Then arrived the chariot of the king. His eyes fell on the dervish in his rags standing boldly in the middle of the road. Instead of waiting for his bow the king bowed himself, and the dervish said, "That is why". There was a young man standing by his side who could not understand the meaning of these words "That is why", spoken by the dervish whatever way he was treated. When he asked the dervish kindly to explain what was meant by these words, the answer was, "They explain all I mean".

There is a great truth in what Christ has said in the sermon on the mount, "Blessed are the meek, for they will inherit the earth". This will always prove true whatever be the time and whatever be the evolution of the world. Be it the time of aristocracy, be it the period of democracy, the value of that nobility of nature which is expressed in graciousness will always command its price. It is easy to know the word, but most difficult to practise graciousness through life, for there is no end to the thought that needs to be given to every action in life. It wants judgment and a fair sense of weighing and measuring all one does. Besides, it needs a fine sense of art and beauty, for in refining the personality one attains to the highest degree of art. Verily, the making of the personality is the highest art there is. The Sufi considers the cultivation of humane attributes, in which lies the fulfilment of the purpose of his life, as his religion.

A young man one day showed a little impatience towards his aged father, who could not hear very clearly and had asked him two, three times to tell him again what he had said. Seeing the disturbed expression on his face the father said, "My son, do you remember that there was a day when you were a little child, and asked me what was the name of a certain bird? I told you: 'a sparrow'. You asked me perhaps fifty times, and I had the patience to repeat it again and again to you without being hurt or troubled about it; I was only pleased to tell you all I knew. Now when I cannot hear you clearly, you can at least have patience with me and, if I did not hear you the first time, explain it twice to me."

It seems that, in order to learn that noble manner of life, what is most needed is patience – sometimes in the form of endurance, sometimes in the form of consideration, and sometimes in the form of forgiveness.

CHAPTER XIII

Conciliation – Ittifaq

ANY EFFORTS made in developing the personality or in character-building must not be made for the sake of proving oneself superior to others, but in order to become more agreeable to those around one and to those with whom one comes in contact. Conciliation is not only the moral of the Sufi, but it is the sign of the Sufi.

This virtue is not always learned and practised easily, for it needs not only good-will but wisdom. The great talent of the diplomat is to bring about by agreement such results as are desirable. Disagreement is easy; among the lower creation one sees it so often. What is difficult is agreement, for it wants a wider outlook, which is the true sign of spirituality. Narrowness of outlook makes the horizon of man's vision small, and he cannot easily agree with another. There is always a meeting-ground for two people, however much they differ in their thought, but the meeting-ground may be far off, and man is not always willing to take the trouble of going far enough – as far as required in order to come to an agreement. Very often his patience does not allow him to go far enough: to where he can meet the other. What generally happens is that everyone wants the other to meet him in the place where he stands, and there is no desire on his part to move from there.

This does not mean that in order to become a real Sufi a person must give up his ideas so as to meet others in agreement. There is no benefit in always being lenient with every thought that comes from another, and there is no benefit in always erasing one's own idea from one's heart. That is not conciliation. The one who is able to listen to another is the one who will make another listen to him. It is the one who agrees easily with another who will have the power of making another agree easily with him. Therefore in doing so one gains in spite of the apparent loss which might sometimes occur. When a man is able to see from his own point of view as well as from the point of view of another, he has a complete vision and a clear insight: he so to speak sees with both eyes.

No doubt friction produces light, but light is the agreement of atoms. When one seeks stimulus to thought it does not matter so much if two people have their own ideas and argue about them, but when a person argues for the sake of argument, the argument becomes his game; he finds no satisfaction in conciliation. Words then provide the means of disagreement, reasons become fuel for that fire. Wisdom is there where the intelligence is pliable, when one understands all things: the wrong of the right, and the right of the wrong. The soul who arrives at the perfect knowledge has risen above right and wrong; he knows them and yet he does not know. He can say much, and yet – what can he say? Then it becomes easy for him to conciliate each and all.

There is a story that two Sufis met after many years, having travelled along their own lines. They were glad to meet each other after all those years of separation, for they were both mureeds of the same Murshid. One said to the other, "Tell me, please, your life's experience. After all this time of study and practice of Sufism I have learned one thing: how to conciliate others. I can do this very well now. Will you, please, tell me what you have learned?" The other one said, "After all this time of study and practice of Sufism I have learned how to master life. All that is here in this world is for me, and I am the master; all that happens, happens by my will". Then came the Murshid whose mureeds they were, and both spoke of their experiences during their journey. The Murshid said, "Both of you are right. In the case of the first one it was self-denial in the right sense of the word which enabled him to conciliate others. In the case of the other one nothing was left of his will any more. If there was any will, it was the will of God".

Question: You said the other day that self-denial in the right sense of the word is "I am not, Thou art". What is self-denial in the wrong sense of the word?
Answer: The right meaning is always one, wrong meanings

are many. Among many wrong meanings the one which is most often understood is that self-denial is denying oneself the pleasures and happiness that the world can offer.

CHAPTER XIV

Consideration – Murawwat

MURAWWAT IS a virtue most delicate to express in words. It is refraining from action out of respect for another, be it in consideration for his age, position, knowledge, goodness or piety. Those who practise this virtue do not necessarily have that respect only for someone who has a high position or who has much piety; when they develop this quality it manifests itself in their dealings with all people.

Murawwat is the contrary of what is called bluntness in English. It is not necessarily respect, it is something more delicate than respect: it is consideration and respect together. This virtue in its full development may even rise to such an extent that, out of consideration and respect, a person may try to sustain the lack of the same virtue in another. But when one arrives at this stage then ordinary manner ends and sage manner begins.

Man in this world is not born only to eat, drink and make merry. He is born to arrive at the fullness of humane character, and he realizes this by a greater thoughtfulness and consideration. If not, with power, position, wealth, learning, and all good things in the world, he remains poor without the riches of the soul which is good manner. All the beauty around man is something outside of him; the only beauty which is dependable is to be found and developed in his own character.

A person may show lack of *murawwat*, if not in words, in his glance. He does not need to speak in order to be rude; in his look, in his turns or twists, in his standing up or walking, in closing the door on leaving the room, he can show his feelings. If man does not speak he makes the door speak. It is not an easy matter to manage oneself when one's mind escapes one's hands. Plainly speaking, *murawwat* is acting with consideration and respect for another in a situation where a rude impulse is called out; it is controlling oneself, refraining from committing an insolence, out of respect for another.

Delicate ideas such as these are most difficult to learn and to practise in life. To-day many may wonder if they are not weaknesses. But nothing in the world can prove to be a weakness when it can only be practised by mastering oneself. There is no loss if thought or consideration is given to someone who does not deserve it; for if such an action does not bring any profit, it is still practice – and it is practice which makes man perfect.

CHAPTER XV

Tact

TACT IS a thread which connects heaven and earth making them one. Tact, therefore, is not learned by worldly cleverness. Earthly qualifications do not make a man really tactful; he may imitate a tactful person, but polish is different from gentleness. Where does tact come from? Tact comes from the profound depth of the human heart, for it is a sense which is developed by human sympathy. A selfish person, therefore, cannot prove to be tactful to the end. He will perhaps begin by being tactful but will end in losing that spirit, because false tact will not endure. It is the real alone – object or person - that can endure.

Tactfulness comes from our consideration for one another, and that consideration comes from our feeling, our sympathy for one another. What is consideration? Consideration is feeling "all that is displeasing, distasteful, disagreeable to me – I must not cause it to another". From this sense tact develops as wisdom. A man may be most learned, most capable, most influential, and yet not be tactful. Tactfulness is the sign of the great ones; great statesmen, kings, leaders, heroes, the most learned men, the great servers of humanity were tactful. They won their enemies, their worst adversaries, by their tact; they accomplished the most difficult things in life by the power of tact.

One never can say, "I have enough tact". It is never enough. A real tactful person, having proved not to be tactful enough in his everyday life, finds more faults with himself than a tactless person. As one becomes more tactful so one finds more fault with oneself, because there are so many shortcomings: actions manifest themselves automatically, words slip off from the tongue, and then the tactful one thinks and sees that he did not do right. But as Sa'adi says, "Once it is done then you, thoughtful one, repent of it. This is not the time to repent, you ought to have controlled yourself first".

One becomes tactful through self-discipline, one develops tact by self-control. A tactful person is subtle, fine, poetic; he shows real learning and fine intelligence. Many say, "How can we be tactful and at the same time truthful?" Many look at the fineness of the tactful person saying, "Hypocritical!" But what is the use of that truth which is thrown at a person's head as a big stone, breaking his head. A truth which has no beauty – what kind of truth is it? The Qur'an says, "God is beautiful", therefore truth must be beautiful. If it were not beautiful then beauty-seeking souls and intelligent beings would not have sought after truth.

It is not always necessary to say things which could just as well have not been said. Very often it is weakness on the part of a person to drop a word which could have been avoided. It is the tactful soul who becomes large, because he does not always express himself outwardly. So his heart, accommodating wisdom, becomes larger; it becomes a reservoir of wisdom, of thoughtfulness. It is the tactful person who becomes popular, who is loved; it is the tactful person whom people listen to. Besides, it is by tact that we maintain the harmony of our lives. If not, life turns into a stormy sea. The influences coming from all around in our everyday life are enough to disturb the peace of our lives, and if we were tactless in addition to it what would then become of us? There would be one continual storm in our lives and there could never be peace. It is by tact that we make a balance against all inharmonious influences which have a jarring effect upon our spirit. When inharmony comes from all sides and we are creative of harmony, we counterbalance it, and this makes life easy for us to bear.

What is goodness, piety, or orthodoxy without wisdom, without tact? What will a good person accomplish by his goodness, if he is not able to give pleasure and happiness by what he says or does? Of what use his piety or spirituality will be, if he is not creative of happiness for those who come in contact with him? It is, therefore, with tact that we begin our work of healing ourselves and others.

The Sufis of all ages have been known for their beautiful personality. It does not mean that among them there have not been people with great powers, wonderful powers and wisdom. But beyond all that, what is most known of the Sufis is the human side of their nature: that tact which attuned them to wise and foolish, to poor and rich, to strong and weak – to all. They met everyone on his own plane, they spoke to everyone in his own language. What did Jesus teach when he said to the fishermen, "Come hither, I will make you fishers of men"? It did not mean, "I will teach you ways by which you will get the best of man". It only meant: your tact, your sympathy will spread its arms before every soul who comes, as mother's arms spread out for her little ones.

The Sufis say, "Neither are we here to become angels"*, nor to live as the animals do. We are here to sympathize with one another and to bring to others the happiness which we always seek". Yes, there are many thorns on the path of life, but looking at ourselves we see the same faults, if not more, as those of others which prick like stings, like thorns. Therefore if we spare others the thorn that comes out of us, we will give that much help to our fellowmen – and that is no small help! It is by being tactful that we accomplish our sacred duty, that we perform our religion. For how do we please God? We please God by trying to please mankind.

---

* cf Note 2

CHAPTER XVI

Spirituality

SPIRITUALITY IS natural nobleness, and the unfolding of this innate nobleness is spirituality. It is a divine heritage which is hidden in every soul, and by the manifestation of this divine heritage a soul shows its divine origin. All striving in the spiritual path is to bring out that nobleness – but one need not strive to bring it out; it will come by itself, if one is conscious of one's divine heritage.

It is this consciousness which brings out the nobleness of spirit. In the Sufi terminology this nobleness is called *akhlaq Allah*, which means the manner of God, a manner which is unlike any other manner known to the world. It is the manner of the mother towards her child, the manner of the father towards his son, the manner of a man towards his friend, the manner of the maiden towards her beloved, it is the manner of the lord towards his servant; it is the manner of the child towards his mother, the manner of a son towards his father, the manner of a slave towards his king – and yet it is above and beyond all manners known to mankind. It is humility, it is modesty, it is pride, it is honour, it is kindness, it is graciousness, it is indifference, it is independence; a manner unconceivable to human mentality, a manner which cannot be learned or taught, a manner which springs up by itself and comes forth as a divine blossom.

It is in this manner that lies the fulfilment of the purpose of man's life. This manner is the highest religion, the true spirituality, real aristocracy, and perfect democracy. All disputes and disagreements, all misunderstandings fall away the moment the human spirit has become noble, for it is the sign of the noble spirit to comprehend all things, to assimilate all things and therefore to tolerate and forgive all things. Of what use is a religion, a philosophy, a mysticism, or whatever you call it, if it does not produce that spirit in you, that inclination which is divine? And if that inclination and that spirit manifest themselves in anything, they show in divine manner. Neither in the graciousness of a king, nor in the subservience of a slave one will find that dignity and that humility which divine manner gives.

Is not man the seed of God? Is it then not his life's purpose to bring forth divine blossoms? It is not by working wonders that man shows his divine origin, nor is it by possessing extraordinary powers. If in anything divine origin is seen it is in the aristocracy of the human soul, it is in the democracy of the human ego. In the world we see that there is aristocracy and that there is democracy, but in spiritual unfoldment these two become one, culminating in real perfection.

A flower proves to be genuine by it fragrance, a jewel proves to be genuine by its radiance, a fruit proves to be genuine by its sweetness, a soul proves to be genuine by its manner. Therefore manner is not to be disregarded. This is something to take notice of first. All studies, practices, silences and meditations aside, this is the main thing: to express God in all one does, especially in the manner one shows towards another.

CHAPTER XVII

Innocence

1

INNOCENCE IS so much idealized that a person may ask whether intellect is not a thing to be avoided. The world has advanced very much in intellect: how to get all for oneself, how to get the best of another diplomatically, how to get the best of another politically, how to get the best of another politely and with charming manners, is thought wisdom. This is not wisdom, it is intellect.

If a person has not developed his intellect, the world will take the best of him and he will not realize it. The Sufi should develop his intellect – not in order to use it in the same way as an intellectual person would use it, but in order to see the world as it is. On all sides you will see the selfishness of the world, and the more you develop spiritually, the more you will see it. Sometimes one may wonder whether there are not only animals in the world and no human beings at all. Sometimes one may wonder whether this is not a world of devils. Everywhere one voice is heard, "I want to eat you! I want to take you!" And you cannot go away, go out of the world. You cannot run away to the mountains and jungles. There are very few wise men in the world, and very many intellectual persons.

Another thing is that you may not be innocent as the child is innocent. The child, if it has a diamond brooch and a thief wants to take it, will give it and not know what it is giving. You should be like the king in a story which tells that a king was sitting in his room in which were carved chairs, made like tigers' heads. The eyes of the tigers were diamonds and very beautiful. The king went to sleep. When he awoke, he saw that a thief had come into the room and was stealing the eyes of the tigers. The thief said, "Hush! Don't tell anyone I am stealing the diamonds". The king was much amused at his boldness and confidence, saying this to the king from whom he was stealing. So, knowing that he was a thief, he let him take the diamonds.

You should not do a kindness to an undeserving person, thinking that he deserves your kindness, for the next day you will discover that he does not deserve it, and you will repent. You should do a kindness to a person knowing that he does not deserve it. Then your kindness is very great and there is no repentance.

2

The way of attaining spiritual knowledge is quite opposite to the way by which one attains worldly knowledge. As the sky is in the direction opposite to the earth, so the source of knowledge of spiritual things is opposite to the knowledge of the world. As a man becomes intellectual he knows things of the world, but this does not mean that he becomes spiritual. He goes, on the contrary, further away from spirituality through the thought, "I understand worldly things".

What is the best way of attaining spiritual knowledge? First one must develop in one's nature that little spark which is divine and which was shining in one's infancy, showing something pure, something of heaven. What attracts us most is innocence. It is innocence which gives an impression of purity, but we must not understand this wrongly. Knowledge of the world is more than necessary; it is needed to live in the world, to make the best of our life, to serve God and humanity – it is not needed to attain spiritual knowledge: innocence is necessary for that.

When one sees among one's friends, one's relatives, something which attracts one most it is perhaps the side of their nature which is innocence. People forgive those who are dear to them, they tolerate their faults. They say, "He is wrong, but he is innocent". There is a purity which is divine and which attracts everyone. Innocence is like a spring of water purifying all that is foreign to heart and soul.

How can we attain innocence? Innocence is not foreign to our nature; we have all been innocent, and by being conscious of that nature we develop it. By admiring, by appreciating that nature we develop it too, for all things which we admire become impressions. Those who have a bad nature but have collected good impressions will in time turn their nature.

During my travels in India, the purpose of which was to pay homage to the sages of that land, what appealed most to me was that the greater the soul, the greater was his innocence. It is innocence one sees in them, not simplicity. The one who is simple does not understand. We see this in everyday life: he closes his eyes. Innocence is to understand and to rise above things. Every person sees another through his own glasses. Prejudice often stands between them; for insight unity is necessary. When innocence is developed one has attained spirituality. A man becomes wise after having been intellectual, when he rises above the intellect. Then he sees cause behind cause and understands the way of his enemy.

Would it be practical to live altogether according to the principle of innocence? A principle is to be used, not to guide our life. When people make a chain out of principles, it becomes captivity. Life is freedom. One cannot force oneself to innocence. But if there is any sign of piety or spirituality, there is no better sign than innocence together with all understanding. (7)

CHAPTER XVIII

Holiness

OFTEN ONE wonders what the word holy means. Sometimes people understand by it spiritual, pious, good, pure, religious. But none of these words can fully explain the meaning of the word holy. Holy is the next degree to pious. God-realizing is pious, self-realizing is holy. The first step to self-realization is God-realization; it is not by self-realization that man realizes God, it is by God-realization that man realizes self.

Holiness is a spark of divinity in man, and no soul must be considered as being deprived of this spark of divinity. This spark is light itself, which also exists in the form of life in the lower creation among animals and birds, in trees and in plants. In man this light has the opportunity to blaze into a flame, but at first this light is buried in the heart of man. From the moment this spark of divinity begins to sparkle from his heart, a man shows the sign of holiness. Therefore holiness is no human heritage, it is inherited by every soul from God. It manifests itself only when the heart is open and when out of that spark, which is divine in man, there rises a tongue of flame which illuminates the path of man in life's journey towards the spiritual goal.

It is lack of understanding of this subject which has made man accept one teacher in whom he, or his friends or ancestors, recognized divinity, and reject another with all his holiness. Holiness does not belong to a particular race, community, or family. It comes naturally in the life of some; in the life of others it requires digging. The fire is there, but it is buried, it wants to be brought to the surface, and sometimes blowing is needed to help the flame to rise.

Is holiness seen in action? Yes, it can be seen in action, but who can judge the action? When it is difficult for a wise man to judge the action of the worst sinner, who with any sense would be ready to judge a holy man? Can holiness be recognized in goodness? Yes, it is possible, and yet no one can fix a standard of goodness, for what is good for one is bad for another; something which is poison for one is a remedy for another, and the goodness of every person is peculiar to himself. The worst person in the world, if he wants to, can accuse the best person of lack of goodness. No man has ever proved, nor will any man ever prove, to be good to the satisfaction of every soul that demands goodness.

Holiness in itself is goodness, even if it is not in accordance with people's standard of goodness. Holiness is a continually rising fountain of light, it is a phenomenon in itself; it is illumination and illuminating. Light has no other proof than itself. Holiness needs no claim, no pleading, no publicity; it is its own claim, it pleads for itself. Light itself is its own publicity.

Many in this world seem to be confused about false and true, but there comes a moment when one can see the difference between false and true without any difficulty, because false cannot stand longer than a moment all the tests that come from all sides. It is the real gold that stands all tests – so it is with true holiness. Holiness is enduring, knowing, forgiving, understanding, and yet it stands beyond all things, above all things. It is unbreakable, unshakable; it is beauty, it is power, and it is divinity when it reaches its perfection.

CHAPTER XIX

Resist not Evil

ONE OFTEN wonders at this saying in the Bible, and it is not always given the right interpretation. To interpret it the first thing is to explain what evil means. Is there any particular action, is there any particular thing that one can point out as being evil? No doubt man is always apt to point out a certain action as evil, but nothing can be evil according to a fixed principle. What then is evil? It is something which is void of harmony, which lacks beauty, something from which love is missing. Beyond and above all, it is something which does not fit into the accommodation of life. What fits into the accommodation that life offers cannot be evil; it is the characteristic of evil that it does not fit into it.

Evil may be likened to fire. The nature of fire is to destroy everything that comes into its fold. The power of evil is as great as the power of fire, and at the same time evil is as weak as fire, for fire does not endure, and so evil does not last. As fire destroys itself, so evil is its own destruction. Why is it said, "Do not resist evil"? Because resistance gives life to evil, non-resistance lets it burn itself out.

In the form of anger, passion, greed, or stubbornness one sees evil, and also in the form of deceit and treachery. But the root of evil is one, and that is selfishness. In one person's heart the evil is perhaps manifest on the surface, in another person it is in the depth.

There is a saying in the East, "Do not invoke the name of Satan or he will rise from his grave". An inconsiderate or tactless person always falls into the error of awakening this evil even if it is asleep, for he does not know the music of life. In order to live in the world one should become a musician of life. Every person therein is a note, and the one who feels this way has an instrument before him: the whole world is an instrument upon which a symphony is to be played.

Even in small things one can observe the same law. Very often the great trouble that one has in life is not due to the difficulty of others, but to a lack of comprehension of human nature. If one knew human nature, not to resist evil would be the first and the last lesson to learn, for resistance becomes fuel to its fire. If one tells someone, "Do not do this", if one asks someone, "Why did you do it?", if one says to someone, "You have done such and such a thing", by all these words one only makes evil stronger; one makes the person firmer in his fault.

Everyone in this world can be a teacher – but not a real teacher. A real teacher is the one who always teaches himself, and the more he teaches himself, the more he finds that there is so much to be taught. This self has so many lacks that a whole lifetime is not enough to teach it. The more the self learns, the more it overlooks the evil in others. It does not mean that the evil is in others; it only means that one finds in oneself the enemy which one was seeing outwardly. And the worst enemy one was faced with in outer life one finds to be in one's own heart. It makes one feel humiliated, but it teaches the true lesson: one finds oneself having the same element which one wishes to resist in another.

Life is a place where gentle movement is necessary. In thought, speech or action, in everything the rhythm must be controlled; the law of harmony should be observed in all that one does. One should know that, when walking barefoot on thorns, even they will not allow one to be free from accusation: the thorns will accuse one of having trampled upon them. If the delicacy of living in this world is to that extent, can anyone say, "I have gained sufficient wisdom", or can anyone say, "I can afford to live in this world without giving a thought to this problem?"

The problem of evil is great. Many cannot tolerate to hear the name of evil, but they are faced with it every moment of their lives and therefore to leave this problem unsolved does not help. Besides this, everyone is ready to judge, to observe, or to take notice of the evil in another, not knowing that sometimes the surface of a thing is quite different from its depth. Maybe what seems evil has something good inside it, or what is good in appearance may have a spark of evil inside. By what standard can we determine evil and good, and who can judge the evil and good of any man? If one can judge something it is one's own evil and good. No one except God has the power to judge another. The sense of justice that is given to man is for judging his own actions, and if he judges himself he uses this sense best, because it is for this purpose that the sense of justice has been given to him.

When we look at life through a telescope, we shall find that it is nothing but a struggle for living, individually and collectively and it appears that, if there is anything worthwhile in this life, it is what is besides this struggle: giving and taking kindness and love, doing any action of unselfishness. However qualified a person in the things of the world, his qualification reaches a certain extent and does not go beyond. The whole qualification required is the understanding of life, the understanding of the law which is working behind it. It is this qualification alone which will diminish man's continual struggle in life. It will diminish his struggle in this way that it will give him less to resist. It will make him more tolerant of the natural condition of human beings. As soon as one realizes that one cannot expect from anyone something of which he is not capable, one becomes tolerant.

The difficulty is that everyone demands more of another person in the way of thought and consideration, of kindness and love, than he does of himself. Man wants more justice and fairness on the part of another than he is himself prepared to give; and his standard may be so high that another person cannot keep up to it, which in turn makes him disappointed. What generally happens is that one does not just remain quiet after being disappointed but one resists, and so the struggle of life continues. One should not expect the pear-tree to bear roses, nor the rose-bush to produce jasmine. Every person is like a certain plant, but not the same plant. We may be fond of roses, but every plant does not bear roses; if we want roses we should seek only the plant on which roses grow, and we must not be disappointed if what we find is not the rose plant. In this way we can correct our own deception.

When people say that someone is bad it really means that the surface has become bad. The depth cannot be bad, however bad a person may seem. For goodness is life itself;

and a person who would be all bad could not live. The very fact that he is living shows that there is a spark of goodness in him. Besides just as there are various objects so there are various persons; some show softness inside; some are very good in the depth and evil on the surface; and some are evil on the surface and good in the depth, for there are as many different varieties as there are souls.

What education, what point of view, what attitude in life is the best and will give the greatest happiness? It is the attitude of overlooking evil instead of resisting it. There are three ways of living one's life, which can be compared with struggling in the sea whose waves are rising and falling all the time. The first will struggle as long as life will permit; but the rising and falling of the waves in the sea continue for ever and ever, and in the end he will be drowned. And so it is with man. He struggles along, intoxicated by his struggle. How long will it go on? As long as his energy will permit it, and in the end he will be drowned. In this struggle he may seem powerful, he may seem to have overcome others, he may seem to have done things greater than others – but what is it after all? In the end that person is drowned.

There is another man who knows how to move his arms harmoniously in the water, and who has got the rhythm of moving his arms and legs. He swims with the rising and falling of the waves, he is not struggling. This man has a hope of arriving at the port, if only the port is near. If his ideal is not too far off, then he is the one to accomplish it.

The third person is the one who walks above and over the water. It is this which is the meaning of Christ's walking upon the sea. Life is just like waves, it is making its way continually. The one who allows himself to be disturbed by it will be more and more disturbed every day. The one who does not take notice of it will keep the quietness which is his own within himself. The one who sees all things and yet rises above things is the one who will walk upon the sea.

No one can reach the highest summit of life, the summit of wisdom, in a moment's time; even a lifetime is too short. Yet hope is necessary. The one who hopes and sees the possibilities walks towards the summit. The one who has no hope has no legs to mount on this hill of wisdom, the summit of which is the desired goal.

Question: How can anyone at the head of a business or institution possibly keep to the rule of not resisting evil?
Answer: I have seen people at the head of certain factories who had won the heart of every worker, and another head of a factory whom every worker was speaking against. It may be that the latter made a greater profit than the former, but in the end he would find the profit of the former more durable than his own.

The manner of wisdom and tenderness cannot be made into principles to which people should be restricted. A brush cannot take the place of a knife, and therefore everyone has to use every manner and action according to the situation. Nevertheless, the thought of not resisting evil should always be at the back of it.

Question: How can one manage a person who is really bad?
Answer: If a person is "really bad" it means that the whole surface has become bad, but still the depth cannot be bad. However bad a person the depth cannot be bad, for goodness is life itself, and a person who is all bad cannot live. The very fact that he is alive shows that there is a spark of goodness. Besides, just as there are various objects, so there are various persons. Some show softness outside, hardness inside; some show hardness outside and softness inside. Some have good in the depth and evil on the surface, and some have evil in the depth and good on the surface, because as many souls there are, so many are the varieties.

Question: Is there a system to take away evil?
Answer: That system is understanding life more and more; it is keeping the love element alive, trying to keep an harmonious attitude as much as possible, and then keeping beauty before oneself.

It is difficult, but it is possible when we have the spirit never to be really grown-up, never to close our heart to learning, always to be ready, whatever be our age, to accept what is harmonious and beautiful. When one thinks, "What I think is right", and one finds arguments and reasons to make it right, and when one thinks, "What the other person thinks is wrong", and one finds reasons to make it wrong, one will always remain in the same place. But when one is ready to accept, even from a child, that something one says may be wrong, one thinks, "Even though it is a child who said it, it is a profit for me to accept it". God has not spoken only through His prophets, He speaks through every person, if we open our hearts to listen. The difficulty is that we become teachers. If throughout our whole life we remain pupils teaching will come all the time from within and without. As soon as we become teachers we close our hearts from Him who alone is our Teacher.

Question: If we want to be kind to a person, how can we prevent him from abusing our kindness?
Answer: Our part is to be kind; that person's part is to use it rightly. It is not our part to see that the other person makes the right use of our kindness. If we think about that we shall forget our part.

Question: How can we help a person who does not understand our kindness and is doing harm?
Answer: Love is a conqueror, and in the end will conquer. It is not only the person outside whom love will conquer, but it will conquer the self of the one who loves. This is the conquering of the kingdom of God. The power of love is penetrating, nothing can resist it in the end, and by giving kindness we have not lost anything. It is an element which is never lessened, it is a treasure which is divine. When we consider whether a person is worthy or unworthy we limit our love to a channel, but when we allow that feeling of kindness to flow it will develop into a continually flowing condition. Then kindness will work out its destiny without any intention on our part.

CHAPTER XX

Resignation

RESIGNATION IS the outcome of the soul's evolution, for it is the result of either love or wisdom.

Man has a free will, but its power is too small in comparison with the all-powerful will of God which stands before him in the form of more powerful individuals, or of conditions which cannot be helped, or in that of many other things. Resignation does not mean giving things up, resignation means being content to give up.

To be resigned means to find satisfaction in self-denial. That self-denial cannot be a virtue which comes as a result of helplessness and culminates in dissatisfaction. The nature of an unevolved ego is to resent everything that comes up in life as a hindrance on his path to the accomplishment of a certain object. When one accepts to become resigned in the face of a difficulty, and when at the same time this gives satisfaction, the resigned person, even without having accomplished his object, has risen. In this way even a defeat of a truly resigned soul, in truth, is success.

Resignation is a quality of saintly souls. It is bitter in taste, but sweet in result. Whatever be the power and position of a person, he always has to meet with a more powerful will, in whatever form it may manifest itself, which in truth is divine will. By standing against the divine will one may break oneself, but by being resigned to the divine will one makes a way. For resignation is the manner of water: if anything is standing in its way it takes another course and runs along. It yet makes its way so as to meet the ocean in the end. Such is the way of the saintly souls who tread the path of resignation and yet keep self-will alive. That will has the power to make its way. A person who is resigned by nature becomes in the end a consolation to the self and a happiness for others.

Resignation is not necessarily weakness, or laziness, or cowardice, or lack of enthusiasm. Resignation is only the expression of mastery over oneself. The tendency to resign to the will of another or to conditions does not always work to the disadvantage of the resigned one. It may sometimes prove to be profitless, but the benefit of such a virtue is realized in the end.

It is lack of power of endurance which is the cause that souls are not ready to resign; they cannot endure their pain, they cannot sustain their loss. The resigned ones practise resignation even in small things of everyday life; they avoid using the power of their will unnecessarily in every little thing they do. Resignation is passivity, and it shows itself sometimes to be disadvantageous in the life of an active person who has an object before him to accomplish. But it may be understood that a continual activity, with power and energy given to it, very often results in disaster. Every activity is balanced by passivity. One must be active when it is time to be active, and passive when the conditions ask one to be passive. It is in this manner that success in life is attained and that happiness, which is the seeking of every soul, is gained.

The truth of this can be seen in the life of the child and that of the grown-up person. As soon as the child becomes attracted to objects, it knows that it wants them, and if it is denied an object the child is dissatisfied. As the child grows, with its evolution in life, it learns resignation. That is the difference between an unripe soul and a soul advanced in the path of wisdom; for the riper the soul the more it shows in its nature the power of resignation.

Question: When should we be active and when passive?
Answer: Suppose a person goes on a bicycle in the streets of Paris and says, "I shall go straight on, because my object is just to keep the line I have taken. If a motor-car comes my way, I shall not mind it, I shall just go on". This person will come against something which is more powerful than he and he will destroy himself. The wise cyclist, therefore, will see that there is a vehicle before him, or that the road is blocked: he will take another way. At the time it is just a little hindrance, yet that resignation makes him safe from disaster and gives him a chance to strike another line by which he will come to the same destination.

Very often people who are strong-headed will not be resigned, and often they will find in their lives that, by not being resigned, they get what they want. That gives them proof of the beneficial nature of their strong-headedness – which means their lack of resignation. But what happens in the end? Their own power sometimes strikes them so hard that it breaks them to pieces, because there is no passivity. Man after all is limited, and there is an unlimited power before him. If he always wishes to fight, he must of necessity break himself. There is the saying: Man proposes, God disposes. If man is conscious of this, he will know when to try and make his way, and when to strike a different way.

Question: In the Bible it is said: If a person wants you to go one mile with him, go two miles.
Answer: Resignation is self-denial. In our everyday life it may happen many times that we meet with people who say something which hurts our feeling, and we wish to answer back. It is a natural tendency which expresses itself spontaneously. However, if at that time our wisdom is awakened, we ask ourselves, "Is it necessary to answer? And if we did not answer?" That is becoming resigned to the will of God. Spontaneity is just giving the answer, but when kindness comes, or the feeling that perhaps the other person did not understand us, or that he had a little more experience than we, it restrains the tendency to speak back, and this is mastery. It is bitter for the time, it shakes one: that force which wanted to express itself is controlled. But by being able to sustain it, one has gained a certain mastery over oneself.

Question: In your example one just stops for a moment, but mostly in life this resignation means going quite another way.
Answer: Both are possible. By resignation is only meant to be resigned to one's own wisdom, to one's own feeling of kindness and dignity, or to be resigned to the person whose will perhaps is better or greater.

Question: There are natures who develop the contrary to resignation.

Answer: Very often we give unnecessary strain to our will and this exhausts us very much. It is consideration which is wanted. Every day there are many cases of this which we can avoid by not using so much will-power to resist them.

CHAPTER XXI

Struggle and Resignation

THERE ARE two distinct paths through which one attains
the spiritual goal, and they are quite contrary to one another:
one is the path of resignation, the other the path of struggle.
No doubt in the path of struggle there is also resignation, and
in the path of resignation there is also struggle. But the one
who is treading the path of resignation has only one thought:
to be resigned; as to the one who strikes the path of struggle,
his main object is to struggle.

These two paths are illustrated in a symbolical way by
the words of Christ, "Take your sword and sheathe it".
The taking of the sword means struggle, the covering of
it is resignation. The necessity of these two paths is so
great that it is not possible that one of them is ignored
and only one of them is accepted. People often think that
Sufism means pacifism, but it is not "passivism", it is activity
and "passivism" both. It is the knowledge of the secret of
man's life on earth, of what he needs for his character, for
his condition.

When we reflect upon these principles, we find that there
are things in life to which we can only be resigned. It is easy
to be resigned to things one cannot help, but if one has the
power to struggle it is difficult to be resigned. A person who
is resigned in easy conditions, not finding it difficult, does not
know resignation. For instance there is a person whose poor
relations want a part of his capital, because they are in great
need, but in spite of all their need he cannot be resigned to
let them have that part. Then during the night robbers break
into his house and go away with his fortune, and the next day
this person resigns himself to it. This resignation is no virtue.
To resign means that one has the power to manage, and yet
resigns.

All the great ones have seen the value of resignation, and
have taught it. Christ said that if someone wants you to walk
a certain distance with him, [you should] walk with him a

longer distance. What does it teach? Resignation. One might think that resignation is unpractical, that this selfish world will take the best of one. Yes, it is true, but the loss is much less when compared to the gain – if only the heart can sustain the loss. If one is not contented with what has been done, it is better not to resign. For instance, an acquaintance comes to your house and asks to take your umbrella, and you say "yes". Then comes the time when you want to go out yourself. It is raining and your umbrella is taken. Now you grumble about that acquaintance, "How stupid of him, how could he have the boldness to ask for my only umbrella!" That resignation was no good; it bears no fruit. That is only virtue of resignation when you went out in the rain, yet you were satisfied, because the other person was safe from it. Only then would resignation be a virtue.

One who is really resigned does not show it. Resignation is not an easy thing. How many people in this world try to learn wonderful spiritual things, but this simple thing, resignation, is miraculous; for this virtue is not only beautiful, it is a miracle. There are little things in which we do not see resignation, and where yet it is. Those around us may ask us to do something that does not please us; those around us perhaps say something that we do not wish to take silently, we wish to talk back; then, in everyday life, there are the little pin-pricks from those around us. If we are not resigned, we shall feel excited every moment. To be resigned, therefore, is not weakness, it is a great strength.

When one goes further one finds that one can be resigned even to cold and heat, to places congenial and uncongenial; one finds that all has a meaning, a benefit. Even if one had not formed a habit of being resigned, one could just as well resign oneself, for not having resigned oneself to an experience is the loss of an occasion.

There are two forces working: the individual power and the collective power. In Sufi terms the former is called *qadr*, the latter *qadha*. Often the individual power will not surrender, but if it does not do so it is crushed. For instance someone is called to arms in his country, but says he will not join the army. In spite of all the beauty of his ideal he is helpless before the might of the whole nation. Here he must resign to the condition in which there is a conflict between a lesser and a greater power; here resignation is the only solution.

No doubt everything must be understood rightly. Resignation preached foolishly is of no benefit. There was a mureed who learned from a Murshid the lesson of resignation, and thinking on this subject the simple mureed was walking in the middle of a road, when a mad elephant came from the other side. As he was walking in the thought of resignation he stayed in the middle of the road. A wise man told him to go out of the way, but he would not do so, because he was resigned to the elephant, until he was pushed away by its strength. They brought him to his Murshid who asked him how he came to be hurt so much. He answered that he was practising resignation. The Murshid said, "Was there not somebody who told you to go away?" "Yes", he answered, "but I would not listen". "But", said the Murshid, "why did you not resign yourself to that person?" Often beautiful principles can be practised to the greatest disadvantage. Nevertheless, resignation has proved to be the path of saints, because it develops patience in man. And what is patience? It is all the treasure there is. Nothing is more valuable, nothing is a greater bliss than patience.

There is a story about a prophet who was very ill. He suffered many years, and through his suffering his insight became clearer. His suffering was so great that those around him became tired of it and so, in order to relieve them from seeing his pain, he had to seek refuge with God in the forest. As his sight was keen and the ears of his heart were open, he heard from the trees, "I am the medicine of your disease". The prophet asked, "Has the time of my cure come?" A voice came answering, "No". So he said, "Why shall I take you then?" Another time he had this experience again; he heard, "I am the medicine of your disease", and asked, "Has the time of my cure come?" The answer came, "Yes". The prophet said, "Why shall I take you then?"

When we think of this extreme ideal we may ask: is it not unpractical, especially at this time where there are so many treatments, so many mechanical means? But a thoughtful person will see how many people have ruined their lives by going from one treatment to another, lacking the patience and resignation in which resides their absolute cure. The remedy is not always the answer to the difficulty; often patience is the answer. It seems as if man becomes more and more impatient every day owing to his superficial life; there is hardly any resignation to little things. Yet it is better to resign than to struggle.

When we throw a mystic light upon this subject we find that we form a harmonious connection with the Infinite by being resigned. How to learn it? Should we learn it by being resigned to God? No, that is a still greater lesson to learn. The first thing to learn is to be resigned to the little difficulties in life. What does this mean? It means not to strike out at everything that comes in our way. If one were able to manage this, one would not need to cultivate great power; then one's presence would be healing. Such a person is in the world more precious than a branch of the rose, which may have many thorns and hardly one flower.

Question: How to attain peace when our life is often so difficult?
Answer: No doubt, life is difficult for many of us, but very often we make it even more difficult for ourselves. When we do not understand the real nature and character of life we make our own difficulties. I can assure you that in every man's life five percent of his difficulties are brought about by the conditions of life, and ninety-five percent are difficulties caused by himself.

Now you will ask: When the difficulties come from ourselves, where do they come from? We do not like struggle in life, we do not like strife, we only want harmony, we only want peace. It must be understood, however, that before making peace war is necessary, and that war must be made with our self. Our worst enemy is our self: our faults, our weaknesses, our limitations. And our mind is such a traitor! What does it? It covers our faults even from our own eyes, and points out to us the reason for all our difficulties: others! So it constantly deludes us keeping us unaware of the real enemy, and pushes us towards those others to fight them, showing them to us as our enemies.

Besides this, we must tune ourselves to God. As high we rise so high becomes our point of view, and as high our point of view so wide becomes the horizon of our sight. When a person evolves higher and higher his point of view becomes wider and wider, and so in all he does he strikes the divine note, the note which is healing and comforting and peace-giving to all souls.

CHAPTER XXII

Renunciation

RENUNCIATION IS in fact denial of the self, and it is that denial which will be of use. As all things in this world can be used and abused, so the principle of renunciation can be used and abused. If renunciation as a principle were a good thing, there would seem to be no purpose at the back of the whole creation. The creation might well not have been manifested if renunciation had been the principle. Therefore renunciation in itself is neither virtue nor sin. It becomes a virtue or a sin according to the use one makes of it.

When one considers renunciation from the metaphysical point of view, one finds that this principle is used as a staircase by which to rise above all things. It is the nature of life in the world that all things we become attracted to in time become not only ties but burdens. If one considers life, one sees that it is an eternal journey. The more one is loaded with burdens on one's shoulders, the heavier the journey becomes. Think how the soul, whose constant desire it is to go forward, is daily retained by ties and continually more burdened. One can see two things: as the soul goes on it finds chains on its legs. It wants to go forward – and at every step it is more attracted; so it becomes more difficult to go forward.

Therefore all the thinkers and the wise who have come to the realization of life have taken renunciation as a remedy. The picture that the sage makes of this life is the fable of the dog and the piece of bread. A dog carrying a loaf in its mouth came to a pool; it saw the reflection of the bread in the water, and thought that there was another dog. It howled and barked, and lost its bread. The more we see our errors in life, our petty desires, the more we find that we are not far from the fable of the dog. Think of the national catastrophes of recent times. How these material things of the world, ever changing and not everlasting, have been pulled at and fought for! It shows that man, blinded by material life, disregards the secret, hidden things behind that life.

When one comes to reason out what one should renounce and in what way one should practise renunciation, there is a lesson to be learned: no virtue is a virtue if it is forced upon the one who is incapable of it. A person upon whom a virtue is forced, who is forced to renounce, cannot make the right renunciation. No virtue which gives pain is a virtue. If it gives pain, how can it be a virtue? It is called virtue because it gives happiness; that which takes away happiness can never be a virtue. Therefore renunciation is rightly practised by those who understand renunciation, and are capable of practising it. For instance, there is a person who has only one loaf of bread. He is travelling in a train and finds somebody who is hungry and in need of his bread. He himself is hungry too, and he has only one piece of bread. If he thinks that it is his *dharma** to give and starve, and is unhappy about it, he would do better not to give it, because it is no virtue. If he did it once, the next time he would surely not do it again because he suffered by it. As the virtue brought him unhappiness, this virtue will never develop in his character. That person alone is capable of renunciation who finds a greater satisfaction in seeing another with his piece of bread.

The person whose heart is full of happiness after his action, that person alone should make a renunciation. This shows that renunciation is not a thing that can be learned or taught; it comes by itself as the soul develops, when the soul begins to see the true value of things. All that is valuable to others a seer-soul begins to see otherwise. This shows that the value of all things, which one sees as precious or not precious, is according to the way one looks at them. For one person the renunciation of a penny is too much, for another the renunciation of all he has is nothing. It depends on how one looks at things.

One rises above all things that one renounces in life. Man is a slave of the thing which he has not renounced; of the things that he has renounced he becomes king. This whole world can become a kingdom in his hand, if a person has renounced it. But renunciation depends upon the evolution of the soul.

* dharma – religion, duty, personal ritual or moral obligation

One who has not evolved spiritually cannot well renounce. For the grown-up person little toys, so valuable to children, are nothing; it is easy to renounce them. So it is for those who develop spiritually: all things are easy to renounce.

Now rises the question: how can one progress in this path of renunciation? By becoming able to discriminate between two things, and to find out which is the better one. A person with the character of the dog in the fable cannot renounce: he loses both things. Life is such that, when there are two things before one's view, it demands the loss of one of them. It depends upon man's discrimination what to renounce and for what; whether to renounce heaven for the world, or the world for heaven; wealth for honour, or honour for wealth; whether to renounce things momentarily precious for everlasting things, or everlasting things for things momentarily precious. The nature of life is such that it always shows two things, and many times it is a great puzzle to choose between them. Very often one thing is at hand and the other further from one's reach, and it is a puzzle which one to renounce, or how to get the other. Very often man lacks the will-power to renounce. It not only requires discrimination between two things but also will-power to do what one wishes to do. It is not an easy thing for a man to do in life as he wishes. Many times he cannot renounce because his own self cannot listen to him. Think how difficult life is; when we ourselves cannot listen to ourselves, how difficult then for others to listen to us!

Renunciation can be learned naturally. One must first train one's sense of discrimination, and discriminate between what is more valuable and what is less valuable. One can learn this by testing, as gold is put to the test by comparing it to imitation gold: that which lasts for a little time and then turns black is imitation, that which always keeps its colour is real. This shows that the value of things can be recognized by their constancy. One might ask: should we not recognize the value of things by their beauty, but we must recognize beauty by its durability. Think of the difference in the price of a flower and a diamond. The flower with all its fineness, beauty of colour and fragrance falls short in comparison with the diamond. The only reason is that the beauty of the flower will fade the next day, while that of the diamond will last.

This shows our natural tendency; we need not learn it. We are always seeking for beauty and also for that which is lasting. Friendship that does not last, however beautiful it may be, what value has it? Position, honour that do not last, what value have they? Although man is like a child, running after all that attracts him and which is always changing, still his soul seeks constancy. In learning the lesson of renunciation one can only study one's own nature, what the innermost being is yearning for, and try to follow one's own innermost being. Wisdom comes by this process of renunciation. Wisdom and renunciation go together: by renunciation man becomes wiser, by being wise he becomes capable of renunciation.

The whole trouble in the lives of people, in their houses, in the nation and everywhere, is always their incapacity of renunciation. If civilization can be explained, it is only a developed sense of renunciation which manifests itself in consideration for each other. Every act of courtesy, of politeness shows renunciation. When a person offers his seat to another, or when he offers something that is good, it is renunciation. Civilization in its real sense is renunciation.

The highest and greatest goal that every soul has to reach is God. As everything wants renunciation, that highest goal wants the highest renunciation. But a forced renunciation – even for God – is not proper, not legitimate. Proper renunciation one can see in those who are capable of doing it. There is a story in the Bible of Abraham sacrificing his son. Man to-day is likely to laugh at some of the ancient stories, reasoning according to his own point of view. But think how many fathers and mothers have given their children as a sacrifice in the war, for their nation, their people, their honour. This shows that no sacrifice can be too great a sacrifice for one's ideal. There is only the difference of ideal: whether it is a material or a spiritual ideal, whether for earthly gain or for spiritual gain; whether for man or for God.

As long as renunciation is practised for spiritual progress, so long it is the right way. As soon as renunciation has become a principle, renunciation is abused. Man, in fact, must be the master of life. He must use renunciation, not go under in renunciation. So it is with all virtues. When virtues control man's life, they become idols. It is not idols that man must worship, it is the ideal he must worship in the idol.

CHAPTER XXIII

Sacrifice

1

SACRIFICE WAS taught to the world at different times, in different degrees suited to the stage of evolution that had been reached, just as we teach a child by its dolls.

At first men were taught to sacrifice a goat or a sheep, because at that time they cared so much for a goat that they were ready to kill another man for the sake of a goat. We see that the same ignorance still exists; for the sake of a trench men killed so many men, and even then they were not sure that the trench would remain theirs.

A man who had so much cruelty in him that he could not refrain from killing and eating a goat was taught, "First sacrifice it. When you kill the goat, do it for God, do it for others". If he had been told, "Sacrifice yourself", he might have said, "How can I sacrifice myself when I cannot even sacrifice my inclination to eat the goat?"

Afterwards self-sacrifice was taught, which Christ explained so well in his life and in the Sermon on the Mount. This sacrifice – to turn the other cheek, to give the cloak away when the coat has been taken – could not be understood by the ordinary person, because it is the moral of sages and saints. This makes it very difficult for them to live in the world, and has made many people turn away from religion altogether. They said, "The teaching of the prophets and saints is too high for us. We cannot understand it". If one says to a business-man in his office, "Give whatever they claim from you, and give more", he will say, "No, I have a thousand claims in the law-courts; I will fight and win".

When Muhammad came, all that had been taught before in the prophetic messages was united in his message. Both sorts of sacrifice were taught: the sacrifice of animals, that is of their property, for those who were in that grade of evolution; self-sacrifice for those who had reached a higher stage.

2

The moral of sacrifice was taught at a time when mankind in general was much nearer to the animal. The dog, even when it has had enough food and there is some remaining on its plate, will not let another dog take it. Even in this time we do not like another to share our profit, our benefit, even if it is our own brother. If he has his profit somewhere else it is all right, but he must not take the best part of ours. The dog does not like to let another dog have even the remains of its food, because it does not know whether it will get more at another time. Where we see our own benefit, there we are blind, and it is only this that keeps us imperfect.

If you see your own benefit, there may be a wife in your house, a child, a sister, a brother, a friend, or a servant, but you will see only yourself. If you consider yourself as being the whole family, then you are the sister, the brother, the wife, the child, the friend, the servant. Then you are a perfect family: by opening yourself you have become a perfect family. If you can say, "I am the nation", you are greater; if you say, "If my nation's honour goes down, I go down", you are the nation. If you can say, "I am my race", that is still greater. And if you say, "I am the whole humanity", that is the greatest. Then everyone who comes before you is your sister or your brother. You are yourself all. When man is his individual self, then he is narrow and imperfect; when he is all, then he is perfect.

I was reading this morning a verse of the Bible and was much touched by its meaning, "Ye are the salt of the earth". The salt is that which in water has the strongest flavour. So in the whole manifestation man is the strongest power on earth, and "if the salt hath lost its savour, wherewith shall it be salted?" If man loses his human quality, where shall it be found? The birds, the animals cannot give it to him; God Himself is helpless to give it to him. All man's perfection is within himself, if only he would uncover it and see it. The Kingdom of God is within man, and his will should rule it.

All godheads were really men, not different from us. What

was in their soul is in our soul also. If we single out one man for our worship, it proves our ignorance, our ignorance of our own soul. We are as they were; it is only that the divine power, the divine wisdom was working through them.

The dog, as I said, does not like to let another dog take even the remains of its food, because it has no confidence in the sustaining power of nature; also its self is always before its eyes, and it is the idea of the self that blinds. We have read in books and we have understood intellectually that God is all, that we are the Whole Being. But when a little insult comes to our self, to our pride, how angry we are! We think the whole world is altered. In reality there was no harm, it was just a little hurt to our pride. But if we are so angry, it is because we have understood only with our intellect that God is all; we have not realized it in our own life.

We cannot easily become saints – they are the great ones; we cannot become prophets – they are greater still. But we can ask ourselves every day whether we have considered the other as ourself, whether we have considered his benefit as our benefit. There are many practices, but this is the greatest practice and the most difficult one. It does not require more study, more learning; but by this practice we can reach perfection.

3

There is a great teaching in the story of Abraham's sacrifice. It has often been misinterpreted and so its meaning has been lost. The great religions have often been misinterpreted by their followers and by historians, and this has caused their downfall for which otherwise there was no reason. I will tell you this legend in which there is a great revelation.

Abraham had a son whom he loved very much. At that time children were prized much more than they are in the present age. Now we have many other possessions besides children, and these other possessions distract our thought from the children. Then a child, a son or a daughter, was all. A son was valued more, because they thought: a son keeps the name and a daughter does not.

Abraham loved his son very much. It is the nature of every human heart to love and especially of one chosen to be a prophet. That Power which draws all and everyone to itself became jealous of this love; for it is our nature that whatever we love is the whole world to us, whether it is a child, a brother, a friend. When we have it we think that we have the whole world, and when we lose it we think that the whole world is lost.

A voice came from the Divinity to Abraham, "Sacrifice your son to Us." Abraham was ready to sacrifice his son to God. He asked the mother's consent; she gave it. Then he asked his son; he also was resigned to the will of God for his own sacrifice. He said, "Yes, I may be sacrificed".(8) Then Abraham took a knife and cut his son's throat. As he cut it his son was taken away and he saw him standing before him, safe. A goat was put in his place.

The meaning of this legend has often been misunderstood; it has been said that the goat, the life, should be sacrificed. The meaning is much greater. Abraham is the spiritual teacher, the father. We still call the priest father; he who shows the way to God is the father of the spirit. Isma'il* is the pupil, the child to whom the Murshid show this way to sacrifice: the sacrifice of the self, of the individuality. This is the greater sacrifice, the annihilation of the self. By *shaghl* and *amal*† and other practices the self is made to disappear, it is lost. When the self is gone from before us then all other selves can come, then illumination comes; then, when the individual self disappears, the spiritual self appears. Only the illusion is lost; the self is not lost, but the beginning is annihilation. This is all the secret of mysticism, all that the prophets and mystics have taught.

4

Sacrifice has been much misunderstood by those who practise it. It is thought that God will be pleased with the life of a

---

* In the Islamic tradition it was Isma'il (Ishmael) rather than Izaac(Ishaq) whom Abraham offered for sacifice
† mystical concentrations with breathing exercices

goat that is offered – and which the sacrificers then keep
for themselves. The bankbook is not sacrificed, property is
not sacrificed, nor the house, nor the furniture, but a goat is
brought and killed, and they make a feast.

It was taught to say when sacrificing: *Allahu akbar, la ilaha
ill' Allahu* – God is great, none exists but God. This shows that
the sacrifice of our animal self is meant by the law of sacrifice.
We should sacrifice our time, our sleep, thinking, "Before my
birth I slept and I do not know where I was. In the grave sleep
is waiting for me. Now only is the time when I can work".
Then the thought comes, "That day I felt as I should not feel,
that time I spoke as I should not speak, that year I acted as I
should not act. So many months and years, so much of my
life is past, and nothing is done that was worthwhile". This
makes us think that it is not too late to awaken.

If we can sacrifice our sleep to work for humanity, we
should do it. If by having not such good food we can share
with another, we should do it. If by having not such a nice
dress we can give a dress to one who needs it, we should do
it. If by having one dish instead of many we can share with
someone who needs it, we should do that. If we can sacrifice
our pleasures, our theatres, to give to others we should do it.
We can sacrifice our anger when anger comes upon us. We can
sacrifice our pride. We can bow to those who think little of us.
There are many sacrifices that do not cost one penny. We can
give some of our time if we cannot afford a great generosity.
We can give our patience to those who need our patience. To
those who want some liberty – very well, we can give liberty.
I think all this is worthwhile sacrifice: we should do it.

5

Sacrifice is only legitimate when, through every cost or loss, it
is willingly done, The one who sacrifices may feel the reward
much more than the cost or pain he has endured or suffered
in sacrificing. The law of sacrifice is that it is only valuable
when it gives pleasure to the one who sacrifices. The sacrifice
must be done whole-heartedly. Sacrifice is like a bath in the
Ganges; it can be more sacred than anything in the world.

When a person does not do it for a principle, but only for the good he may receive in return, then it is useless. When it is done for the joy of sacrifice, in that case the joy is great.

The law of sacrifice depends upon the degree of evolution. One sees this among children. A child who grows up understands life better and is perhaps more ready to make a sacrifice than the child who knows only the object he wants and nothing else. In this world it is not the difference of years, but the evolution of every soul which keeps it young: the more grown-up the more ready to sacrifice, and the younger the less ready for the joy of sacrifice.

Apart from the point of view of the benefit hidden in the idea of sacrifice, it is not a thing that every soul can understand. One person will do something and consider that there is great wisdom in his sacrifice, while another who is not evolved enough to understand it will say, "How very foolish!". Remember therefore that not only to the wise person the man of little sense seems foolish, but even to the foolish person the wise one seems foolish. The points of view of both are different: one looks from the top of the tower, the other standing on the ground. So there is a vast difference in the range of their sight.

It is a man's outlook on life which makes him broad or narrow, and it is the grade of his evolution which gives man the illumination of sacrifice. What a man was not inclined to do last year, he may be inclined to do this year; the sacrifice one could not make yesterday, one can make today, for the rate of speed of man's evolution cannot be limited to a particular standard. A broad outlook enriches man and a high point of view ennobles the soul.

CHAPTER XXIV

Ambition

THIS WHOLE manifestation has ambition as its underlying motive and, as everything in the world has two swings, it also has a forward swing and a backward swing. When a race or a nation has reached the furthest point of the forward swing, it recognizes that all is valueless, and it begins the backward swing which means annihilation, the return to God.

We can see this in the East. The wish of every person there is to do without. They will rather eat with their fingers than with fork and knife; they will rather eat on the floor than at a table; they will rather go bareheaded than wear a hat, and they will rather go barefoot than wear shoes. All their present backwardness is because they have lost ambition for advancement. When they had ambition they too progressed, and at one time they were first in civilization.

When the wise people had reached that point the time of renunciation began, and the reflection of the wise fell upon the foolish. Not only the wise men who had some reason for it practised renunciation, but also the foolish. They had no reason for it, but the influence of the wise affected them. They are all in a dream, without ambition, lazy. If one would say to them, "You are always dreamy and lazy. Have some ambition, be active!", they would answer, "I am happy in my dream. What else could you teach me?" If anyone wishes to walk over their head, they allow it; they say, "There will be a third one, stronger than he, who will one day walk over his head". There are many in India who do not kill insects, as the Jains. A Brahmin does not kill a snake. How then could he take a weapon in his hand and stand against a man?

I have met a Brahmin, a great musician, and I was much astonished for he was in his *dhoti* wearing only a towel which covered his back. But when he began to speak it was evident that his knowledge was so great that he was the greatest musician of his time. In the West the ambition for worldly things drives a man so far that he often forgets his parents, he neglects his duties. His self is always before his eyes. I have seen that it is always so in the life of business, of commerce, of trade. The worldly ambitions are so strong that a man has no time for spiritual knowledge. Very often he would have a tendency to realize the truth through his intelligence, but the ambitions of the world are too strong.

If one says, "Shall we renounce and become as they are in the East, living in a dream, and rather lazily? Shall we allow whatever nation to walk into our country?" – I shall answer that there cannot be one principle for everyone, because everyone is not in the same stage of evolution. Therefore the Sufi prescribes no common principle for all. He does not say, "Renounce. Do not be cruel". The Sufi has been blamed for this many times, because to have no principles in ordinary language means to be very bad. We recognize that what is a right principle for one is not always right for another. To a lord who has so many millions of pounds we shall not say, "Do not give a great dinner or a ball in your house". He would say, "All the other lords do it". He cannot have the same principles that a Murshid prescribes for himself. My Murshid once refused initiation to the Nizam of Hyderabad because the Nizam could not follow the principles that the Murshid would prescribe.

A person must not choose the way of renunciation as long as any ambition within him remains unfulfilled. *Vairagya*, the thought of renunciation, comes to every wise person, to every righteous person. Sometimes a man thinks, "I want to renounce all, because I am disgusted". Another time he thinks, "But if I were given a little bungalow and a little garden, I would not renounce it". Sometimes he thinks, "I will renounce the whole world", and another time he thinks, "But if I were Mr Asquith"*, or Mr Asquith's secretary, I would not renounce". If one says, "I have renounced the Tsar's throne", what does that mean? Only the Tsar may say, "I renounce the throne that has been given to me".

* Liberal prime minister of Great Britain who led Britain into World War I

It is only when every ambition has been satisfied that a person should take the way of renunciation. Until then let him use his power. Whilst any desire remains he must not renounce it; it is not right. You might ask, "Then shall we never renounce?" Yes, when your ambition is unjust, when it is cruel, then renounce.

CHAPTER XXV

Satisfaction

THE SATISFACTION of every soul lies in its recognition. Every person desires that there would be someone in the world who understands him well, at least as well as he understands himself. A wife says, "I have a comfortable home and a good husband; I only wish that he would understand me better". The servant says, "I get good pay and the master is kind; I only wish that he would know me well". An artist is satisfied when his art is admired by the knower. This is the usual seeking of every soul.

There is a story about a mimic who was performing his skill of imitating different birds and animals in the street in front of the window of a palace from where the king was looking on. At the end of his performance a golden shawl was thrown to him from the palace-window as a reward from the king, and an old blanket was presented to him by a shepherd. The mimic adorned himself with the ragged blanket of the shepherd and kept the shawl of the king under his arm. The king disliked this behaviour on the part of the mimic and asked him why he insulted the palace by adorning himself with the shepherd's gift, hiding the reward of the king. He answered, "Because the shawl was given as a token of your Majesty's greatness, and the blanket was given purely in deep admiration for my imitation of the cow twitching its skin, which no one but the shepherds could understand so well".

From this story we learn that there is no greater reward given or love shown than in recognition. As this is the desire of every soul, so it is also the desire of the Soul of souls. He puts forward His hand to such suitor who comes before Him with full recognition.

Harmlessness

HARMLESSNESS IS a good moral, but the difficulty is that we cannot be good to one without being harmful to another. For instance, we are good to our cat and we give it the lamb's meat to eat; so we are harmful to the lamb. Or we sacrifice the vegetable for the sake of being good to the lamb. We harm the mineral when for the sake of some flowers we put clay in water, bend and knead it and then put in the fire in order to make a bowl to hold the flowers. How many things do we make out of iron, how much do we torment it in order to make ourselves comfortable? How many things do we make out of wood? The lives of how many animals do we sacrifice in order to make ourselves comfortable and happy? As to ourselves, how much do we sacrifice the benefit, the comfort of our fellow-beings for our own benefit? We do not ponder upon it, but it is so.

How many things do we make out of the bones of animals? Our shoes are made out of the skin of animals; the furs of animals cover us warmly. The flesh of animals we use for our food. Fishes, which never dreamed of harming us, we catch in nets. We load burdens upon horses, camels and elephants, and we take from the calf its share in the form of milk and butter upon which our everyday's livelihood depends. This shows that what we have built up and have comforted ourselves with is nothing else than tyranny – of which we never stop to think for a while.

We are so placed that we cannot live one instant without being harmful. In Persian it is said: *Bandagi becharagi* – bondage is helplessness. Man cannot help being harmful, and without being that he is helpless. It is this dependence, this helplessness, which makes him the servant of God. The Qur'an speaks of *abd'Allah*, servant of God, and this is the highest title that can be given to man.

The moral is rather to be harmful to the lower creation for the sake of the higher, rather to be harmful to the animal than to man. If a man has stolen your dog, rather let him have the dog, than have him sent to prison, because the man is more valuable than the dog. If your child has hurt the cat a little, and if you shake the child and hurt it, it is a mistake, because the child is of more value than the cat. If an animal has eaten your corn, your flowers and fruits, let the corn go, do not break the back of the animal. By this moral a person becomes so harmless that in the end he is not harmful any more – not even to the mineral. Harmlessness is the essence of moral.

CHAPTER XXVII

A Question about Vegetarianism

Question: Is vegetarianism advisable for the sake of not killing animals?

Answer: There are two things to be considered in this connection. One is harmlessness. It is a human tendency to hurt and harm; man has inherited it from the lower creation. It is this tendency which prompts him to kill poor creatures and make his food out of them in spite of all the vegetables and cereals, fruits and nuts which are provided for him by nature. The other point is that for the purification of the blood, for the health of the muscles, and for general purity of the body the vegetable diet is far preferable to flesh food.

At the same time the training of the Sufi is a spiritual treatment and, as a physician sees in every case what is best for that particular person, so the Murshid prescribes for his mureeds what is best for them. There may be a person for whom a vegetable diet is not sufficient or not good; meat for him may be like a medicine. There is no such restriction, therefore, in Sufism; the need of every individual is according to his health. We do not make a dogma out of vegetarianism.

In connection with the same question I may make another remark. In ancient times shepherds used to clothe themselves with tiger skins in order to secure their lives from the danger of wild animals, when taking care of their herds they moved about in the forests. When a wise person who is good and kind lives in this world of different natures, it is more difficult for him to live in the gross vibrations than for others who perhaps are more or less of the same kind. Very often therefore one hears people say of a person who has died young that he was good – and there is some truth in it too. Many souls, fine, good and beautiful, come on earth and cannot withstand the coarseness of the ordinary human nature.

What is diet? Diet is not for the soul, it is only for the body. The body is a cover, a blanket, and if the body is covered with armour, then it can stand the struggle of life. If ever the great ones allow themselves to partake of flesh food, which in reality is meant for the average person, it is for that reason.(9)

CHAPTER XXVIII

Unselfish Actions

A PERSON is apt to think, "Why should I perform actions that bring me no return? Why should I be kind, where no kindness is shown to me, where there is even no appreciation?" In this way he commercializes his kindness: he gives in order to receive. This blindness comes upon man, and it makes him blind even towards God. He thinks, "Why should I be grateful to God? There is nothing to be grateful for. If the sun shines, it is natural. If I have what I need for my living, I work for it all day"; or else, "I belong to such a family where it is natural that everything should be provided for me".

Man never sees how helpless he is in himself. If there were no ground, he could not stand. If there were no air, he could not breathe. If there were no parents, he could not have been brought up. All things that keep him alive are those upon which his existence depends, for which an unbounded amount of thanks is due. But he thinks, "If I perform any kind action, God should do a thousand kindnesses to me. If I do anything for others, God should do a thousand times as much for me." Then he wishes to give only when there is a return. He speaks a kind word in order that kind words may be spoken to him; this is flattery. He says, "I like you because you like me. I am your friend, because you can help me. I am your enemy, because you have done me harm".

The Sufi says, "*Ishk Allah, Mahboob Allah* – God is love and Beloved". This word love we have so altered, so degraded in our ordinary life. We say, "I love you, because you love me. I am your friend, your well-wisher, because you are my friend and well-wisher". This friendship lasts a short time and then it is gone. It is as if we say: "I like this flower because it is beautiful", and when its beauty is gone, it is thrown away.

Question: What is the best way to learn not to look for appreciation and reciprocity?

Answer: To develop independence in nature. When one loves one must love for the sake of love, not for a return. When one serves one must serve for the sake of service, not for acknowledgement. In everything a person does, if he does not think of reciprocity or appreciation in any manner or form, he may perhaps seem a loser in the beginning, but in the end that person will be the gainer, for he has lived in the world and yet held himself above the world; it cannot touch him.

Furthermore the tendency to doubt, to be depressed, the tendency towards fear, suspicion and confusion, the tendency to puzzle – where does it all come from? It all comes from the thought of getting something in return: "will another give me back what I have given him? Shall I get the just portion back, or less?" If that is the thought behind one's acts there will be fear, doubt, suspicion, puzzle and confusion. For what is doubt? Doubt is a cloud that stands before the sun, keeping its light from shining. So is doubt: gathering around the soul it keeps its light from shining out, and man becomes confused and perplexed. Once selflessness is developed, it breaks through the cloud saying, "What do I care whether anyone appreciates it; I only know to give my service, and that is all my satisfaction. I do not look forward to get it back. I have given it and it is finished; this is where my duty ends". That person is blessed, because he has conquered, he has won.

Then it is lack of knowledge of the divine justice when man doubts whether he will get his just portion, or whether the other will get the best of him. If he looked up and saw the perfect Judge, God Himself, whose justice is so great that in the end the portions are made equal and even – there is only a question about the beginning, not about the end – if only he saw the justice of God, he would become brave, he would trust and not trouble about a return. God is responsible for returning a thousandfold what man has ever given.

CHAPTER XXIX

Expectations

THE QUR'AN says, "Man is cruel and man is foolish". He is cruel because he is harmful at each move he makes throughout life, and he is foolish because he does not know his true benefit.

Whatever you wish to obtain, live only for that, think only of that. If you wish to be rich, think only of riches, be with rich people, be always playing with money: then you will certainly be rich. But if, when you have ten pounds, you think I want a dinner party, and a theatre party and a new dress, you cannot be rich. If you want fame think only of fame; work and praise and flatter, think only how your name and fame may come out.

Man does not know what he really wants, what his true benefit is. Sometimes he thinks that satisfying the senses is his benefit; sometimes he thinks that material comforts are his benefit; sometimes he thinks that fame or money will satisfy him. His true benefit is to be independent of all these momentary satisfactions, but great renunciation is needed for this. He must renounce even what is necessary for life, as food, sleep, praise and attention. Then he sees, "I can live without this, I can live without what is needed for life". Then comes the realization that he is not a physical being but a higher being, and by this realization he is liberated and exalted.

Resignation to the will of God is the highest stage. A person must first work with the idea of benefit for the self, before he can arrive at that stage. This means that he must pass through selfishness in order to arrive at unselfishness. You might say, "The world is full of people working for the self"; but those have not realized what is the real benefit of the self. That which gives a momentary pleasure, a pleasure that lasts a few days, is no benefit for the self. To abuse another gives a pleasure for a moment; it is not of real benefit to the self. Those actions are not even selfish actions, they are foolish: the intelligence has not understood what the self is.

CHAPTER XXX

Be a Lion Within

LIFE IS such that if we lay our hand here, there is a stone, if we lay our hand there, there are thorns. We can rely upon no one, not upon a relation, nor upon a friend. Whether friend or relative, whether master or servant, husband or wife, they do not care how we fare, they want so much work done by us. Whether it is a friend or a brother, he wants his own benefit from us, however near he may be. How could we expect the contrary, when we cannot rely upon our own mind and our own body to be always the same? After many experiences a person learns this. It takes a long time, because hope always remains. Man always thinks, if I cannot rely upon this one, then upon that one, if not upon this friend, then on that other one.

Then, from a lion, man must become a sheep. In the world each one is a lion, and behind each lion there is a bigger lion, and a machine gun ready to devour him. Man becomes a sheep; he becomes humble, meek. You might think, "The lion is greater than the sheep. Why, from a lion, should I become a sheep, from better become worse?" The lion is lion outside; to others he is a lion, in his own soul he is a sheep, because he has not the courage to fight his own passions. His anger rules him, he does not control his anger.

In order to be the lion of God you must be a lion within, towards yourself. Then you are brave enough to stand against any evil, any power, because there is no guilt, there is no weakness. Great humility is needed for this way.

CHAPTER XXXI

Humility

THERE IS a story of Khwaja Moin-uddin Chishti, whose fame is still so great that, although he died hundreds of years ago, thousands come to his tomb every year, and the power of his holiness is so great that everyone who goes there falls into a trance.

One of his mureeds once wrote him a letter and, as we write "yours sincerely", "yours truly", he signed "faqir". *Faqir* means one who has renounced, one who is spiritual. Khwaja Moin-uddin Chishti read the letter and said, "Thank God, I have a mureed who is *faqir*, what I myself, all my life following this way, have not become". He answered the mureed saying, "I am very glad to read that you have become *faqir*". The mureed was much dismayed. He thought, "What have I done? I have written a very wrong thing". *Faqir* also means a humble person, which was what he meant.

He went to his Murshid and said, "I have made a great fault". The Murshid replied, "It is all right. I wish that you should be greater than I. I shall show you how I am considered". He took the mureed out in the wilderness where the hermits were living, a long, long way from any town. They knocked at a door, and a voice came from within, "Will the dogs of the world not leave us in peace even here?". Khwaja Moin-uddin Chishti said, "I am your Murshid, and you see in what sort of respect I am held".

CHAPTER XXXII

Moral Culture

1

WE DISTINGUISH between good and evil, right and wrong by our own experiences. One man has a good experience from a certain thing and at once calls it good; another has a bad experience from the same thing and calls it bad. A person who may seem very bad to some is called good by his friend. In a person who leads a merry life one may be sure, by looking carefully, to find some good, such as may not be found in persons of great repute for their holiness and spirituality.

Man is born with such a critical tendency and has so much developed this tendency that he easily seeks what is bad in everything. The Sufi takes the contrary way; he seeks for what is good in everyone and everything. The way of morality is to think that if someone has done us some good it is very great, and if we have done good to someone to think that it is very little and that we might have done more. If a person has done something bad to us we should forget it as soon as possible, and if we have done something bad we should think that a great fault. If we see something that seems bad to us we should overlook it, disregard it, forgive it. This is the only way of happiness and peace.

We must never think, "You did so much good to me, I do so much good to you". That makes all goodness and kindness a commercial transaction: you give me a hat, and I give you a pair of gloves!

If someone finds fault with another, he will try to get us to agree with him. He will say, "That person is doing this. Is it not dreadful?". If we say, "Yes, yes, it is terrible", our fault will be as great, or greater, than his.

Whatever is said or done echoes in the world as in a dome, and what good or bad a person does comes back to him. It may not always come back from the same person to whom he did good or harm. It may come from quite another side, because the universe is not many beings, but one Being. If a man does harm to a person who did nothing to him, that person is receiving back what bad he once did to another. However, that does not justify you, as an individual, in doing harm. When good is done, it also comes back as good, maybe from another side.

Only the Murshid who is responsible for his mureeds, or the father who is responsible for his children, may say to the face of the mureed or the child, "My child, this is not right for you", but he may not tell it to others.

2

The morals of humanity have three aspects: morality with regard to God, morality regarding friends, and morality with regard to those whom we do not like and to enemies.(10)

Morality with regard to God has three parts. The first is to idealize, to see all the good attributes in God, all the beautiful qualities, all His mercy and kindness. You may ask, "Why should we not also see the bad attributes in God. Why should we not say that God is cruel?" For instance, a child may be ill and the mother may say, "I pray God to make my child well". Then, if the child is not better, the mother may say, "God is unjust, God has no justice. This little child, what has it done that it should suffer so much?". In reality the child is not our property; we have no right to it. It belongs to the Spirit. The moral is: if you are sorry – not to complain of God; if you are sick – not to blame God; if you are unfortunate – not to say that it is God's fault. This is called *adab*.

The second part is praise. Wherever we see something beautiful – to give the credit to God. Wherever we see some kindness – to say that it is the kindness of God. When we perform some act of mercy – to give the credit to God.

The third part is thanks. God does not need man's worship or man's thanks. Nothing can be given to Him by man's worship, nor can anything be taken from Him. If one goes to King George's Palace and says, "I wish to thank the king", the sentry will say, "Thank him at home. You cannot thank the king here". Man's worship, man's praise are needed for man himself in order to produce in him the attributes of humanity.

The morality regarding those we like, our friends, firstly is to be sincere, not to say what is not true. In the world everybody says, "How kind you are. How good you are", and not a word of it is meant. People in towns are polite and polished, but the heart does not feel much. If one goes to villages where there are two or three hundred houses, one will find people not so polished but with more heart, more ready to sympathize. This is so all over the world. I used to think that it was so in India, but now I have seen that it is so everywhere.

Secondly, always be a friend. If once you have formed a friendship, keep it up. However circumstances and cases may change, keep up the friendship. Do not be one day a friend and the next day an enemy. Do not expect your friend to do what you do. He may not be worthy, or he may not be able to do what you do, and if you expect a kindness in return for a kindness it becomes commercial: I give you a book, you give me a pencil. That is not friendship, it is trade.

Thirdly, do not increase the friendship. If one increases it, friendship becomes so heavy that it cannot last. It becomes a spell, an intoxication; when the intoxication is gone the love and friendship are gone, and hatred remains. A story is told about the emperor Mahmud Ghaznavi. He was riding his horse outside the city where a drunken man was sitting by the roadside. When he saw the emperor on his horse he said, "O man, will you sell me that horse?". The emperor was amused at his confidence and boldness; he smiled at him and rode on. Later, when the emperor came back, he saw the man still sitting by the roadside, his drunkenness gone. The emperor said to him, "Are you the man who wants to buy the horse?" The man replied, "The buyer of the horse has gone, the servant of the horse remains". This was a very good and nice answer, and the emperor was pleased with it. The moral is: have a little friendship and keep it up.

The morality towards those whom we dislike, towards enemies, is more difficult, and it is much greater. For it is easy to be kind to those whom we like, who please us. In those whom we dislike even merits do not seem merits; we cannot see their merits because of our dislike. We should pity those who cannot attract our liking, and we should not think that we are different from them. We can see on the face of a man who takes a dislike to another that his own soul despises him, because in disliking the other he dislikes his own soul. His own soul is not a different soul; it is the same soul as that of the other, the same soul as the soul of the prophet, the same soul as the soul of the greatest sinner, the same soul as the Soul of the whole world.

3

The most essential lines of a poem of Hafiz are these: "To friends be faithful and loving, to enemies serviceable and courteous. This is the secret of the two worlds".

This was taught in all ages by all the prophets, saints and those who have served the world, and it is because we have forgotten it that we suffer all the ills we suffer; all our lacks come from our forgetting it. It is the secret of happiness and peace. What is done for a return is not service, otherwise all the people in the city working with their machines would be called servants of God. That which is done, not for fame or name, not for the appreciation or thanks from those for whom it is done, but only for love, is service of God.

Muhammad's claim was: Muhammad *Abduhu wa ar-Rasuluh*, Muhammad, His servant and prophet. He was prophet because he was servant. Mahmud Ghaznavi, the emperor, says in a poem, "Mahmud Ghaznavi, who has a thousand slaves, since love gushed from his heart, feels that he is the slave of slaves". No one can be master who has not been servant.

Someone went to Muhammad and asked him, "How long must I serve my mother before I have fully repaid her what she has done for me?". The Prophet said, "If you served her all her life you could not do enough, unless in her last days she said, 'I forgive you what you owe me'". When he asked for more explanation the Prophet added, "You serve your mother thinking that she will live for some years and then it will be over. She served you thinking 'May my child grow and prosper and live after me.' The mother is much greater".

You should ask your soul whether you have always been kind to enemy and friend. If your soul will answer "Yes", then I will say that you are a saint. Although you may not know any mysticism or philosophy, although you may not be a very spiritual person, although you may not see any phenomena or work wonders, this kindness in itself is enough to make you a saint. This kindness is the moral taught by all religions.

You must see in the heart of another the temple of God. God is peeping through the heart of another. In whatever way you can, in act, in speech, in feeling, at whatever sacrifice, you should please the heart of the other and do nothing that can hurt it.

CHAPTER XXXIII

Hope

1

THE WORD 'hope' to those who are broken-hearted is start-ling, to them it is poison. If you speak of hope to the broken-hearted they say, "Do not speak of it, I do not wish to hear of it!". The state of the broken-hearted is worse than death; they are without ambition, without hope, without life. The one who is broken-hearted is dead while he is alive; the breath is still there, but his heart is dead, life has gone with the hope that was lost. He may not be old in years, but he has become old.

To him who is heartless hope is a ridiculous word. The heartless, he whose heart is incapable of feeling, will say, "Hope? What is it? See what you can do, and do it. Do not dream". This is the material person who can see no further than the material possibilities.

In the life of Christ we see that enemies, difficulties and helplessness were all around – and confidence in the truth of the message gave hope to carry it through. If there had not been hope, the thought "I will bring the message", what material possibility was there of spreading the message? This whole manifestation has hope as its underlying motive. Nature first hoped to produce the world and then produced it.

In the Orient people have the habit of depending upon *kismet*, fate, and this is a source of weakness. If an astrologer tells a Brahmin, "After so many years such and such a calamity will come upon you", the Brahmin does not even make an effort to fight against misfortune; he awaits it and accepts it. If a man is told, "In such a year you will become very ill", he does not even try to avoid the illness. They do not consider that hope can avert misfortune and can turn aside even the influence of the planets. Where no possibility of attaining the object is given, a strong hope can attain it.

Without going to the mystics this can be seen in the history of kings. Mahmud Ghaznavi was a slave. What possibility was there for him to become a king? With only hope he started from Turkistan and founded a kingdom in Afghanistan. Of Timur is told that once he was lying asleep in the jungle. He was going through such a hard time that he did not even have a place to lie down, hardly any clothes, nothing. A dervish happened to pass that way and saw Timur lying in the hot sun where not even an animal would lie. He went nearer and saw about this man some signs of greatness. He also saw a sign of bad luck, and that sign was that Timur, while asleep, was lying with his legs crossed. He saw that this man himself was the hindrance to his undertakings. The dervish had a stick and hit him so hard that the bone of his leg broke. Timur woke up feeling a great pain. He said, "O dervish, this is very unkind! I already have such hard luck, and you break my bone". The dervish replied, "My son, your bad luck is gone. You will be emperor". There seemed to be no possibility for it; Timur had no army, no clothes even, and now his bone was broken. But after great striving and after many years he became the emperor Timur Leng.

All works that have been accomplished have been accomplished by hope. Without hope the engineer could not have built a bridge across the Thames; he hoped, and then he built it. Without hope the Suez Canal, a thing that seemed impossible, could not have been cut.

One may ask, "How long shall I hope? I have hoped once and I have been disappointed; I have hoped a second time and I have been disappointed; I have hoped a third time and I have been disappointed". I will say "Hope until the last breath. While there is breath in the body, hope".

A person may lose hope in his profession or trade. For instance he may have gone to a singer to take singing lessons for one or two months, or for one or two years, and then he may think, "I am not getting on with this, I should stop singing. I believe I have no voice". Or he may think, "I am not getting on in my business. I cannot make it a success, I should give it up". The ill is not changing of profession or business, but giving up altogether. If the person thinks, "Now I wish to be a poet", and becomes a poet, then he is not hopeless; or if he thinks, "Now I wish to compose", and

becomes a composer; or "I should be a teacher", and becomes
a teacher, then he is not hopeless.

People say that doctors now have found remedies for so
many diseases, but I say that the cause of most illnesses is
loss of hope. In the pharmacy there is no such great remedy
for all diseases as hope is. Even when the disease is incurable,
hope cures it.

The question arises: What hope is right, and what hope
is not right? A wise person will never hope for what is
impossible. Hoping to be a queen, when there are no means
of being a queen, is hoping the impossible. First we must
know what is possible – this is wisdom – and then we must
hope. The Qur'an speaks of *khawf*, hope with consideration.
This word does not mean fear, as it has sometimes been
translated, but consideration, conscientiousness. Hope with
the consideration of the purpose for which the manifestation
was made, with the consideration of God – that hope is always
right. Hope without consideration is wrong.

Why with consideration? Because we must not hope for
what is wrong, for what is bad. We must hope with the
fear of God before us. The hope must be so strong that, if
to-day we are penniless, we must think that there is every
possibility that tomorrow we may be a millionaire. If to-day
our own relations do not know us, we must think that there
is every possibility that to-morrow we may be known to the
whole world.(11)

2

There is no stain so great as the stain of hopelessness.
Sometimes weakness is the cause of hopelessness. During
an illness a person thinks, "I am so weak, I cannot get
better". Or weakness is caused by old age; a person thinks,
"I am old, there is little left for me to do", and he becomes
sad and discouraged. He really may have the strength to do
much more, but the loss of hope makes him old. A man may
be given to drink, or he may be a gambler, or have any other
vice, and may think, "I am too weak, I cannot be cured".

Besides physical weakness or the weakness that comes with

old age the hurt of the heart may cause hopelessness. This shows us how careful we should be not to hurt the heart of another and not to let our own heart be hurt. In India we are most careful of this; *diljoi*, not to hurt the heart of another is taught as the greatest moral: not to hurt the heart of the parent, of the friend, even of the enemy. Also our own heart must be protected by forts around it.

A story is told about a man who went to the Sharif of Mecca and said to him that the camel the Sharif rode was his and had been stolen from him. The Sharif asked whether he had any witnesses. He had none. Then the Sharif asked, "What proof have you that the camel is really yours? How can you recognize it?" The man answered, "On my camel's heart are two black spots". "On its heart?", said the Sharif, "How do you know that?" The man replied, "The animals feel as we do. My camel – it is a she-camel–had two young ones, and at different times both died. Each time I saw that the camel looked up to heaven and gave a cry like a sigh, a deep great sigh, and that was all. So I know that on her heart are two black spots". The Sharif held out two gold coins and said, "Either take back your camel, or take the price for your discovery". If the heart of an animal can feel like this, how much can the heart of man feel!

Man was made with a most feeling heart. A Hindustani poet has said, "The heart of man was made for feeling. For praise and worship the angels in heaven are many". Man's heart has a great capacity for feeling, it is most sensitive to any touch. How careful we must be to touch it, lest we may wound it. The greatest fault is to hurt the heart of another, the greatest virtue is to please the heart of another. He who has learned this moral has learned all morality.

If we do not protect our own heart from harm, we can be killed at every moment. Amir, the poet, says, "Why did you not kill me before you wounded my heart? It would have been better to kill me first". We must consider what the world is and what it can give. We must give and not expect to take the same as we give. A kick for a kindness, a blow for a mercy is what the world gives. We must not expect the world to be as we are expected to be. If we receive some good, it is well. If

not, it does not matter. The world does not understand in the
same way as we do. Material interest has so blinded people
that when a question of money comes, of interest, of a share,
of a territory, of property, even a child, a wife, a relative, or
the closest friend will turn against us. A Sanskrit poem says
that, when the question of money arises, no consideration for
father or brother remains.

We must fortify our heart, so that we always may be the
same, always kind, merciful, generous, serviceable. When a
person has understood this, then comes that inner hope which
is within every heart, the hope in another life. If one asks
anyone why a man must go out and work all day long and
have no time to give to what he likes, why a man must leave
his parents and go to work, why lovers must part, the answer
is always the same: "It is the struggle for life". If this life is so
valuable, how great must be the value of that other life. The
hope of another life is in man, of a life that is unchanging,
immortal and everlasting. It is only because our consciousness
is so bound to the self that we are not conscious of it, and it
is very bad that the external self always is before us, because
it always makes us think, "I have been offended, I have been
badly treated, I have been neglected" – always I, I, and I.

There was a dervish who used to say, "Knife upon the
throat of man". *Man** in Hindustani means I. People asked
the dervish what he meant, and he said, "The goats and sheep
say 'man, man, man'. I say: a knife upon their throat for this!"
A man who says "I" deserves to be killed like the goats and
sheep who are slaughtered because they say "man".

When that "I" is killed, when the consciousness of this
"I" is lost, then comes the consciousness that in the whole
existence there is only I – no you, no he, no she. The illusion
makes us distinguish you, he she and it; in reality there is
only I. When the external I is lost, then a fragrance comes
into the personality, a beauty, a magnetism. Then he sees in
every being the manifestation of God, he bows before every
being. In the Sufi poems we may read of the tyranny of the
beloved. This is the tyranny of the beloved, the opposition

---

* pronounced as *my* followed by a nasal *n*.

of manifestation. It is the grade of worship. There is still the grade of realization, of merging in God, but that is beyond it. The grade of worship comes first. If a priest sees a foolish person doing something foolish, he may say with authority, "He is a sinner". But the Sufi says, "I am much worse than he, I have no right to condemn him. I am a worshipper, I must see here the manifestation of God. I must worship it; I must revere it, serve it, and therein accomplish my life's purpose".

Aphorism

I have always hope. Hope is my greatest strength. I do not require that my hopes are fulfilled, as fuel is needed to keep the fire burning. My hopes are kept alive in my faith.

CHAPTER XXXIV

Patience

PATIENCE, THE word itself, is the heaviest thing that is. To one who is in difficulties and troubles, to one who is in sorrow, to one who lives in the wish of obtaining his desire, the word patience has a dreadful sound. The sound is dreadful, the thought is terrible, the idea is frightful to us. Yet all our difficulties in life, all our failures come from lack of patience. All the results of life often are lost through impatience. A person may have patience for forty years, and then lose patience, and so lose the result of all his endeavours during so many years.

The impatient person will show his impatience in his speech. When you ask him something, he will not let you finish your sentence; he answers before you have finished because he thinks, "Why should you still say that half sentence?" The impatient person eats very fast, and all the veins and tubes of his body cannot drink so fast as he drinks. If he walks across the room he will stumble ten times; he walks into chairs, into the table, into the door and does not look into whom he walks. If he intends to take some action, he starts, and three times before he reaches the door he will say, "I am going, I am not going, I am going", because he does not give time to his decision.

All our errors and faults come from impatience. It is not that the soul wants something which is wrong, but we do not stop to weigh our acts. We seize upon the first thought that comes to us without weighing or considering it. Nowadays the wish for variety has grown so strong that we always wish for new surroundings, new friends, new faces, and our thoughts change every moment. If we could hold our thought, we should increase its power. We think, "It is only a thought, it will pass". In reality, by our thought we create a spirit, a *jinn*, a genius, that acts and works and achieves. The more patiently we think a thought, the stronger the thought becomes.

The lesson of patience is much less taught nowadays as the influence of religion has become much less, and education is mostly given for commercial purposes. So we must look upon the lesson of patience as a lesson we give to ourselves; we must think of all the beautiful results we gain by patience, and be sure that, if we have conquered patience, we have conquered the whole world.

CHAPTER XXXV

Confidence

1

PATIENCE IN perseverance is a very good thing, but it can only be possessed by those who have confidence. Each Sura of the Qur'an is addressed to those who have patience, and great importance is given to confidence: *iman*.

Muslims perform *namaz*, their prayers, five times a day. If you ask an old Muslim whether he has gained anything by it, he will answer, "What do you know about it? I have gained what I wanted: my satisfaction". If he is ill he does not care, he does not blame God. If he loses his fortune, he does not blame God. He does not say, 'After so many years of *namaz* this illness, this trouble has come!"

Everything that has been done, has been done by confidence, and nothing can be done without confidence. You cannot dig the earth for gold, if you do not have confidence that the gold is there; you cannot watch the cooking pan, if you do not have confidence that there is something in the pan which the fire has the power to cook.

If I were to tell you to work three hours in the night repeating the name of Allah, you would say, "My Murshid has told me so, and I must do it, but . . ." Then when you repeated Allah, Allah for half an hour, you would think, "Here I am sitting for half an hour in this cold, and I do not see what I have gained by it. If I were to write some music now, to-morrow I could sell it for five pounds. Then I would have worked and I would have gained something".

It has been the difficulty of all prophets, of all who have come with a message, that people said, "Show us something that these eyes can see. Show that the sun comes down, or the moon, or that the earth cleaves. But the message of God – what is it? Show us something". That is why, if there is a suffrage meeting, at once there is a subscription for a thousand pounds, because people know that by fighting the government they can get laws passed. If someone comes with a message from God and says, "We need money to spread this message", people say, "Why do you need money? Money is needed for a scheme. Have you engineered a scheme?"

To have patience, to have confidence, we must see an object before us. We can have confidence in obtaining any material object. It is much more difficult to have patience where there is nothing to show – only the satisfaction of the soul; to have patience enough to acquire virtue, to merge in the illumination, to gain the light. It is the same with fire: at first there is smoke mixed with it and, if it had no patience until it would become a flame, there would only be smoke and then it would go out. If it has patience it will become a flame that illumines the whole room so that everything can be seen and known. More than all else this patience is the greatest gift and blessing.

2

Every success in life is brought about by confidence, *iman*, and all our lacks are due to want of confidence. It is so with material as well as spiritual things.

In India many things are thought lucky or unlucky. If you go out on an undertaking and a cat crosses your road, it is thought that you cannot be successful then. If you go out and at once meet a person carrying flowers, then you will be successful. It is easy to understand the reason. If you first meet something that gives you pleasure, you have a good impression, and that gives you confidence. If you receive a bad impression your confidence disappears. A man, an ordinary sort of man, once came to my Murshid and asked him, "Give me your blessing for good luck. I have built a carriage and I want to make some money with it". My Murshid said, "Every morning when you get up count your money".

Whatever we undertake, we should say, "I shall accomplish it, or lose my life". Failure comes from lack of confidence, lack of confidence comes from doubt, doubt comes from reasoning, and reasoning comes from thinking of the means.

If you think, "I will go to Brighton, but perhaps, if I do, the Zeppelins will come and I shall be killed"*, then you lose your confidence. There was no need to think of the Zeppelins. They might come, but if they came you would be one among the many inhabitants of Brighton, and you might not be killed.

Whether in our own undertakings, or in what we may do to help another, confidence is needed. You may do everything to help another, but if he has no confidence, if he does not work also, there cannot be success. God also needs your confidence and your effort for success.

---

* Hazrat Inayat Khan lived in London during World War I

CHAPTER XXXVI

Faith

1.

BY FAITH in God hopelessness can be turned into hopefulness. The spirit draws its power inspirationally from the divine Source. Every impulse, every desire comes from there, and in accomplishment the law of perfection is realized. But when a person doubts about everything and says that there is no inspiration then, by denying this power, he gives away that which he already possessed. By recognizing the divine Fatherhood of God one becomes conscious of one's divine heritage and one knows that there is no lack in the divine Spirit, and no lack in life. Then there is certainty of fulfilment, which is only a matter of time.

Some good people have almost arrived at the fulfilment of their desire, and then just at the last moment have failed, while others attain ultimate success in everything. One will always find that the souls of the former were influenced by great power but lacked faith, while the others had power supported by faith. If faith is lacking one may attain ninety-nine percent of success and miss the last one, and so in the end the loss takes away all that was previously gained.

Question: What is more necessary for a student of mysticism, faith or intelligence?
Answer: For absolute faith the first step is the ideal. The next step brings man into the presence of God. For the intelligence the way goes from intellect to wisdom, and there are obstacles at every step.

Faith – faith in the greatness, the mercy, the power of God – is the greatest thing. It also is the most difficult thing. For the one who has faith all difficulties, all responsibility rest upon Him in whom he has faith. The intelligence takes its own responsibility. But if there is the least chance of the intellect rebelling against faith, it is a sign that the intellect asks to be fed, and it should be given its food: all knowledge.

2

Faith is a word that has been so little understood, and often it is considered to be a religious term. Really speaking faith is not only something which is required in religion, but in all aspects of life it is the one thing that is required most. It is the misinterpretation of faith that has taken away the value that could be attached to the word. Otherwise, if I am to say one word, the sense of which is most valuable in the world, it is faith. In the Orient they call faith *yaqin* and another Arabic word used for it is *iman*.

There are many things sacred in the world, but faith is the most sacred; not faith in something, but faith in itself. Faith comes from above, doubt rises from below, from the earth. Therefore one is heavenly, the other earthly. When a person is more worldly he is more doubting; the less worldly he is the more faith he has. You may find a person who once had a great faith and then lost it, and you will observe that at the same time his life went from a less worldly condition to a more worldly one. Being more absorbed in the life of this world makes one void of faith. This shows that faith is innate in human nature; doubt is something of which man partakes.

The sun is light, the light which always is light; clouds may cover it, but they do not really cover the sun, they only cover the sun from our eyes. When a person has no faith, it does not mean that in the depth of his being there is no faith. There is faith, but that sun is covered by clouds. When the heart is exposed to the things of the world, there are always doubts rising from the earth, and they will cover the heart.

Doubt gives a pessimistic attitude. One questions, "Will it be, or will it not be? Do I think rightly, or do I think wrongly? Am I on the right path, or on the wrong path? Shall I succeed, or shall I fail throughout life? Will conditions be better, or worse?" When there are two possibilities the earth impresses a person with doubt against the good one. He wants to conquer the good one, to have it, he desires that things should be better, but what he finds, rising from the earth, is doubt, and for his faith therefore he does not get proper support from the earth. As man does not see God, he does not look up, he only looks at the earth and wants support from there. The great lesson that the blessed ones have taught to humanity was to raise one's vision upwards and to find faith in something which is free from all doubt. Pessimism and optimism, therefore, are two different attitudes: the one looks downwards, the other looks upwards.

Very few of us know what miracle is hidden in faith, what power and inspiration. We only think, "I can believe in some things, and in some things I cannot believe". But for what we believe we want proof from the earth. In order to sustain our faith we need sustenance from an unlimited source, but we look for sustenance to the earth which is a limited source. When a person looks at a tank full of water and says, "Oh, what a small supply, what shall I do for next year?", he is right – but he is looking at the tank. When he looks above he will see that the source from which the rain falls is there and can fill many such tanks, and even rivers. Blessing of all kind is there, if only we prepare our heart to receive it. If the heart is small like a glass, it can only fetch a glass of water even if it is taken to the sea. But if the heart is larger then it will bring that much more water.

No doubt, patience is the first lesson to learn in the path of faith, because it is patience which gives one strength to hope. My spiritual teacher used to say as his benediction, "May your faith be strengthened". As a youth I thought that he would say, "May you live long, may you be happy, prosperous, may you gain wisdom". The meaning of this blessing I realize now more and more every moment of my life, for in faith there is all. All that one wants, all that one needs, all that one wishes to attain through life – it is all hidden in one's faith.

It is most interesting and sometimes laughable to see how easy it is for a man to fix his faith on small things, while on large things he cannot fix it: he fixes his faith on an object, not on a person. For instance if one says to somebody, "Here is a medicine for you, a medicine that will cure you", it is

easy for him to have faith. And when one says, "Well, I will
think of you for your cure; you will be cured"(12), the first
thing that will come to his mind will be doubt. What is the
reason? The reason is that he sees the object, he does not see
the thought.*

I once met a very great healer who had much success,
and I asked him the secret of his working. He said, "The
secret of my way of working is first that I have taken a
religious shrine where people come and sit; they certainly
come with faith in this particular shrine. Then I give them
some kind of mixture of powder. Really speaking I heal
them by myself, but they have no faith in that; so I give
them some powder or something to drink, and then they
feel better." The whole effort of different religions has been
to make man see what is hidden in a human being. Rituals,
ceremonies and all different forms teach the same thing: find
the secret and the mystery of life not only in the objects
but, when you have passed through them, in the human
being.

It is the same thing to see that one can easily have faith
in a man, while it is difficult to have faith in God, for the
reason that one can see a human being before one, but one
cannot see the greatest Power and Perfection, which is in
the abstract. Faith is as a substance: if one does not possess
that substance, one cannot raise it to the highest ideal which
alone merits faith.

Medical science is now coming to the realization of the
importance of psychology, although it is as yet only considering the thought waves and thought power. Faith is still
something else to be considered and studied. My experience
with numerous students in this line has shown me that a
person may be able to concentrate and maintain a thought,
but often is not capable to do it fully, because there is no
faith at the back of it. Faith, therefore, is not something
which may be called a thought; faith is the ground itself:
it is a ground from which thoughts spring up as plants. If
the land is not fertile the plants cannot come up. And so,

* i.e. he can see the medicine, he cannot see the thought of the healer

if there is no faith at the root of a thought, the thought is not beneficial. Besides this there is another thing: something that can be accomplished by the power of thought in a year's time, is accomplished with the power of faith behind it in one day.

Someone said to a Brahmin who was worshipping an idol made of stone, "God is formless. He should not be worshipped in an idol of rock". The Brahmin answered, "It is a question of faith. If I have faith in this stone, God who is everywhere will speak through this stone. But if one has no faith, even the God of the abstract, of heavens, will not be able to speak". If this is so, is there anything that cannot be accomplished, that cannot be realized by faith?

When we look at it from a metaphysical point of view we shall find that the secret of the whole creation is faith, and the perfection of faith is attained when it has risen to that ideal, that height, where it can hold itself without any support. Faith therefore after having accomplished all that is to be accomplished, will be the one thing – and that will prove to be all things.

Question: How do we gain that faith?
Answer: By fighting doubt. It is a continual fight, because doubts are the inheritance of the earth. We are walking on the earth, so it is a continual fight.

Question: But faith can be mastered?
Answer: Of course faith can be mastered. As one will fight doubts, so one will gain one's victory over doubts.

Question: Can there be a religious faith without being attached to any religion?
Answer: Certainly. The religion of every soul is his own. Outwardly one may belong to a religion, but inwardly everyone has his own religion, and that is his true religion. By faith I do not at all mean faith in a particular religion or gospel, or idea. I say that faith is within a person.

Question: Can one obtain the spiritual plane by an earthly fight?

Answer: We say in the East that a teacher is most helpful for that. A person, who in his scientific attainment has arrived for instance at the stage of Edison, is there already; he only has to turn his face and he is already there. There is perhaps a business-man who all his life has done nothing but gain wealth. A religious, orthodox, or pious person will look upon him as most materialistic, but he does not know what fight this man had to go through in his life in order to gain that much money, and what sacrifice, what struggle and consideration he had to give to it. It is not always easy to become a man of wealth. Therefore if he has struggled along and has arrived at a point where he can be called rich, he just has to change his attitude and he is there already.

Question: Can faith have an effect on things that are not religious?

Answer: Oh yes, faith can be used in every direction, just like light. By light you can study religion and fare forth to heavens and do anything. No one in the world has been able to accomplish a great thing without the power of faith, whether he was a general, a business-man, an inventor, or a religious man. The power that faith gives is beyond words. The weakness and the poverty that exist in the absence of faith are most deplorable. A person may have everything in life, youth, wealth, comfort, position and power – if faith lacks he is poverty-stricken.

Question: So if our object is right we are bound to get it unless our faith fails?

Answer: Yes, that is true. It depends upon our attitude – if our heart, just like a compass, is always seeking the right direction. The heart is just like a compass: you can take it to any side, it always points in the same direction. So the heart, wherever one turns it to, will always point to the same direction. In other words for him who does right it is most difficult to do wrong – and for the wrongdoer it is most difficult to do right.

Question: Can the wrongdoer come to right one day?

Answer: Right is the might, and right is the depth, and right is the ideal of every soul. A person who tells a lie, who deceives people, who is treacherous, will do so to others, but he does not want his friends to do the same to him. This shows that he prefers it to be different.

CHAPTER XXXVII

Faith and Doubt

FAITH AND doubt are as light and darkness. The moments of faith are like the moments of the day and the moments of doubt are like those of the night. As both day and night come in life, so hours of faith and hours of darkness also come. It is the seeking of the soul to reach that stage where it feels faith, and it is the nature of the soul to gather doubts around itself. Therefore the soul attracts both faith and doubt. If it happens to attract doubts more, then more doubts will be gathered; if it attracts faith, then more and more faith will come.

Doubts are likened to clouds. If there is one cloud, it will attract others and, if many clouds are gathered, still more will be attracted to join them. If there is one current of the sun shooting through the clouds it will scatter them, and once they are scattered they will be scattered more and more, and more and more light will manifest itself to view. Doubts cover faith but faith breaks doubt. Therefore faith is more dependable: doubts only come and go.

It would not be an exaggeration if I said that doubt is a disease – a disease that takes away faith. Perhaps it would be more appropriate to say that doubt is the rust that eats the iron, the iron-like faith. It is very easy to allow doubts to work, and it is difficult to keep faith. However much evolved a person may be, there comes a time when doubts take hold of him, and the moments he is in doubt the light of intelligence disappears. Therefore there is a constant conflict between doubt and faith. If there was not this enemy who always fights with faith, man could do great things, wonderful things; every man would perform miracles, every man would be perfect. This shows that the greater your faith, the greater person you are; the more deeply rooted your faith, the higher you reach.

One might ask: Is it possible to develop faith? Is it possible to find faith? Yes, in every person a spark of faith is hidden somewhere, but sometimes it is so covered, clouded and buried, that it needs digging, it needs being dug out. What is it buried with? With the sand of doubts. As soon as the sand is removed, the faith-like water springs up.

One can study this principle in a child: a child is born with faith. When one says, "This is water, this is bread, this is father, this is mother", the child does not refuse to believe it; it does not say, "It is not so". The child at once takes it to be so. It is afterwards that doubts begin to come. When the infant grows up, when it begins to hear a story and asks, "But is it real?", then doubt begins. Very often worldly knowledge gives more and more doubts; the experiences of worldly life make one doubt more and more, and when doubt becomes predominant in a person's nature, then he doubts everything and everyone. He doubts those who should not be doubted and he doubts those who can be doubted; there is always a doubt before his eyes. No sooner does he cast his glance upon a person than the cloud of doubt stands between them. In this way inspiration is lost, power is lost, the personality is lost; man has become a machine, a mechanism.

In the business world, in the world of industry, a person does not care what your feelings are, what your being is, how much evolved you are, how deeply you feel, what your principles are, what your thoughts. What this person is concerned with is if the other will sign the paper, whether he will stamp that paper at once, and whether there are two witnesses who watch it at the same time. It does not matter what you are, who you are, as long as the paper is perfect. We are coming to mechanical perfection, we seek after worldly, earthly perfection.

Five hundred years ago – this shows how gradually the world has changed – a Hindustani poet has written: "Those days have passed when a value was attached to man's personality". That is so; it is some centuries since the world went downward. It seems that man has no trust, no faith in another man; what he trusts is the written word.(13)

Faith should be continued to the end. One may have faith when climbing stairs of a hundred steps; one may climb ninety-six steps with faith, and then one may lose it. Before the four steps that are still to be climbed one may lose faith; doubt has come and the whole journey is spoiled. This happens very often in the lives of so many people who are face to face with their success and yet fail. They have just approached what they wanted and then they lose it. In nearly every person's life one sees this, and the greater the person the more one sees it; for the greater the person the more powerful his faith, and therefore he is able to see the play of faith. It is just like sending a kite so far into the sky – and before it reaches higher it drops down. The enemy which causes this is doubt.

One may do something during one's whole life and accomplish it to a great extent, but through lack of a little more faith one will lose it, and all that was done will be spoiled in a moment's time. How long does it take for a house to be built, and how long does it take to destroy it? How long does it take to make a business really prosperous? How long does it take to fail? One moment. When one learns this principle and thinks about it, one begins to see that the whole world, with all that we hear and see and touch and feel, is all illusion in the face of faith. Faith alone is reality, and compared with faith all else is unreal. But since we do not see faith with our own eyes, it is very difficult to call faith real and all else unreal; our eyes cannot see faith and we do not know where it is.

Now arises the question: how can one find faith in oneself, how can one develop it? One can find faith by practising self-confidence as the first thing, by having self-confidence even in the smallest things. To-day most people have the habit to say with everything "perhaps". It seems as if a new word has come in use; they say "perhaps it will happen". It is a kind of polite expression, or a word of refined people to show themselves pessimistic. I can see their reason; they think that it is fanatic, presumptious, and simple to say, "It will be", or "It will come", or "It will be accomplished", or "It will be fulfilled". To say "perhaps", – so they think – makes them free from the responsibility of having committed themselves. The more pessimistic a person, the more "perhaps" he uses, and this "perhaps" has gone so deep in souls to-day that they cannot find faith.

After self-confidence is developed, the second step is to trust another with closed eyes. One might think that this is not always practical, and one might think that it might lead to great loss. But at the same time even that loss would be a gain, and a thousand gains compared with the loss of faith would be as nothing. A person is richer if he has trusted someone and lost something than if he had not trusted someone and preserved something – that one day will be taken away from him! He could just as well have given it up.

One might say that every simple person is inclined to trust another. Yes, but the difference between the wise person who trusts bravely and the simple person who trusts readily is great. The wise man who trusts, if he is influenced by another that he may not, or must not, trust a certain person, even if he is given a certain proof, even then that habit of trusting will remain with him. As to the simple man, as soon as anyone says, "Oh, what are you doing, you trust somebody who is not trustworthy", his trust will change. That is the difference between the wise and the foolish person. The foolish person trusts because he does not know better; the wise person trusts because he knows that to trust is best.

The third step towards the development of faith is trust in the unseen, to trust in something which one does not see. Reason does not show what it is, where it is, how it is, how it should be gained, how it can be brought about, how it should be obtained, how it can be reached. One does not see the reason, one only sees: it will be done, it must be done, it must come. It is that trust in the unseen which is called trust in God. When you do not see any sign before you of something that should happen, and yet you think, "Yes, it must happen, it will happen, it certainly must happen", and you have no doubt, then your trust is in God.

The first principle of the Sufi message is faith. It is not only occult study, nor is it scientific analysis, nor psychic phenomena. The first lesson of the message is faith, and it is with faith that the message will be spread. We each shall work in our own way in serving, in spreading the message, and it is with faith that the message of God will be fulfilled.

CHAPTER XXXVIII

The Story of Orpheus(14)

THERE IS is always a deep meaning in the legends of the ancient Greeks, as in those of the Indians, Persians and Egyptians, and it is most interesting to watch how the art of the Greeks, with its beautiful structure as well as with its legends, had a much deeper meaning than would appear on the outside. Seeing and studying this art we find the key to the ancient culture, and the further we explore it the more we shall be acquainted with its depth and its profound meaning.

From the first part of the story of Orpheus we learn that no object a person has once desired from the depth of his heart will ever be lost. Even if the object of love that a person has once desired is in the deepest depth of the earth – where reason, but not the eye, can see it – even then it can be attained if he pursues it sufficiently.

The next thing we learn is that in order to attain an object the love element alone is not sufficient, but besides love wisdom is necessary. It is wisdom, which awakens in harmony and harmonizes with the cosmic forces, which helps one to attain one's object. There is a saying that the one who possesses the knowledge of sound knows the science of the whole life, and this will be admitted by the wise ones of all ages and of all countries. The invoking of the gods by Orpheus was his coming in touch with all the harmonious forces which, united together, brought him that object which he wanted to attain.

But the most fascinating part of the story is the last one, both as a picture and as to the sense. As Orpheus was proceeding, Euridice following him, the promise was that he was not to look back. The moment he would look back Euridice would be taken away from him. The meaning of this is that the secret of all attainment is faith. If the faith of a person endures as far as ninety-nine miles and one mile remains before gaining the object, even then, if doubt comes, attainment is no more to be expected.

From this we learn a lesson, a lesson which can be used in everything we do, in every walk of life: in order to attain anything we need faith, and if faith is lacking – even if there is the slightest lack of faith in the form of doubt – it will spoil all we have done.

"Verily faith is light and doubt darkness".

CHAPTER XXXIX

Happiness

OUR HAPPINESS and unhappiness depend upon one thing: how we look at life, whether we appreciate and value all we have or depreciate and underestimate all we have. If we think of what we have not in life, we shall find that there is so much that we have not got, and it will then seem that what we have got is not even as big as a bubble in a vast sea. And if we try to realize what we have, there also will come a time when we shall see that what we have not is like a little bubble in a vast sea. It is a matter of looking at it. The general tendency is to see what we have not got in life, and rarely a soul is so blessed that he is awakened to appreciate all he has in life and to be thankful for it. When we think of what we lack, there comes a flood of that lack and it drowns the whole universe; we find ourselves entirely lacking everything that it is possible to have. If we begin to realize what we have, it will be increased and be completed by abundance, so that in the end of our realization we shall be able to find that, really speaking, we have all. It is in this that lies the secret of spiritual attainment. The saying of Christ, "Seek ye first the kingdom of God and all these things shall be added unto you", has the same meaning: when by our thankfulness, by our appreciation of life we arrive at the fullness of life, in that bliss we shall find the kingdom of God, and once the kingdom of God is realized all else will be added.

Once a dervish came before Sekandar, the great king, with the bowl of a beggar and asked him if he could fill it. Sekandar looked at him and thought, "What is he asking of an emperor like me? To fill that little bowl?" The dervish asked, "Can you fill this little bowl?" The emperor immediately said, "Yes", but the bowl was a magic bowl. Hundreds and thousands and millions were poured into it but it would not fill, it always remained half empty, its mouth wide open to be filled. When Sekandar began to feel poor while filling this bowl he said, "Dervish, tell me if you are not a magician. You have brought a bowl of magic; it has swallowed my whole treasure and it is empty still". The dervish answered, "Sekandar, if the whole world's treasure was put into it, it would still remain empty. Do you know what this bowl is? It is the want of man".

Be it love, be it wealth, be it attention, be it service, be it comfort, be it happiness, be it pleasure, be it rank, position, power, honour or possession in life, the more man can receive the more he wants. He is never content, he will never be content. The richer man becomes – richer with everything, with anything – the poorer he becomes, for the bowl that he has brought with him, the bowl of want, can never be filled, and is never filled.

The only secret of attaining happiness therefore is to learn how to appreciate our privileges in life. If we cultivate that sense of appreciation we shall be thankful, we shall be contented, and every moment we shall offer our thanks to God, for His gifts are many and enormous. When we do not see them it is because our wants cover our eyes from seeing all with which we are blessed by Providence. No meditation, no study, nothing can help in that direction, except one thing and that is to keep our eyes open to appreciate every little privilege in life, to admire every glimpse of beauty that comes before us, being thankful for every little love, kindness or affection shown to us by young or old, rich or poor, wise or foolish. In this way, continually developing the faculty of appreciating life and devoting it to thanksgiving, we arrive at a bliss which no words can explain, a bliss which is beyond imagination: the bliss that we find ourselves having already entered the kingdom of God.

CHAPTER XL

The Privilege of Being Human

MANKIND IS so absorbed in life's pleasures and pains that a man has hardly a moment to think what a privilege it is to be human. Life in the world contains, no doubt, more pain than pleasure and that which one considers to be pleasure costs so much that, when it is weighed against the pain it costs, it also becomes pain. As man is so absorbed in his worldly life he traces nothing but pain and complaint in life and, until he changes his outlook, he cannot understand the privilege of being human.

Yet, however unhappy a person may be in his life, if he were asked, "Would you prefer to be a rock rather than a human being?", his answer would be that he would rather suffer and be a human being than be a rock. Whatever be the condition of a man's life, if he were asked, "Would you rather be a tree than a man?", he would choose to be a human being. And although the life of the birds and beasts is so free from care and troubles, so free in the forest, yet if a man were asked whether he would prefer to be one of them and be in the forest, he would surely prefer to be a man. This shows that when human life is compared with the other different aspects of life it proves its greatness and its privilege, but when it is not compared with them man is discontented and his eyes are closed to the privilege of being human.

Another thing is that man is mostly selfish, and what interests him is that which concerns his own life. Not knowing the troubles of the lives of others he feels the burden of his own life even more than the burden of the whole world. If only man in his poverty could think that there are others who are poorer than he, in his illness that there are others whose sufferings are perhaps greater than his, in his troubles that there are others whose difficulties are perhaps greater than his! Self-pity is the worst poverty. It overwhelms man and he sees nothing but his own troubles and pains, and it seems to him that he is the most unhappy person in the world, more so than anyone else.

A great thinker of Persia, Sa'adi, writes in an account of his life, "Once I had no shoes, I had to walk barefoot in the hot sand, and I thought how very miserable I was. Then I met a man who was lame, for whom walking was very difficult. I bowed down at once to heaven and offered thanks that I was much better off than he who had not even feet to walk upon." This shows that it is not a man's situation in life, but his attitude towards life that makes him happy or unhappy. This attitude can even make such a difference between men that one living in a palace could be unhappy and another living in a humble cottage could be very happy. The difference is only in the horizon that one sees: one person looks only at the condition of his life, another looks at the lives of many people; it is a difference of horizon.

Beside this, the impulse that comes from within has its influence on one's affairs: there is an influence always working from within. If it is a discontent and dissatisfaction in life, one finds its effect in one's affairs. For instance, a person impressed by illness can never be cured by a physician or medicines. A person impressed by poverty will never get on in life. A person who thinks, "Everybody is against me, everybody troubles me, everybody has a poor opinion of me", wherever he goes will always find that it is so. There are many people in the world – in business, in professions – who before going to their work bear in their mind as a first thought, "Perhaps I shall not be successful".

The masters of humanity, in whatever period they came to the world, always taught faith as man's first lesson to learn: faith in success, faith in love, faith in kindness, and faith in God. This faith cannot be developed unless man is self-confident. It is very essential that man should learn to trust another. If he does not trust anyone, life will be hard for him. If he doubts, if he suspects everyone he meets, then he will not trust the people nearest to him in the world, his closest relations, and this will soon develop to such a state of distrust that he will even distrust himself. But the trust of the one who trusts another and does not trust himself is profitless.

It is he who trusts another because he trusts himself who has the real trust, and by this trust in himself he can make his life happy in whatever condition he may be.

In the traditions of the Hindus there is a well-known idea: that of the tree of the fulfilment of desires. There is a story in India of a man who was told that there was a tree of the fulfilment of desires, and who went in search of it. After going through forests and across mountains he arrived at last at a place where he lay down and slept without knowing that the tree of the fulfilment of desires was there. Before he went to sleep he was so tired that he thought, "What a good thing it would be if I had just now a soft bed to rest upon and a beautiful house with a courtyard around it and a fountain, and people waiting on me!" With this thought he went to sleep, and when he opened his eyes from sleep he saw that he was lying in a soft bed, and there was a beautiful house and a courtyard and a fountain, and there were people waiting on him. He was very much astonished and remembered that before going to sleep he had thought of all that. But then, as he went further on his journey and thought about this subject, he found, "The tree that I was looking for – it was under that tree that I slept, and it was the miracle of the tree that was accomplished."

The interpretation of this legend is a philosophy in itself. It is man himself who is the tree of fulfilment of his desire, and the root of this tree is in the heart of man. The trees and plants with their fruits and flowers, the beasts with their strength and power, and the birds with their wings are unable to arrive at the stage which man can attain. The trees in the forest await that blessing, that freedom, that liberation in stillness, in quietude; the mountains and the whole of nature seem to await that unfoldment, the privilege of which is given to man. That is why the traditions say that man is made in the image of God. Thus one may say that the most fitting instrument for the working of God is the human being; from a mystical point of view, one may also say that the Creator takes the heart of man as His means of experiencing the whole creation.

That shows that no being on earth is more capable of happiness, of satisfaction, of joy, of peace, than man and it is a pity when man is not aware of this privilege of being human. Every moment in life that he passes in this error of unawareness is a waste and is to his greatest loss.

Man's greatest privilege is to become a suitable instrument of God, and until he knows this he has not realized his true purpose in life. The whole tragedy in the life of man is his ignorance of this fact. From the moment a man realizes this he lives the real life, the life of harmony between God and man. When Jesus Christ said, "Seek ye first the kingdom of God", this teaching was an answer to the cry of humanity: some crying, "I have no wealth", others crying, "I have no rest", others crying, "My situation in life is difficult", "My friends are troubling me", or, "I want a position, wealth". The answer to them all is, "Seek ye first the kingdom of God, and all these things shall be added unto you".

How can we understand this from a practical, a scientific point of view? All that is external is not in direct connection with you and is therefore unattainable in many cases. Therefore sometimes you can attain your wish, but many times you fail. By seeking the kingdom of God you seek the centre of all that is within and without, and all that is in heaven and on earth is directly connected with the centre. So, from the centre, you are able to reach all that is on earth and in heaven but, when you reach what is not at the centre, all may be snatched away from you.

In the Qur'an it is written, "God is the light of the heavens and of the earth". Beside the desire to obtain the things of the earth there is that innermost desire, unconsciously working at every moment of life, to come into touch with the Infinite. When a painter is painting, when a musician is singing or playing, if he thinks, "It is my painting, my playing, my music", perhaps he has some satisfaction but it is like a drop in the ocean. If he connects his painting, his music, with the consciousness of God, if he thinks, "It is Thy painting, Thy music, not mine", then he connects himself with the centre, and his life becomes the life of God.

There is much in life that one can call good, and there is much to be contented with; there is much that one can admire, if one can only bring about that attitude, and it is that attitude that can make man contented and his life happy.

Another thing is that God is the painter of all this beautiful creation, and if we do not connect ourself with the painter we cannot admire his painting. When one goes to the house of a friend whom one likes and admires, every little thing is so pleasant, but when one goes to the house of an enemy, everything is disagreeable. So our devotion, or love, our friendship for God can make this whole creation a source of happiness to us. In the house of a dear friend a loaf of bread, a glass of milk is most delicious, and in the house of the one we dislike all the best dishes are useless. As soon as one begins to realize that the many mansions in the house of the Father are this world with its many religions, many races, many nations, which yet are in the house of God then, however humble and difficult our situation in life, it must sooner or later become happier and better; for we feel that we are in the house of the One we love and admire, and all that we meet with we take with love and gratitude, because it comes from the One we love.

Think for a moment of the condition of the world just now: how nations, communities, churches, religions, all divide humanity – the children of one Father who loves them all without distinction! Man with all his claims of civilization, of progress, seems to have fallen into the greatest error. For centuries the world has not been in such a state as it is just now: one nation hating another, looking with contempt on another. What can we call it? Is it progress, or is it stand-still? Or is it worse than that? Is this not the time when thinking souls should open their eyes from sleep and devote themselves to the effort of doing what good they can to humanity in order to better the conditions of the world and, when each one is thinking only of his own interest, to think of the interest of all?

Sufism brings to the world the message of unity, of uniting in the Fatherhood of God beyond all differences and distinctions. The chief object of the Sufi is to bring about a friendly understanding between people of different nations and races, to bring people of different religions closer together in one understanding, the understanding of truth.

One may ask, "Is it then not the message of Christ which brought the tiding of the love of God and the unity of mankind in the love of God?" There cannot be two religions, there is always one religion only and there cannot be a new one, as Solomon said that there is nothing new under the sun. Whenever the message of love and wisdom is given it is not a new religion, it is the revivification of religion, in order to bring to man the realization of the truth of the religion he follows. Sufism therefore does not bring a new religion, it brings that life and light which are necessary to revivify that religion that has always existed.

NOTES

Health and Order of Body and Mind

(Some parts of the original manuscripts, omitted to avoid either duplication or subjects leading away from the main theme or line of thought, have here been included as notes as well, in order to preserve the integrity of those texts in this edition.)

1. In the original text here follows an instance of the witty caricature of themselves with which Hazrat Inayat Khan delighted his audiences as much as himself. (cf. also note 5 below) These mostly call for a more perceptively experienced ear. It was Europe's "belle époque", which an elder relation had lived in and very thoroughly absorbed during the eighteen-nineties, that had caused his family to turn their eyes West with the sympathy, even affection, of a certain identification. And so here it is also the landowning and courtly India that is poked fun at in unmistakable overtones. Fun, not social criticism, as earnest younger generations more unsmilingly ideological, might be led to infer, is therefore the portée of a fragment such as the following:
Self-pity is a great cause of disease. This is particularly the case with rich people who have no occupation. We should expect to find most illness among poor people who have no very good houses, no very good surroundings, nor enough clothes, nor the means to have regularity in their lives and habits, but they have much less diseases. In the palace, when the weather changes, everybody has a cold, and they lie in bed for fear that they might get a worse cold; the ladies more, the gentlemen less.

2. See further on the subject of purification Volume XIII of this series, The Gathas: *Everyday Life.*

3. Farid Shakr Ganj – one of the most ascetic of early Chishti Sufis, d. Pakpatan (Panjab) 1265. He was a successor of Muin-ud-Din Chishti's khalifa Qutb-ud-Din Bakhtiyar Kaki, of Ferghana, and himself the Murshid of Nizam-ud-Din Auliya, through whom continued the Chishtia Order's line of Sufis to which belonged Hazrat Inayat Khan's own spiritual teacher, Syed Abu Hashim Madani of Hyderabad.

4. More on the treatment of criminals in Volume XIII of the present series, Gatha *Pasi Anfas – Breath,* Series II, No 2.

5. There was one more question (n.b. the date, 1922): What must we do before an invading enemy, German or Bolshevic? *Answer*: I think that this saying must be blown with a trumpet through all parts of the world: Fight with another is war, struggling with oneself is peace.

6. This lecture was given in 1925, at the opening of the Suresnes Summerschool during which Hazrat Inayat Khan gave lectures and other addresses. His first words at this occasion were:

My blessed mureeds and friends, it gives me a great happiness to welcome you this day, on the first day of our Summerschool, in this new hall. Thanks to Providence that brings us all together to think about spiritual ideals and to practise them.

7. Hazrat Inayat Khan had added here the following words:

Now I would like to tell my mureeds treading the spiritual path that during the days they are here in the Summerschool – beside their studies and practices – it would be worthwhile trying to have a practice of self-discipline in some form or other; it does not matter in what way. I shall be glad to prescribe to each the way best suited to each, and when my mureeds are here in presence of Murshid, it is easier to practise it.

8. This chapter Self-control was dictated by Hazrat Inayat Khan and afterwards much amended by him; the authentic document shows the alterations in his own handwriting. Some sentences of the first draft seem worth mentioning. For instance:

Those who by the power of their strong will can scatter these gathered clouds, they alone find the way toward the eternal Sun, and to them is disclosed the divine Light which is hidden under the clouds.

And the last sentence of the next paragraph:

That is the absorption in the light: to become so lost in it that the light itself would turn into darkness, in other words, the state of Eternal Consciousness.

9. The subject of Breath is extensively treated in Volume XIII of this series, Gatha: *Pasi Anfas – Breath*.

10. Hazrat Inayat Khan ended his answer with the following anecdote:

Once a man came to me and said, "What is the reason that everything I do in my business goes wrong?" I asked him, "How long has this been going on?" "For three years", said he. I told him to go to a doctor to have his nose examined. He was very

astonished about this advice; he had gone to a mystic to ask a
spiritual advice and was sent to a nose-specialist. His nose was not
in a good condition and could not breathe rightly; so naturally the
rhythm of the breath went wrong and he lost his balance. Since the
nostrils were made in good condition he learned how to breathe.
To-day he is such a successful businessman that he never comes to
see me any more.

11. This answer also ended with an anecdote, which was then
followed by another question:
The other day in New York a man came to see me who said, "I
am in great trouble, because I see so many colours, blue and black
and red and white, and I am beginning to see different entities which
manifest to my view. I am getting so afraid, I don't know what to
think about it. Others do not see it, but I see it". He was in an office
where he had to do with many people. I told him, "After having
seen each person who brings a certain problem before you, you
must write down what colour you saw at that time". The man was
first very surprised, thinking, "Why is Murshid interested in other
people's affairs?" But he wrote down the colours he had seen after
his different interviews, and I told him, "With the first problem it
will go wrong; the second one will come right, the third problem
will take time, the fourth will not be considered". He saw that all
this came quite true and asked, "How did you know this?" I replied,
"From the colours. Every colour you saw has a relation with the
affair, and in this way you can make use of such manifestations
and experiences, provided you have the knowledge of the science
of breath". These colours are nothing but a manifestation of breath.
Colour is visible breath; in other words, when a person sees colours
he sees himself, his own inner condition.

Question: Does the colour one sees depend upon one's own
condition, or upon the condition of the other person?
Answer: On the combination of the other's condition and one's
own. It depends upon the strength, the power and the clearness
of the breath. Sometimes one's own breath colours the condition
of another. Therefore one must be able to purify one's breath so
well that it is just like a mirror. Then the other person will be
reflected in it; otherwise he will not be reflected. In this way seers
see the mystery of life.

12. See Volume IV of this series: Mental Purification, Chapter XV:
The perceptible breath which the nostrils can feel as air drawn in
and air going out is only an effect of breathing. It is not breath. For
the mystic breath is that current which carries the air out and brings
the air in. The air is perceptible, not the current.

13. A circle through the traditional fourteen earthly and heavenly planes – See Hazrat Inayat Khan in "The Way of Illumination" (Volume I of this series):

When the consciousness begins to look within, the world unseen is disclosed and *Choudatabaq*, the fourteen planes consisting of seven heavens and seven earths, are revealed.

14. The lecture ended with the following words:

There is a Sura in the Qur'an explaining that sleep is a temporary state of death, which makes us understand how important sleep is for our life. In absence of it all wealth, power, luxuries and comforts are as nothing. After sleep, however much tired a person may have been before, he regains his energy.

15. *Miraj* – the ascension of the Prophet from Jerusalem to the Heavens. This visionary mystical experience of the Prophet is reported in the Tradition (Hadith) and usually related to Qur'an, Sura 17: "Limitless in His glory is He who transported His servant from the Inviolable House of Worship to the Remote House of Worship." According to Hazrat Inayat Khan the Prophet was taken to the Temple of Peace which was an initiation into the higher spheres. See Volume IX of this series, the Symbology of Religious Ideas.

16. Questions in India often tend to be interpreted as implicitly reproachful, rather than as an expression of polite interest. In the case of "Where are you going?" the intrusion of privacy, when moving from or through a normally gregarious society, is felt so strongly that the question has generally come to be regarded as of ill omen, and hence as all the more objectionable and discourteous.

17. The following two lectures, though covering the same ground, proceed along very different, even if complementary, lines. In the first lecture emphasis is on the practical and psychological implications of thought, imagination and feeling. Although these in part recur in the second lecture, in the latter it is rather the spiritual and mystical implication of all faculties of mind and heart – hence now defined as spirit – that is elaborated in much further detail. The preceding paragraphs combine the introductory sections of the first and second lectures in order to avoid duplication.

Volume IV of this series also includes in the book: Mental Purification a chapter on *The Control of the Mind*, which is mainly constituted by two of Hazrat Inayat Khan's other lectures on this same subject; it also includes some small parts of the two chapters integrally published here.

18. In order to give another example Hazrat Inayat Khan told the following story of a dervish, omitted in the text as it is also to be found in "Graciousness", Part III, p. 199:

There is an old story of a dervish. Dervishes are those wanderers who think deep, and whose life is to wander about. A dervish was standing in a street of Delhi. The emperor was about to pass by that road. First came the pages who ran before the bodyguard. They pushed the dervish saying, "Away, O dervish, don't you see the emperor is coming!" The dervish being moved away said, "That is why". Then he came back and stood where he was before. The bodyguard came saying, "Away, away, dervish!" So he took two steps backward and said, "That is why". He then again came forward. Some noblemen arrived on horseback. They only moved their horses from the place where the dervish stood, and he said, "That is why". Then the emperor came while the dervish was standing in the same place. The emperor saw the dervish, without a hat, with a patched robe, and he himself greeted him. And the dervish said, "That is why. Such is life".

The Privilege of Being Human

1. It is told in the Qur'an that God ordered the angels to make an image out of clay. God breathed into that image which then became living, and asked the angels to bow down before it. All the angels bowed except Iblis, who thus brought God's displeasure upon himself.

2. To be human, to live a really human life on earth, is man's first objective. Then, in order to become perfect and to attain "self-realization", two further grades are to be reached: the angelic stage and finally union with the divine Being. This is explained in the chapters Self-Realization, 1, 2, 3.

3. According to esoteric tradition *Nabi, Ghawth, Qutb* are high degrees in the spiritual hierarchy. See Volume IX of this series: The Unity of Religious Ideals.

4. The following lines have been omitted in order to avoid duplication:

To become an angel is not very difficult; to be as the world is easy. It is greatest and most difficult to be human.

5. Hazrat Inayat Khan told here the same story already included in The Art of Being 1, ((p. 72)) in the following words:

Once a woman went to a healer and said, "Can you help me? I am in distress". The healer asked her what was the matter, and she told him, "When my husband comes home he is in such a state that there is always disagreement between us". "Oh", said the healer, "that is the easiest thing to remedy. I shall just give you these magnetic lozenges. When your husband comes home you take one of these in your mouth and keep it". When the husband came home, tired and fatigued, he was inclined to war as usual, but she was quiet and did not answer. He was grumpy for a little while, but then became quiet too, and so home became more harmonious. When the lozenges were nearly finished the woman went to the healer and asked, "Give me one more packet of these", but he answered, "Lady, learn from this that it is not the lozenges, it is the keeping quiet, it is the closed lips. When your husband is tired he does not know his mind, and when you do not encourage him to quarrel he will not quarrel".

6. Two kinds of intoxication are to be distinguished: "the intoxication which enriches the soul", mentioned here, which is spiritual ecstasy, and the blinding intoxication caused by the agitation of earthly life.

7. The lecture was rounded off with the following additional remarks:

The Brahmins were so very great and knew the science of everything. Their eating out of leaves shows that they knew the nature of everything, and they thought that no spoon which had been in the mouth of one person should go to the mouth of another person. And why are they now down, and others, such as the Japanese and Chinese, whose philosophy cannot touch the Vedanta, are placed before them? Because their science led them to think that "I am different, because I understand more. The *Kshatrya* understands rather less, let him be separate from me. The *Vaishya* understands less. The *Shudra* understands much less. He must not touch me. I am different from my brother. Therefore I should cook in a different kitchen and he should cook in a different kitchen."

This is why Sa'adi says, "Every head has its craze". The political person calls the business person crazy. The artist calls the scientist crazy. The intellectual person calls the wise person crazy. Because each has his view. We must meet here for unity. The Sufi uses his intellect to see the unity. This leads to friendship which will never cease. The business friendship will cease as soon as interest ceases. The political friendship will cease. This friendship is the best, and it will never cease, because it is the friendship in God.

8. Throughout the Muslim Orient and the Indian Subcontinent a rich oral tradition of stories concerning the Biblical – Quranic Prophets and heroes takes many colourful shapes: simplifying, elaborating and adjusting ancient lore to current notions. Particularly beloved figures such as Ibrahim (Abraham) and Musa (Moses), Khizr Ilyas (Elijah) and Isa (Jesus), appear in a lively variety of anecdotes, similes and teachings. And not in popular story-telling only, but as well and above all in great classical works such as Rumi's Mathnavi-i-Manavi. In different contexts Hazrat Inayat Khan is clearly happy to use such oral versions of ancient stories so as to enliven his discourses all the more zestfully.

9. More on the subject of vegetarianism in Volume XIII, of this series, Gatha: *Everyday Life*, I, 6.

10. This subject is treated more extensively in Hazrat Inayat Khan's book: Moral Culture, included in Volume III of the present series.

11. The original manuscript still shows the following passage:
Sometimes a person may think, "So many lords and millionaires drink a whole bottle. If I drink one glass there can be no harm. They are not turned out of their houses!" But we must remember that there is the possibility that all the people in the world may be released from all the evil they have done, and we may not be released from a small wrong we have done. The finer a person becomes the stricter account is demanded of him. A holy person, a *wali*, is called to account for his thoughts and feelings. An ordinary person does foolish things from morning till night and is never called to account. Only he who has signed the contract is held accountable by the judge. The foolish one who does not know how to write is released.

12. More on the subject of spiritual healing by thought in Volume IV of this series in the book: Health and Healing.

13. The story of Orpheus and Euridice, which recurs in the next chapter, was told here in the following words:
In the Greek story of Orpheus and Euridice there is a beautiful teaching on this subject. In the first part of the story Orpheus lost Euridice who was among the people of the underworld. This shows that love tries even to bring up, to raise a soul who is thrown down so far into the depths of the earth. When Orpheus learned that Euridice was taken to the other world, he began to sing the song by the power of which he won the gods of the lower worlds. That shows us what power the word has, what power sound has and how it appeals to cosmic forces. The gods of the lower world were

the cosmic forces, planetary influences, the conditions which were destined, the spirits, the powers that held in their hands the reign of destiny. This also shows how Orpheus according to the Arabic means the knower, the one who has the knowledge of life. In Arabic the knowledge of life is called *'arifah*, and the knower is called *'arif*. The real knowledge is the knowledge of sound and of rhythm, of word and of note. It is this knowledge which gives mastery in the higher or mystical or psychological music, as there is a saying of Wagner that he who has the knowledge of sound knows everything.

So Orpheus pleased the gods of the lower worlds and they gave him the promise that Euridice would follow him on the condition that he should not look back. As long as Orpheus went on by the power of faith, Euridice was drawn to him; his faith was drawing her. As he was going forward in faith, so Euridice was following him. He could have gone to the other side of the world and she would have followed him; as long as he had faith, so long she followed him. But then came doubt, the worst enemy of man, and said, "Look if she is really there". As soon as Orpheus turned back Mercury was there to lift Euridice up and take her away.

(Orpheus – 'Arif: This remarkably happy association of sounds – of the consonants which predominate in the grammatical structure of semitic languages – has of course no etymological intent. Even so it may be worth noting here that the origin and significance of the name of Orpheus has never yet convincingly been explained. It certainly was not Greek. The Greeks have always regarded Orpheus as a Thracian, a "barbarous" non-Hellene, and considered that it was from ancient Egypt that he introduced the Mysteries carrying his name into Greece.)

14. Hazrat Inayat Khan was asked to give an interpretation of the story of Orpheus before a musical performance of Gluck's opera Orpheo ed Euridice.

LIST OF DOCUMENTS
THAT ARE THE SOURCES OF VOLUME VIII

(Hazrat Inayat Khan lived in London during and immediately after World War 1. Many of his addresses and lectures given between 1916 and 1921 were noted down without indication of place and date. These are referred to below as "manuscripts from the early London period".)

Health and Order of Body and Mind

Health –1–	– an undated manuscript under the heading "Sufism"
–2–	– Magazine the "Sufi Quarterly", December, 1925
–3–	– manuscripts from the early
Physical Condition	London period
Physical Culture –	a compilation of manuscripts from the early London period
Control of the Body	
Balance –1–	– manuscripts from the early
–2–	London period
–3–	Paris, October, 1925
– in Solitude	– manuscripts from the early London period
– in Greatness	
Life's Mechanism –	Paris, May, 1924
Harmony –	Paris, December 1922
Mastery –	a manuscript from the early London period
Self-Mastery –	England, 22nd January, 1920
Self-Discipline –	Suresnes, 14th June, 1925
A Question about Fasting	
–	asked after a lecture on "The Tuning of the Heart", Chicago, 3rd May, 1926
Self-Control –1–	manuscripts from the early London
–2–	period
–3–	

Self-Control –4–	London, probable date 1916/1917; a manuscript with corrections in Hazrat Inayat Khan's handwriting
Physical Control	San Francisco, 5th April, 1926
Questions about Vaccination and Inoculation:	1st question – Suresnes, 19th August, 1923
	2nd and 3rd questions – Suresnes, 21st July, 1923
	4th question – Paris, 11th October, 1923
Questions about Breathing	– San Francisco, 5th April, 1926
The Mystery of Breath	– Magazine "Sufism", March, 1924
The Science of Breath	– London, approximate date 1916/1917
The Philosophy of Breath The Control of the Breath –1– –2–	manuscripts from the early London period
The Power of Silence Feelings –	a manuscript from the private collection of one of Hazrat Inayat Khan's first disciples, approximate date 1916–1920
The Control of the Mind –1– –2–	San Francisco, 7th April, 1926 Chicago, 1st May, 1926
The Mystery of Sleep, –1– –2–	manuscripts from the early London period
The Nature of the Dream How Dreams are Formed	compiled with manuscripts from the early London period
Dreams are of Three Kinds Spiritual Healing	March, 1924

The Priviledge of Being Human

Man, the Purpose of Creation	– originally "The Privilege of being Human" Southampton, 24th May, 1921
Character-Building 1	– An answer given after a lecture of the series "Character Building", Suresnes, 11th Aug. 1923
Character-Building 2	– a manuscript from the early London period

Human Nature 1, 2, 3 — different manuscripts from the early London period, the third one corrected in Hazrat Inayat Khan's handwriting

Self-Realization 1, 2, 3 — different manuscripts from the early London period

The Art of Personality — Detroit, 4th February, 1926 In transscribing the shorthand report, the reporter omitted the two passages placed between brackets. These have recently been deciphered from the stenogram; some words, however, remain illegible. To that extent the exactitude of those passages as reproduced cannot entirely be vouched for.

Man Likened to the Light — Paris, 27th November, 1923

Truth — London, 13th May, 1921

Selflessness-*Inkisar* — Suresnes, summer 1922

Indifference-*Vairagya* — a manuscript from the early London period

Indifference and Independence — Suresnes, 20th August, 1922 question asked after a lecture on Divine Manner, Suresnes, 11th Oct. 1923

Overlooking-*Darquza* — Suresnes, 15th July, 1923

Graciousness-*Khulq* — Suresnes, 14th July, 1923

Conciliation-*Ittifaq* — originally "Reconciliation", Suresnes, 16th July, 1923

Consideration-*Murawwat* — Suresnes, 15th July, 1922

Tact — Suresnes, 5th August, 1924

Spirituality — Suresnes, 2nd September, 1924

Innocence 1 — 7th January, 1923
2 — a manuscript from the early London period

Holiness — Suresnes, summer, 1922

Resist not Evil — Paris, 20th Febrary, 1924

Resignation — Suresnes, 4th August, 1923

Struggle and Resignation — Geneva, 4th April, 1924 question asked after a lecture on "Divine Manner", Suresnes, 9th Oct. 1923

Renunciation — 3rd April, 1922

Sacrifice 1, 2, 3, 4 — different manuscripts from the early London period

Sacrifice 5	– from the private collection of one of Hazrat Inayat Khan's first disciples, approximate date 1916–1920
Ambition Satisfaction	different manuscripts from the early London period
Harmlessness A Question about Vegetarianism	– Geneva, 9th October, 1923
Unselfish Actions	
Expections	
Be a Lion Within	different manuscripts from the
Humility	early London period
Moral Culture 1, 2, 3	
Hope 1, 2	
Aphorism "Hope"	– Magazine "Sufism", June 1923
Patience Confidence 1, 2	different manuscripts from the
Faith 1	early London period
Faith 2	– Paris, 27th February, 1924
Faith and Doubt	– Suresnes, 17th August 1926
The Story of Orpheus	– originally "An Interpretation of the Story of Orpheus", Paris, 14th June, 1924
Happiness	– Suresnes, 26th August, 1924
The Privilege of being Human	– 20th June, 1921

INDEX

Abraham 205–6
abstract plane 48
Abu Hashim Madani 158
activity 190–1, 193
adab 224
advaita 134
akhlaq Allah 176
Allah *see* God
amal 41, 206
ambition 209–11
Amir 231
angels 120, 131–3
art of life 2–3
astral plane 46, 47
at-one-ment 102

balance, between activity and
    repose 9, 13
  in life 14–15, 16, 24
  in nature 16–17
  maintaining 17–19, 174
beauty 25, 28
Bhavasaga 33
Bible 13, 21, 67, 121, 134, 140,
    145, 184, 191, 201, 204
    (*see also* Jesus Christ)
Brahma, dream of 102
breath, centralizing 58, 59
  control of 68–70
  direction of 68
  far-reaching 58, 60
  mastery of 71–2
  mystery of 60–4
  philosophy of 66–8
  rhythm of 58, 61
  science of 64–6
  volume of 58
breathing, depth of 58

positive and negative 59
Buddha 20, 126, 141
burag 70

character 34–5, 125–7, 171
charity 121
Christian Science 29
circulation 9
communion 102
compassion 128
concentration 15, 23, 41, 84
conciliation 168–9
confidence 236–8
consciousness 48, 102
consideration 171–2, 173, 230
criminals 28

darquza 164–5
dhikr 10, 15
diljoi 231
discipline 34
disease 113–14 (*see also* illness)
dream plane 46, 108
dreams, formation of 106–7
  in *Nasut* condition 99–101
  nature of 95, 104–5
  three kinds of 107–9
doubt 240–1, 246–8

ecstasy 15–16, 43
ego 92–3, 122
emotions, control of 45
environment 22–3, 37
Eternal Consciousness 47, 76, 96
    (*see also* God)
evil 183–8, 223